"......it was too deep for them......"
Chapter XXV p. 190

THE WAYFARER'S LIBRARY

The
INNOCENTS ABROAD
and
Jumping Frog

Mark Twain

J. M. DENT & SONS Ltd.
LONDON

CONTENTS

CHAPTER I

A

The Innocents Abroad

Contents

3

The Innocents Abroad

Contents

The Innocents Abroad

Contents

LIST OF ILLUSTRATIONS

"..saddles....green spectacles and umbrellas.....veils........"

THE INNOCENTS ABROAD

CHAPTER I

FOR months the great Pleasure Excursion to Europe and the Holy Land was chatted about in the newspapers everywhere in America, and discussed at countless firesides. It was a novelty in the way of Excursions—its like had not been thought of before, and it compelled that interest which attractive novelties always command. It was to be a picnic on a gigantic scale. The participants in it, instead of freighting an ungainly steam ferry-boat with youth and beauty and pies and doughnuts, and paddling up some obscure creek to disembark upon a grassy lawn and wear themselves out with a long summer day's laborious frolicking under the impression that it was fun, were to sail away in a great steamship

9

The Innocents Abroad

with flags flying and cannon pealing, and take a royal holiday beyond the broad ocean, in many a strange clime and in many a land renowned in history! They were to sail for months over the breezy Atlantic and the sunny Mediterranean; they were to scamper about the decks by day, filling the ship with shouts and laughter—or read novels and poetry in the shade of the smoke-stacks, or watch for the jelly-fish and the nautilus, over the side, and the shark, the whale, and other strange monsters of the deep; and at night they were to dance in the open air, on the upper deck, in the midst of a ball-room that stretched from horizon to horizon, and was domed by the bending heavens and lighted by no meaner lamps than the stars and the magnificent moon—dance, and promenade, and smoke, and sing, and make love, and search the skies for constellations that never associate with the " Big Dipper " they were so tired of: and they were to see the ships of twenty navies—the customs and costumes of twenty curious peoples—the great cities of half a world—they were to hobnob with nobility and hold friendly converse with kings and princes, Grand Moguls, and the anointed lords of mighty empires!

It was a brave conception; it was the offspring of a most ingenious brain. It was well advertised, but it hardly needed it: the bold originality, the extraordinary character, the seductive nature, and the vastness of the enterprise provoked comment everywhere and advertised it in every household in the land. Who could read the programme of the excursion without longing to make one of the party? I will insert it here. It is almost as good as a map. As a text for this book, nothing could be better:

The Innocents Abroad

EXCURSION TO THE HOLY LAND, EGYPT, THE
CRIMEA, GREECE, AND INTERMEDIATE POINTS
OF INTEREST

BROOKLYN, *February 1st, 1867.*

The undersigned will make an excursion as above during
the coming season, and begs to submit to you the following
programme:—

A first-class steamer, to be under his own command, and
capable of accommodating at least one hundred and fifty
cabin passengers, will be selected, in which will be taken a
select company, numbering not more than three-fourths of
the ship's capacity. There is good reason to believe that
this company can be easily made up in this immediate
vicinity, of mutual friends and acquaintances.

The steamer will be provided with every necessary comfort, including library and musical instruments.

An experienced physician will be on board.

Leaving New York about June 1st, a middle and pleasant
route will be taken across the Atlantic, and passing through
the group of Azores, St. Michael will be reached in about ten
days. A day or two will be spent here, enjoying the fruit
and wild scenery of these islands, and the voyage continued,
and Gibraltar reached in three or four days.

A day or two will be spent here in looking over the wonderful subterraneous fortifications, permission to visit these
galleries being readily obtained.

From Gibraltar, running along the coasts of Spain and
France, Marseilles will be reached in three days. Here ample
time will be given not only to look over the city, which was
founded six hundred years before the Christian era, and its
artificial port, the finest of the kind in the Mediterranean, but
to visit Paris during the Great Exhibition; and the beautiful
city of Lyons, lying intermediate, from the heights of which,
on a clear day, Mont Blanc and the Alps can be distinctly
seen. Passengers who may wish to extend the time at Paris
can do so, and, passing down through Switzerland, rejoin the
steamer at Genoa.

From Marseilles to Genoa is a run of one night. The
excursionists will have an opportunity to look over this, the
" magnificent city of palaces," and visit the birthplace of
Columbus, twelve miles off, over a beautiful road built by
Napoleon I. From this point, excursions may be made to
Milan, Lakes Como and Maggiore, or to Milan, Verona (famous
for its extraordinary fortifications), Padua, and Venice. Or,
if passengers desire to visit Parma (famous for Correggio's

The Innocents Abroad

frescoes), and Bologna, they can by rail go on to Florence, and rejoin the steamer at Leghorn, thus spending about three weeks amid the cities most famous for art in Italy.

From Genoa the run to Leghorn will be made along the coast in one night, and time appropriated to this point in which to visit Florence, its palaces and galleries; Pisa, its Cathedral and "Leaning Tower," and Lucca and its baths, and Roman amphitheatre; Florence, the most remote, being distant by rail about sixty miles.

From Leghorn to Naples (calling at Civita Vecchia to land any who may prefer to go to Rome from that point) the distance will be made in about thirty-six hours; the route will lay along the coast of Italy, close by Caprera, Elba, and Corsica. Arrangements have been made to take on board at Leghorn a pilot for Caprera, and, if practicable, a call will be made there to visit the home of Garibaldi.

Rome, [by rail] Herculaneum, Pompeii, Vesuvius, Virgil's tomb, and possibly the ruins of Pæstum, can be visited, as well as the beautiful surroundings of Naples and its charming bay.

The next point of interest will be Palermo, the most beautiful city of Sicily, which will be reached in one night from Naples. A day will be spent here, and leaving in the evening, the course will be taken towards Athens.

Skirting along the north coast of Sicily, passing through the group of Æolian Isles, in sight of Stromboli and Vulcania, both active volcanoes, through the Straits of Messina, with "Scylla" on the one hand and "Charybdis" on the other, along the east coast of Sicily, and in sight of Mount Ætna, along the south coast of Italy, the west and south coast of Greece, in sight of ancient Crete, up Athens Gulf, and into the Piræus, Athens will be reached in two and a half or three days. After tarrying here awhile, the Bay of Salamis will be crossed, and a day given to Corinth, whence the voyage will be continued to Constantinople, passing on the way through the Grecian Archipelago, the Dardanelles, the Sea of Marmora, and the mouth of the Golden Horn, and arriving in about forty-eight hours from Athens.

After leaving Constantinople, the way will be taken out through the beautiful Bosphorus, across the Black Sea to Sebastopol and Balaklava, a run of about twenty-four hours. Here it is proposed to remain two days, visiting the harbours, fortifications, and battle-fields of the Crimea; thence back through the Bosphorus, touching at Constantinople to take in any who may have preferred to remain there; down through the Sea of Marmora and the Dardanelles, along the coasts of ancient Troy and Lydia in Asia, to Smyrna, which will be reached in two or two and a half days from Constanti-

The Innocents Abroad

nople. A sufficient stay will be made here to give opportunity of visiting Ephesus, fifty miles distant by rail.

From Smyrna towards the Holy Land the course will lay
through the Grecian Archipelago, close by the Isle of Patmos,
along the coast of Asia, ancient Pamphylia, and the Isle of
Cyprus. Beirout will be reached in three days. At Beirout
time will be given to visit Damascus; after which the steamer
will proceed to Joppa.

From Joppa, Jerusalem, the River Jordan, the Sea of
Tiberias, Nazareth, Bethany, Bethlehem, and other points
of interest in the Holy Land can be visited, and here those
who may have preferred to make the journey from Beirout
through the country, passing through Damascus, Galilee,
Capernaum, Samaria, and by the River Jordan and Sea of
Tiberias, can rejoin the steamer.

Leaving Joppa, the next point of interest to visit will be
Alexandria, which will be reached in twenty-four hours. The
ruins of Cæsar's Palace, Pompey's Pillar, Cleopatra's Needle,
the Catacombs, and ruins of ancient Alexandria, will be found
worth the visit. The journey to Cairo, one hundred and
thirty miles by rail, can be made in a few hours, and from
which can be visited the site of ancient Memphis, Joseph's
Granaries, and the Pyramids.

From Alexandria the route will be taken homeward, calling
at Malta, Cagliari (in Sardinia), and Parma (in Majorca), all
magnificent harbours, with charming scenery, and abounding
in fruits.

A day or two will be spent at each place, and leaving Parma
in the evening, Valencia in Spain will be reached the next
morning. A few days will be spent in this, the finest city of
Spain.

From Valencia, the homeward course will be continued,
skirting along the coast of Spain. Alicant, Carthagena, Palos,
and Malaga, will be passed but a mile or two distant, and
Gibraltar reached in about twenty-four hours.

A stay of one day will be made here, and the voyage continued to Madeira, which will be reached in about three days.
Captain Marryatt writes: " I do not know a spot on the
globe which so much astonishes and delights upon first
arrival as Madeira." A stay of one or two days will be made
here, which, if time permits, may be extended, and passing
on through the islands, and probably in sight of the Peak of
Teneriffe, a southern track will be taken, and the Atlantic
crossed within the latitudes of the north-east trade winds,
where mild and pleasant weather, and a smooth sea, can
always be expected.

A call will be made at Bermuda, which lies directly in this
route homeward, and will be reached in about ten days from

The Innocents Abroad

Madeira, and after spending a short time with our friends the Bermudians, the final departure will be made for home, which will be reached in about three days.

Already applications have been received from parties in Europe wishing to join the Excursion there.

The ship will at all times be a home, where the excursionist, if sick, will be surrounded by kind friends, and have all possible comfort and sympathy.

Should contagious sickness exist in any of the ports named in the programme, such ports will be passed, and others of interest substituted.

The price of passage is fixed at $1250, currency, for each adult passenger. Choice of rooms and of seats at the tables apportioned in the order in which passages are engaged, and no passage considered engaged until ten per cent. of the passage money is deposited with the treasurer.

Passengers can remain on board of the steamer, at all ports, if they desire, without additional expense, and all boating at the expense of the ship.

All passages must be paid for when taken, in order that the most perfect arrangements be made for starting at the appointed time.

Applications for passage must be approved by the committee before tickets are issued, and can be made to the undersigned.

Articles of interest or curiosity, procured by the passengers during the voyage, may be brought home in the steamer free of charge.

Five dollars per day, in gold, it is believed, will be a fair calculation to make for *all* travelling expenses on shore, and at the various points where passengers may wish to leave the steamer for days at a time.

The trip can be extended, and the route changed, by *unanimous* vote of the passengers.

CHAS. C. DUNCAN,
117 WALL STREET, NEW YORK.
R. R. G——, Treasurer.

COMMITTEE ON APPLICATIONS.

J. T. H——, ESQ.   R. R. G——, ESQ.   C. C. DUNCAN.

COMMITTEE ON SELECTING STEAMER.

CAPT. W. W. S——, *Surveyor for Board of Underwriters.*
C. W. C——, *Consulting Engineer for U.S. and Canada.*
J. T. H——, ESQ.
C. C. DUNCAN.

P. S.—The very beautiful and substantial side wheel steamship "*Quaker City*" has been chartered for the occasion, and will leave New York, June 8th. Letters have been issued by the government commending the party to courtesies abroad.

What was there lacking about that programme to make it perfectly irresistible? Nothing that any finite mind could discover. Paris, England, Scotland, Switzerland, Italy—Garibaldi! The Grecian archipelago! Vesuvius! Constantinople! Smyrna! the Holy Land! Egypt and "our friends the Bermudians!" People in Europe desiring to join the Excursion—contagious sickness to be avoided—boating at the expense of the ship—physician on board—the circuit of the globe to be made if the passengers unanimously desired it—the company to be rigidly selected by a pitiless "Committee on Applications"—the vessel to be as rigidly selected by as pitiless a "Committee on Selecting Steamer." Human nature could not withstand these bewildering temptations. I hurried to the Treasurer's office and deposited my ten per cent. I rejoiced to know that a few vacant state-rooms were still left. I *did* avoid a critical personal examination into my character by that bowelless committee, but I referred to all the people of high standing I could think of in the community who would be least likely to know anything about me.

Shortly a supplementary programme was issued which set forth that the Plymouth Collection of Hymns would be used on board the ship. I then paid the balance of my passage money.

I was provided with a receipt, and duly and officially accepted as an excursionist. There was happiness in that, but it was tame compared to the novelty of being "select."

This supplementary programme also instructed the excursionists to provide themselves with light musical instruments for amusement in the ship; with saddles for Syrian travel; green spectacles and umbrellas; veils for Egypt; and substantial clothing to use in rough pilgrimising in the Holy Land. Furthermore, it was suggested that although the ship's library would afford a fair amount of reading matter, it would still be well if each passenger would provide himself with a few guide-books, a Bible, and some standard works of travel. A list was appended, which consisted chiefly of books relating to the Holy Land, since the Holy Land was part of the excursion, and seemed to be its main feature.

Rev. Henry Ward Beecher was to have accompanied the expedition, but urgent duties obliged him to give up the idea. There were other passengers who could have been spared better, and would have been spared more willingly. Lieut.-Gen. Sherman was to have been of the party also, but the Indian war compelled his presence on the plains. A popular actress had entered her name on the ship's books, but something interfered, and *she* couldn't go. The " Drummer Boy of the Potomac " deserted, and lo, we had never a celebrity left!

However, we were to have a " battery of guns " from the Navy Department (as per advertisement), to be used in answering royal salutes; and the document furnished by the Secretary of the Navy, which was to make " Gen. Sherman and party " welcome guests in the courts and camps of the old world, was still left to us, though both document and battery, I think, were shorn of somewhat of their original august proportions. However, had not we the seductive programme still, with its Paris, its Constantinople, Smyrna, Jerusalem, Jericho, and " our friends the Bermudians? " What did we care?

The Innocents Abroad

CHAPTER II

OCCASIONALLY during the following month I dropped in at 117 Wall Street to inquire how the repairing and refurnishing of the vessel was coming on; how additions to the passenger list were averaging; how many people the committee were decreeing not " select," every day, and banishing in sorrow and tribulation. I was glad to know that we were to have a little printing-press on board and issue a daily newspaper of our own. I was glad to learn that our piano, our parlour organ and our melodeon were to be the best instruments of the kind that could be had in the market. I was proud to observe that among our excursionists were three ministers of the gospel, eight doctors, sixteen or eighteen ladies, several military and naval chieftains with sounding titles, an ample crop of " Professors " of various kinds, and a gentleman who had " COMMISSIONER OF THE UNITED STATES OF AMERICA TO EUROPE, ASIA, AND AFRICA " thundering after his name in one awful blast! I had carefully prepared myself to take rather a back seat in that ship, because of the uncommonly select material that would alone be permitted to pass through the camel's eye of that committee on credentials; I had schooled myself to expect an imposing array of military and naval heroes, and to have to set that back seat still further back in consequence of it, may be; but I state frankly that I was all unprepared for *this* crusher.

I fell under that titular avalanche a torn and blighted thing. I said that if that potentate *must* go over in our ship, why, I supposed he must—but

The Innocents Abroad

that to my thinking, when the United States considered it necessary to send a dignitary of that tonnage across the ocean, it would be in better taste, and safer, to take him apart and cart him over in sections, in several ships.

Ah, if I had only known then that he was only a common mortal, and that his mission had nothing more overpowering about it than the collecting of seeds, and uncommon yams and extraordinary cabbages and peculiar bullfrogs for that poor, useless, innocent, mildewed old fossil, the Smithsonian Institute, I would have felt *so* much relieved.

During that memorable month I basked in the happiness of being for once in my life drifting with the tide of a great popular movement. Everybody was going to Europe—I too was going to Europe. Everybody was going to the famous Paris Exposition —I too was going to the Paris Exposition. The steamship lines were carrying Americans out of the various ports of the country at the rate of four or five thousand a week, in the aggregate. If I met a dozen individuals during that month who were not going to Europe shortly, I have no distinct remembrance of it now. I walked about the city a good deal with a young Mr. Blucher, who was booked for the excursion. He was confiding, good-natured, unsophisticated, companionable; but he was not a man to set the river on fire. He had the most extraordinary notions about this European exodus, and came at least to consider the whole nation as packing up for emigration to France. We stepped into a store in Broadway one day, where he bought a handkerchief, and when the man could not make change, Mr. B. said:

" Never mind, I'll hand it to you in Paris."

" But I'm not going to Paris."

18

The Innocents Abroad

" How is—what did I understand you to say? "

" I said I am not going to Paris."

" Not going to *Paris!* Not g—— Well then, where in the nation *are* you going to? "

" Nowhere at all."

" Not anywhere whatsoever?—not any place on earth but this? "

" Not any place at all but just this—stay here all summer."

My comrade took his purchase and walked out of the store without a word—walked out with an injured look upon his countenance. Up the street a piece he broke silence and said, impressively: " It was a lie—that is my opinion of it! "

In the fullness of time the ship was ready to receive her passengers. I was introduced to the young gentleman who was to be my room mate, and found him to be intelligent, cheerful of spirit, unselfish, full of generous impulses, patient, considerate, and wonderfully good-natured. Not any passenger that sailed in the *Quaker City* will withhold his indorsement of what I have just said. We selected a state-room forward of the wheel, on the starboard side, " below decks." It had two berths in it, a dismal deadlight, a sink with a wash-bowl in it, and a long, sumptuously cushioned locker, which was to do service as a sofa— partly, and partly as a hiding-place for our things. Notwithstanding all this furniture, there was still room to turn around in, but not to swing a cat in, at least with entire security to the cat. However, the room was large for a ship's state-room, and was in every way satisfactory.

The vessel was appointed to sail on a certain Saturday early in June.

A little after noon on that distinguished Saturday,

The Innocents Abroad

I reached the ship and went on board. All was bustle and confusion. [I have seen that remark before, somewhere.] The pier was crowded with carriages and men; passengers were arriving and hurrying on board; the vessel's decks were encumbered with trunks and valises; groups of excursionists, arrayed in unattractive travelling costumes, were moping about in a drizzling rain and looking as droopy and wobegone as so many moulting chickens. The gallant flag was up, but it was under the spell too, and hung limp and disheartened by the mast. Altogether, it was the bluest, bluest spectacle! It was a pleasure excursion—there was no gainsaying that, because the programme said so—it was so nominated in the bond —but it surely hadn't the general aspect of one.

Finally, above the banging, and rumbling, and shouting, and hissing of steam, rang the order to " cast off! "—a sudden rush to the gangways—a scampering ashore of visitors—a revolution of the wheels, and we were off—the picnic was begun! Two very mild cheers went up from the dripping crowd on the pier; we answered them gently from the slippery decks; the flag made an effort to wave, and failed; the " battery of guns " spake not—the ammunition was out.

We steamed down to the foot of the harbour and came to anchor. It was still raining. And not only raining, but storming. " Outside " we could see ourselves that there was a tremendous sea on. We must lie still, in the calm harbour, till the storm should abate. Our passengers hailed from fifteen States; only a few of them had ever been to sea before; manifestly it would not do to pit them against a full-blown tempest until they had got their sea-legs on. Towards evening the two steam-tugs that had accompanied us with a rollicking champagne-party of young New Yorkers on board who wished to bid farewell to one of our number in due and ancient form, departed, and we were alone on the deep. On deep five fathoms, and anchored fast to the bottom. And out in the solemn rain, at that. This was pleasuring with a vengeance.

It was an appropriate relief when the gong sounded for prayer-meeting. The first Saturday night of any other pleasure excursion might have been devoted to whist and dancing; but I submit it to the un-prejudiced mind if it would have been in good taste for *us* to engage in such frivolities, considering what we had gone through and the frame of mind we were in. We would have shone at a wake, but not at anything more festive.

However, there is always a cheering influence about the sea; and in my berth, that night, rocked by the measured swell of the waves, and lulled by the mur-mur of the distant surf, I soon passed tranquilly out of all consciousness of the dreary experiences of the day and damaging premonitions of the future.

CHAPTER III

ALL day Sunday at anchor. The storm had gone down a great deal, but the sea had not. It was still piling frothy hills high in air "outside," as we could plainly see with the glasses. We could not properly begin a pleasure excursion on Sunday; we could not offer untried stomachs to so pitiless a sea as that. We must lie still till Monday. And we did. But we had repetitions of church and prayer-meetings; and so, of

course, we were just as eligibly situated as we could
have been anywhere.

I was up early that Sabbath morning, and was
early to breakfast. I felt a perfectly natural desire
to have a good, long, unprejudiced look at the passengers at a time when they should be free from self-
consciousness—which is at breakfast, when such a
moment occurs in the lives of human beings at all.

I was greatly surprised to see so many elderly people
—I might almost say, so many venerable people. A
glance at the long lines of heads was apt to make one
think it was *all* grey. But it was not. There was a
tolerably fair sprinkling of young folks, and another
fair sprinkling of gentlemen and ladies who were non-
committal as to age, being neither actually old or
absolutely young.

The next morning we weighed anchor and went
to sea. It was a great happiness to get away after
this dragging, dispiriting delay. I thought there
never was such gladness in the air before, such brightness in the sun, such beauty in the sea. I was satisfied with the picnic then, and with all its belongings.
All my malicious instincts were dead within me; and
as America faded out of sight, I think a spirit of charity
rose up in their place that was as boundless, for the
time being, as the broad ocean that was heaving its
billows about us. I wished to express my feelings—
I wished to lift up my voice and sing; but I did not
know anything to sing, and so I was obliged to give up
the idea. It was no loss to the ship though, perhaps.

It was breezy and pleasant, but the sea was still
very rough. One could not promenade without
risking his neck; at one moment the bowsprit was
taking a deadly aim at the sun in mid-heaven, and
at the next it was trying to harpoon a shark in the

bottom of the ocean.   What a weird sensation it is to feel the stem of a ship sinking swiftly from under you and see the bow climbing high away among the clouds! One's safest course that day was to clasp a railing and hang on; walking was too precarious a pastime.

By some happy fortune I was not sea-sick.   That was a thing to be proud of.   I had not always escaped before.   If there is one thing in the world that will make a man peculiarly and insufferably self-conceited it is to have his stomach behave itself the first day at sea, when nearly all his comrades are sea-sick.   Soon, a venerable fossil, shawled to the chin and bandaged like a mummy, appeared at the door of the after deck-house, and the next lurch of the ship shot him into my arms.   I said—

"Good-morning, sir.   It is a fine day."

He put his hand on his stomach and said, "*Oh my!*" and then staggered away and fell over the coop of a sky-light.

Presently another old gentleman was projected from the same door with great violence.   I said—

"Calm yourself, sir; there is no hurry.   It is a fine day, sir."

He also put his hand on his stomach and said, "*Oh my!*" and reeled away.

In a little while another veteran was discharged abruptly from the same door, clawing at the air for a saving support.   I said—

"Good morning, sir.   It is a fine day for pleasuring. You were about to say—"

"*Oh my!*"

I thought so.   I anticipated *him*, anyhow.   I stayed there, and was bombarded with old gentlemen for an hour perhaps; and all I got out of them was "*Oh my!*"

The Innocents Abroad

I went away then, in a thoughtful mood. I said, this is a good pleasure excursion. I like it. The passengers are not garrulous, but still they are sociable. I like those old people, but somehow they seem to have the " Oh my " rather bad.

I knew what was the matter with them. They were sea-sick; and I was glad of it. We all like to see

"Calm yourself Sir — There is no hurry."

people sea-sick when we are not, ourselves. Playing whist by the cabin lamps when it is storming outside is pleasant; walking the quarter-deck in the moonlight is pleasant; smoking in the breezy foretop is pleasant, when one is not afraid to go up there; but these are all feeble and commonplace compared with the joy of seeing people suffering the miseries of sea-sickness.

I picked up a good deal of information during the afternoon. At one time I was climbing up the quarter-deck when the vessel's stern was in the sky.

The Innocents Abroad

I was smoking a cigar and feeling passably comfortable. Somebody ejaculated—

"Come, now, *that* wont answer. Read the sign up there—NO SMOKING ABAFT THE WHEEL!"

It was Captain Duncan, chief of the expedition. I went forward of course. I saw a long spy-glass lying on a desk in one of the upper-deck state-rooms back of the pilot-house, and reached after it—there was a ship in the distance.

"Ah, ah—hands off! Come out of that!"

I came out of that. I said to a deck-sweep—but in a low voice—

"Who is that overgrown pirate with the whiskers and the discordant voice?"

"It's Captain Bursley—executive officer—sailing-master."

I loitered about awhile, and then, for want of something better to do, fell to carving a railing with my knife. Somebody said, in an insinuating, admonitory voice—

"Now *say*, my friend, don't you know any better than to be whittling the ship all to pieces that way? *You* ought to know better than that."

I went back and found the deck-sweep.

"Who is that smooth-faced animated outrage yonder in the fine clothes?"

"That's Captain L——, the owner of the ship—he's one of the main bosses."

In the course of time I brought up on the starboard side of the pilot-house, and found a sextant lying on a bench. Now, I said, they "take the sun" through this thing; I should think I might see that vessel through it. I had hardly got it to my eye when some one touched me on the shoulder and said, deprecatingly—

" I'll have to get you to give that to me, sir. If there's anything you'd like to know about taking the sun, I'd as soon tell you as not—but I don't like to trust anybody with that instrument. If you want any figuring done— Ay, ay, sir! "

He was gone, to answer a call from the other side. I sought the deck-sweep.

" Who is that spider-legged gorilla yonder with the sanctimonious countenance? "

" It's Captain Jones, sir—the chief mate."

" Well. This goes clear away ahead of anything I ever heard of before. Do you—now I ask you as a man and a brother—*do* you think I could venture to throw a rock here in any given direction without hitting a captain of this ship? "

" Well, sir, I don't know — I think likely you'd fetch the captain of the watch, maybe, because he's a-standing right yonder in the way."

I went below—meditating, and a little down-hearted. I thought, if five cooks can spoil a broth, what may not five captains do with a pleasure excursion.

CHAPTER IV

WE ploughed along bravely for a week or more, and without any conflict of jurisdiction among the captains worth mentioning. The passengers soon learned to accommodate themselves to their new circumstances, and life in the ship became nearly as systematically monotonous as the routine of a barrack. I do not mean that it was dull, for it was not entirely so by any means—but there was a good deal of sameness about it. As is always the fashion at sea, the passengers shortly began to pick up sailor terms—a sign that they were beginning to feel at home. Half-past six was no longer half-past six to these pilgrims from New England, the South, and the Mississippi Valley, it was " seven bells; " eight, twelve and four o'clock were " eight bells; " the captain did not take the longitude at nine o'clock, but at " two bells." They spoke glibly of the " after cabin," the " for'rard cabin," " port and starboard " and the " fo'castle."

At seven bells the first gong rang; at eight there was breakfast, for such as were not too sea-sick to eat it. After that all the well people walked arm-in-arm up and down the long promenade deck, enjoying the fine summer mornings, and the sea-sick ones crawled out and propped themselves up in the lee of the paddle-boxes and ate their dismal tea and toast, and looked wretched. From eleven o'clock until luncheon and from luncheon until dinner at six in the evening, the employments and amusements were various. Some reading was done; and much smoking and sewing, though not by the same parties; there were the monsters of the deep to be looked after and wondered at; strange ships had to be scrutinised through opera-glasses, and sage decisions arrived at concerning them; and more than that, everybody took a personal interest in seeing that the flag was run up and politely dipped three times in response to the salutes of those strangers; in the smoking-room there were always parties of gentlemen playing euchre, draughts, and dominoes, especially dominoes, that delightfully harmless game; and down on the main deck, " for'rard "—for'rard of the chicken-coops and the cattle—we had what was called " horse-billiards." Horse-billiards is a fine game. It affords good, active

The Innocents Abroad

exercise, hilarity, and consuming excitement. It is a mixture of " hop-scotch " and shuffle-board played with a crutch. A large hop-scotch diagram is marked out on the deck with chalk, and each compartment numbered. You stand off three or four steps, with some broad wooden discs before you on the deck, and these you send forward with a vigorous thrust of a long crutch. If a disc stops on a chalk line, it does not count anything. If it stops in division No. 7, it counts 7; in 5, it counts 5, and so on. The game is 100, and four can play at a time. That game would be very simple, played on a stationary floor, but with us, to play it well required science. We had to allow for the reeling of the ship to the right or the left. Very often one made calculations for a heel to the right and the ship did not go that way. The consequence was that that disc missed the whole hop-scotch plan a yard or two, and then there was humiliation on one side and laughter on the other.

When it rained the passengers had to stay in the house, of course—or at least the cabins—and amuse themselves with games, reading, looking out of the windows at the very familiar billows, and talking gossip.

By seven o'clock in the evening dinner was about over; an hour's promenade on the upper deck followed; then the gong sounded and a large majority of the party repaired to the after cabin (upper), a handsome saloon fifty or sixty feet long, for prayers. The unregenerated called this saloon the " Synagogue." The devotions consisted only of two hymns from the Plymouth Collection, and a short prayer, and seldom occupied more than fifteen minutes. The hymns were accompanied by parlour organ music when the sea was smooth enough to allow a performer

The Innocents Abroad

to sit at the instrument without being lashed to his chair.

After prayers the Synagogue shortly took the semblance of a writing-school. The like of that picture was never seen in a ship before. Behind the long dining-tables on either side of the saloon, and scattered from one end to the other of the latter, some twenty or thirty gentlemen and ladies sat them down under the swaying lamps and for two or three hours wrote diligently in their journals. Alas! that journals so voluminously begun should come to so lame and impotent a conclusion as most of them did! I doubt if there is a single pilgrim of all that host but can show a hundred fair pages of journal concerning the first twenty days' voyaging in the *Quaker City;* and I am morally certain that not ten of the party can show twenty pages of journal for the succeeding twenty thousand miles of voyaging! At certain periods it becomes the dearest ambition of a man to keep a faithful record of his performances in a book; and he dashes at this work with an enthusiasm that imposes on him the notion that keeping a journal is the veriest pastime in the world, and the pleasantest. But if he only lives twenty-one days, he will find out that only those rare natures that are made up of pluck, endurance, devotion to duty for duty's sake, and invincible determination, may hope to venture upon so tremendous an enterprise as the keeping of a journal and not sustain a shameful defeat.

One of our favourite youths, Jack, a splendid young fellow, with a head full of good sense, and a pair of legs that were a wonder to look upon in the way of length, and straightness, and slimness, used to report progress every morning in the most glowing and spirited way, and say:

The Innocents Abroad

"Oh, I'm coming along, bully!" (he was a little given to slang, in his happier moods). "I wrote ten pages in my journal last night—and you know I wrote nine the night before, and twelve the night before that. Why, it's only fun!"

"What do you find to put in it, Jack?"

"Oh! everything. Latitude and longitude, noon every day; and how many miles we made last twenty-four hours; and all the domino-games I beat, and horse-billiards; and whales and sharks and porpoises; and the text of the sermon, Sundays (because that'll tell at home, you know); and the ships we saluted, and what nation they were; and which way the wind was, and whether there was a heavy sea, and what sail we carried, though we don't ever carry *any*, principally, going against a head wind always—wonder what is the reason of that?—and how many lies Moult has told—Oh, everything! I've got everything down. My father told me to keep that journal. Father wouldn't take a thousand dollars for it when I get it done."

"No, Jack; it will be worth more than a thousand dollars—when you get it done."

"Do you?—no, but do you think it will, though?"

"Yes, it will be worth at least as much as a thousand dollars—when you get it done. May be, more."

"Well, I about half think so myself. It ain't no slouch of a journal."

But it shortly became a most lamentable "slouch of a journal." One night in Paris, after a hard day's toil in sight-seeing, I said:

"Now I'll go and stroll around the *cafés* awhile, Jack, and give you a chance to write up your journal, old fellow."

His countenance lost its fire. He said:

The Innocents Abroad

" Well, no, you needn't mind.   I think I wont run
that journal any more.   It is awful tedious.   Do you
know—I reckon I'm as much as four thousand pages
behind hand.   I haven't got any France in it at all.
First I thought I'd leave France out and start afresh.
But that wouldn't do, *would* it?   The governor would
say, ' Hello, here—didn't see anything in France? '
That cat wouldn't fight, you know.   First I thought
I'd copy France out of the guide-book, like old Badger
in the for'rard cabin who's writing a book, but there's
more than three hundred pages of it.   Oh, *I* don't
think a journal's any use—do you?   They're only a
bother, *ain't* they? "

" Yes, a journal that is incomplete isn't of much
use, but a journal properly kept is worth a thousand
dollars—when you've got it done."

" A thousand!—well I should think so.   *I* wouldn't
finish it for a million."

His experience was only the experience of the
majority of that industrious night-school in the cabin.
If you wish to inflict a heartless and malignant
punishment upon a young person, pledge him to keep
a journal a year.

A good many expedients were resorted to to keep
the excursionists amused and satisfied.   A club was
formed, of all the passengers, which met in the writing-school after prayers and read aloud about the
countries we were approaching, and discussed the
information so obtained.

Several times the photographer of the expedition
brought out his transparent pictures and gave us a
handsome magic lantern exhibition.   His views were
nearly all of foreign scenes, but there were one or two
home pictures among them.   He advertised that he
would " open his performance in the after-cabin at

The Innocents Abroad

' two bells ' (9 p.m.), and show the passengers where
they shall eventually arrive "—which was all very
well, but by a funny accident the first picture that
flamed out upon the canvas was a view of Greenwood
Cemetery!

On several starlight nights we danced on the upper
deck, under the awnings, and made something of a
ball-room display of brilliancy by hanging a number
of ship's lanterns to the stanchions. Our music consisted of the well-mixed strains of a melodeon which
was a little asthmatic and apt to catch its breath
where it ought to come out strong; a clarionet which
was a little unreliable on the high keys and rather
melancholy on the low ones; and a disreputable
accordion that had a leak somewhere and breathed
louder than it squawked—a more elegant term does
not occur to me just now. However, the dancing
was infinitely worse than the music. When the ship
rolled to starboard the whole platoon of dancers
came charging down to starboard with it, and brought
up in a mass at the rail; and when it rolled to port,
they went floundering down to port with the same
unanimity of sentiment. Waltzers spun around
precariously for a matter of fifteen seconds, and then
went skurrying down to the rail as if they meant to go
overboard. The Virginia reel, as performed on board
the *Quaker City*, had more genuine reel about it than
any reel I ever saw before, and was as full of interest
to the spectator as it was full of desperate chances
and hairbreadth escapes to the participant. We
gave up dancing, finally.

We celebrated a lady's birthday anniversary with
toasts, speeches, a poem, and so forth. We also had
a mock trial. No ship ever went to sea that hadn't
a mock trial on board. The purser was accused of

stealing an overcoat from stateroom No. 10. A judge was appointed; also clerks, a crier of the court, constables, sheriffs; counsel for the State and for the defendant; witnesses were subpoenaed, and a jury empanelled after much challenging. The witnesses were stupid, and unreliable and contradictory, as witnesses always are. The counsel were eloquent, argumentative, and vindictively abusive of each other, as was characteristic and proper. The case was at last submitted, and duly finished by the judge with an absurd decision and a ridiculous sentence.

The acting of charades was tried, on several evenings, by the young gentlemen and ladies in the cabins, and proved the most distinguished success of all the amusement experiments.

An attempt was made to organise a debating club, but it was a failure. There was no oratorical talent in the ship.

We all enjoyed ourselves—I think I can safely say that—but it was in a rather quiet way. We very, very seldom played the piano; we played the flute and the clarionet together, and made good music, too, what there was of it, but we always played the same old tune; it was a very pretty tune—how well I remember it—I wonder when I shall ever get rid of it. We never played either the melodeon or the organ, except at devotions—but I am too fast: young Albert *did* know part of a tune—something about " O Something-Or-Other How Sweet it is to Know that he's his What's-his-Name " (I do not remember the exact title of it, but it was very plaintive, and full of sentiment); Albert played that pretty much all the time, until we contracted with him to restrain himself. But nobody ever sang by moonlight on the upper deck, and the congregational singing at church and prayers was not of a superior order of architecture. I put up with it as long as I could, and then joined in and tried to improve it, but this encouraged young George to join in too, and that made a failure of it; because George's voice was just "turning," and when he was singing a dismal sort of base, it was apt to fly off the handle and startle everybody with a most discordant cackle on the upper notes. George didn't know the tunes, either, which was also a drawback to his performances. I said:

"Come, now, George, *don't* improvise. It looks too egotistical. It will provoke remark. Just stick to 'Coronation,' like the others. It is a good tune— *you* can't improve it any, just off-hand, in this way."

"Why I'm not trying to improve it—and I *am* singing like the others—just as it is in the notes."

And he honestly thought he was, too; and so he had no one to blame but himself when his voice caught on the centre occasionally, and gave him the lockjaw.

There were those among the unregenerated who attributed the unceasing head-winds to our distressing choir-music. There were those who said openly that it was taking chances enough to have such ghastly music going on, even when it was at its best; and that to exaggerate the crime by letting George help, was simply flying in the face of Providence. These said that the choir would keep up their lacerating attempts at melody until they would bring down a storm some day that would sink the ship.

There were even grumblers at the prayers. The executive officer said the Pilgrims had no charity:

"There they are, down there every night at eight bells, praying for fair winds—when they know as well as I do that this is the only ship going east this time of the year, but there's a thousand coming west—

what's a fair wind for us is a *head* wind to them—the Almighty's blowing a fair wind for a thousand vessels, and this tribe wants Him to turn it clear around so as to accommodate *one*,—and she a steamship at that! It ain't good sense, it ain't good reason, it ain't good Christianity, it ain't common human charity. Avast with such nonsense! "

CHAPTER V

TAKING it " by and large," as the sailors say, we had a pleasant ten days' run from New York to the Azores islands—not a fast run, for the distance is only twenty-four hundred miles—but a right pleasant one in the main. True, we had head-winds *all* the time, and several stormy experiences which sent fifty per cent. of the passengers to bed, sick, and made the ship look dismal and deserted—stormy experiences that all will remember who weathered them on the tumbling deck, and caught the vast sheets of spray that every now and then sprang high in air from the weather bow and swept the ship like a thunder-shower; but for the most part we had balmy summer weather, and nights that were even finer than the days. We had the phenomenon of a full moon located just in the same spot in the heavens at the same hour every night. The reason of this singular conduct on the part of the moon did not occur to us at first, but it did afterwards when we reflected that we were gaining about twenty minutes every day, because we were going east so fast—we gained just about enough every day to keep along with the moon. It was becoming an old moon to the friends we had left behind us, but to us Joshuas it stood still in the same place, and remained always the same.

Young Mr. Blucher, who is from the Far West, and is on his first voyage, was a good deal worried by the constantly changing " ship-time." He was proud of his new watch at first, and used to drag it out promptly when eight bells struck at noon, but he came to look after a while as if he were losing confidence in it. Seven days out from New York he came on deck, and said with great decision:

" This thing's a swindle! "

" What's a swindle? "

" Why, this watch. I bought her out in Illinois— gave \$150 for her—and I thought she was good. And, by George, she *is* good on shore, but somehow she don't keep up her lick here on the water—gets sea-sick, may be. She skips; she runs along regular enough till half-past eleven, and then, all of a sudden, she lets down. I've set that old regulator up faster and faster, till I've shoved it clear around, but it don't do any good; she just distances every watch in the ship, and clatters along in a way that's astonishing till it is noon, but them eight bells always gets in about ten minutes ahead of her any way. I don't know what to do with her now. She's doing all she can—she's going her best gait, but it won't save her. Now, don't you know, there ain't a watch in the ship that's making better time than she is: but what does it signify? When you hear them eight bells you'll find her just about ten minutes short of her score—sure."

The ship was gaining a full hour every three days, and this fellow was trying to make his watch go fast enough to keep up to her. But, as he had said, he had pushed the regulator up as far as it would go, and the watch was " on its best gait," and so nothing was left him but to fold his hands and see the ship beat the race. We sent him to the captain, and he explained to him the mystery of "ship-time," and set his troubled mind at rest. This young man asked a great many questions about sea-sickness before we left, and wanted to know what its characteristics were, and how he was to tell when he had it. He found out.

We saw the usual sharks, blackfish, porpoises, &c., of course, and by-and-by large schools of Portuguese men-of-war were added to the regular list of sea-wonders. Some of them were white and some of a brilliant carmine colour. The nautilus is nothing but a transparent web of jelly, that spreads itself to catch the wind, and has fleshy-looking strings a foot or two long dangling from it to keep it steady in the water. It is an accomplished sailor, and has good sailor judgment. It reefs its sail when a storm threatens or the wind blows pretty hard, and furls it entirely and goes down when a gale blows. Ordinarily it keeps its sail wet and in good sailing order by turning over and dipping it in the water for a moment. Seamen say the nautilus is only found in these waters between the 35th and 45th parallels of latitude.

At three o'clock on the morning of the 21st of June we were awakened and notified that the Azores islands were in sight. I said I did not take any interest in islands at three o'clock in the morning. But another persecutor came, and then another and another, and finally, believing that the general enthusiasm would permit no one to slumber in peace, I got up and went sleepily on deck. It was five and a half o'clock now, and a raw, blustering morning. The passengers were huddled about the smoke-stacks, and fortified behind ventilators, and all were wrapped in

wintry costumes, and looking sleepy and unhappy in
the pitiless gale and the drenching spray.

The island in sight was Flores. It seemed only a
mountain of mud standing up out of the dull mists of
the sea. But as we bore down upon it, the sun came
out and made it a beautiful picture—a mass of green
farms and meadows that swelled up to a height of
fifteen hundred feet, and mingled its upper outlines
with the clouds. It was ribbed with sharp, steep
ridges, and cloven with narrow cañons, and here and
there on the heights, rocky upheavals shaped themselves into mimic battlements and castles ; and out
of rifted clouds came broad shafts of sunlight, that
painted summit, and slope, and glen with bands of
fire, and left belts of sombre shade between. It was
the aurora borealis of the frozen pole exiled to a
summer land!

We skirted around two-thirds of the island, four
miles from shore, and all the opera-glasses in the ship
were called into requisition to settle disputes as to
whether mossy spots on the uplands were groves of
trees or groves of weeds, or whether the white villages
down by the sea were really villages or only the clustering tombstones of cemeteries. Finally, we stood to
sea and bore away for San Miguel, and Flores shortly
became a dome of mud again, and sank down among
the mists and disappeared. But to many a sea-sick
passenger it was good to see the green hills again, and
all were more cheerful after this episode than anybody
could have expected them to be, considering how
sinfully early they had gotten up.

But we had to change our purpose about San
Miguel, for a storm came up about noon that so tossed
and pitched the vessel that common sense dictated a
run for shelter. Therefore we steered for the nearest

island of the group—Fayal (the people there pronounce it Fy-all, and put the accent on the first
syllable). We anchored in the open roadstead of
Horta, half a mile from the shore. The town has
8000 to 10,000 inhabitants. Its snow-white houses
nestle cosily in a sea of fresh green vegetation, and no
village could look prettier or more attractive. It
sits in the lap of an amphitheatre of hills which are
300 to 700 feet high, and carefully cultivated clear to
their summits—not a foot of soil left idle. Every
farm and every acre is cut up into little square in-
closures by stone walls, whose duty it is to protect the
growing products from the destructive gales that blow
there. These hundreds of green squares, marked by
their black lava walls, make the hills look like vast
chequer-boards.

The island belongs to Portugal, and everything in
Fayal has Portuguese characteristics about it. But
more of that anon. A swarm of swarthy, noisy, lying,
shoulder-shrugging, gesticulating Portuguese boat-
men, with brass rings in their ears, and fraud in their
hearts, climbed the ship's sides, and various parties
of us contracted with them to take us ashore at so
much a head, silver coin of any country. We landed
under the walls of a little fort, armed with batteries
of twelve and thirty-two pounders, which Horta
considered a most formidable institution, but if we
were ever to get after it with one of our turreted
monitors, they would have to move it out in the
country if they wanted it where they could go and
find it again when they needed it. The group on the
pier was a rusty one—men and women, and boys and
girls, all ragged, and barefoot, uncombed and unclean,
and by instinct, education, and profession, beggars.
They trooped after us, and never more, while we

tarried in Fayal, did we get rid of them. We walked up the middle of the principal street, and these vermin surrounded us on all sides, and glared upon us ; and every moment excited couples shot ahead of the procession to get a good look back, just as village boys do when they accompany the elephant on his advertising trip from street to street. It was very flattering to me to be part of the material for such a sensation. Here and there in the doorways we saw women, with fashionable Portuguese hoods on. This hood is of thick blue cloth, attached to a cloak of the same stuff, and is a marvel of ugliness. It stands up high, and spreads far abroad, and is unfathomably deep. It fits like a circus tent, and a woman's head is hidden away in it like the man's who prompts the singers from his tin shed in the stage of an opera. There is no particle of trimming about this monstrous *capote*, as they call it—it is just a plain, ugly, dead-blue mass of sail, and a woman can't go within eight points of the wind with one of them on; she has to go before the wind or not at all. The general style of the capote is the same in all the islands, and will remain so for the next ten thousand years, but each island shapes its capotes just enough differently from the others to enable an observer to tell at a glance what particular island a lady hails from.

The Portuguese pennies or *reis* (pronounced rays) are prodigious. It takes 1000 reis to make a dollar, and all financial estimates are made in reis. We did not know this until after we had found it out through Blucher. Blucher said he was so happy and so grateful to be on solid land once more, that he wanted to give a feast—said he had heard it was a cheap land, and he was bound to have a grand banquet. He invited nine of us, and we ate an excellent dinner

The Innocents Abroad

at the principal hotel. In the midst of the jollity
produced by good cigars, good wine, and passable
anecdotes, the landlord presented his bill. Blucher
glanced at it and his countenance fell. He took
another look to assure himself that his senses had not
deceived him, and then read the items aloud, in a
faltering voice, while the roses in his cheeks turned
to ashes:—

" ' Ten dinners, at 600 reis, 6000 reis! ' Ruin and
desolation! "

" ' Twenty-five cigars, at 100 reis, 2500 reis! ' Oh,
my sainted mother! "

" ' Eleven bottles of wine, at 1200 reis, 13,200 reis! '
Be with us all! "

" ' TOTAL, TWENTY-ONE THOUSAND SEVEN HUN-
DRED REIS! ' The suffering Moses! — there ain't
money enough in the ship to pay that bill! Go—
leave me to my misery, boys. I am a ruined community."

I think it was the blankest-looking party I ever saw.
Nobody could say a word. It was as if every soul
had been stricken dumb. Wine-glasses descended
slowly to the table, their contents untasted. Cigars
dropped unnoticed from nerveless fingers. Each
man sought his neighbour's eye, but found in it no
ray of hope, no encouragement. At last the fearful
silence was broken. The shadow of a desperate
resolve settled upon Blucher's countenance like a
cloud, and he rose up and said:—

" Landlord, this is a low, mean swindle, and I'll
never, never stand it. Here's a hundred and fifty
dollars, sir, and it's all you'll get—I'll swim in blood
before I'll pay a cent more."

Our spirits rose and the landlord's fell—at least we
thought so; he was confused at any rate, notwith-

standing he had not understood a word that had been said. He glanced from the little pile of gold pieces to Blucher several times, and then went out. He must have visited an American, for, when he returned, he brought back his bill translated into a language that a Christian could understand—thus:—

10 dinners, 6000 reis, or	.	.	.	$6.00
25 cigars, 2500 reis, or	.	.	.	2.50
11 bottles of wine, 13,200 reis, or		.	.	13.20
Total 21,700 reis, or	.	.	.	$21.70

Happiness reigned once more in Blucher's dinner party. More refreshments were ordered.

CHAPTER VI

I THINK the Azores must be very little known in America. Out of our whole ship's company there was not a solitary individual who knew anything whatever about them. Some of the party, well read concerning most other lands, had no other information about the Azores than that they were a group of nine or ten small islands far out in the Atlantic, something more than half way between New York and Gibraltar. That was all. These considerations move me to put in a paragraph of dry facts just here.

The community is eminently Portuguese—that is to say, it is slow, poor, shiftless, sleepy, and lazy. There is a civil governor, appointed by the King of Portugal; and also a military governor, who can assume supreme control and suspend the civil govern-ment at his pleasure. The islands contain a popula-tion of about 200,000, almost entirely Portuguese.

The Innocents Abroad

Everything is staid and settled, for the country was one hundred years old when Columbus discovered America. The principal crop is corn, and they raise it and grind it just as their great-great-great-grand-fathers did. They plough with a board slightly shod with iron; their trifling little harrows are drawn by men and women; small windmills grind the corn, ten bushels a day, and there is one assistant superintendent to feed the mill and a general superintendent to stand by and keep him from going to sleep. When the wind changes they hitch on some donkeys, and actually turn the whole upper half of the mill around until the sails are in proper position, instead of fixing the concern so that the sails could be moved instead of the mill. Oxen tread the wheat from the ear, after the fashion prevalent in the time of Methuselah. There is not a wheelbarrow in the land—they carry everything on their heads, or on donkeys, or in a wicker-bodied cart, whose wheels are solid blocks of wood and whose axles turn with the wheel. There is not a modern plough in the islands, or a threshing-machine. All attempts to introduce them have failed. The good Catholic Portuguese crossed himself and prayed to God to shield him from all blasphemous desire to know more than his father did before him. The climate is mild; they never have snow or ice, and I saw no chimneys in the town. The donkeys and the men, women, and children all eat and sleep in the same room, and are unclean, are ravaged by vermin, and are truly happy. The people lie and cheat the stranger and are desperately ignorant, and have hardly any reverence for their dead. The latter trait shows how little better they are than the donkeys they eat and sleep with. The only well-dressed Portuguese in the camp are the half a dozen well-to-do families, the Jesuit priests, and the soldiers of the little garrison. The wages of a labourer are twenty to twenty-four cents a day, and those of a good mechanic about twice as much. They count it in reis at a thousand to the dollar, and this makes them rich and contented. Fine grapes used to grow in the islands, and an excellent wine was made and exported. But a disease killed all the vines fifteen years ago, and since that time no wine has been made. The islands being wholly of volcanic origin, the soil is necessarily very rich. Nearly every foot of ground is under cultivation, and two or three crops a year of each article are produced, but nothing is exported save a few oranges—chiefly to England. Nobody comes here, and nobody goes away. News is a thing unknown in Fayal. A thirst for it is a passion equally unknown. A Portuguese of average intelligence inquired if our civil war was over?—because, he said, somebody had told him it was, or at least it ran in his mind that somebody had told him something like that! And when a passenger gave an officer of the garrison copies of the *Tribune*, the *Herald*, and *Times*, he was surprised to find later news in them from Lisbon than he had just received by the little monthly steamer. He was told that it came by cable. He said he knew that they had tried to lay a cable ten years ago, but it had been in his mind, somehow, that they hadn't succeeded!

It is in communities like this that Jesuit humbuggery flourishes. We visited a Jesuit cathedral nearly two hundred years old, and found in it a piece of the veritable cross upon which our Saviour was crucified. It was polished and hard, and in as excellent a state of preservation as if the dread tragedy on Calvary had occurred yesterday instead of eighteen centuries ago. But these confiding people believe in that piece of wood unhesitatingly.

In a chapel of the cathedral is an altar with facings of solid silver—at least they call it so, and I think myself it would go a couple of hundred to the ton (to speak after the fashion of the silver miners), and before it is kept for ever burning a small lamp. A devout lady who died, left money and contracted for unlimited masses for the repose of her soul, and also stipulated that this lamp should be kept lighted always, day and night. She did all this before she died, you understand. It is a very small lamp, and a very dim one, and it could not work her much damage, I think, if it went out altogether.

The great altar of the cathedral, and also three or four minor ones, are a perfect mass of gilt gimcracks and gingerbread. And they have a swarm of rusty, dusty, battered apostles standing around the filigree work, some on one leg and some with one eye out, but a gamey look in the other, and some with two or three fingers gone, and some with not enough nose left to blow—all of them crippled and discouraged, and fitter subjects for the hospital than the cathedral.

The walls of the chancel are of porcelain, all pictured over with figures of almost life size, very elegantly wrought, and dressed in the fanciful costumes of two centuries ago. The design was a history of something or somebody, but none of us were learned enough to read the story. The old father, reposing under a stone close by, dated 1686, might have told us if he could have risen. But he didn't.

As we came down through the town, we encountered a squad of little donkeys ready saddled for use. The saddles were peculiar, to say the least. They consisted of a sort of saw-buck, with a small mattress on it, and this furniture covered about half the donkey. There were no stirrups, but really such supports were not needed—to use such a saddle was the next thing to riding a dinner-table—there was ample support clear out to one's knee-joints. A pack of ragged Portuguese muleteers crowded around us, offering their beasts at half a dollar an hour—more rascality to the stranger, for the market price is sixteen cents. Half a dozen of us mounted the ungainly affairs, and submitted to the indignity of making a ridiculous spectacle of ourselves through the principal streets of a town of 10,000 inhabitants.

We started. It was not a trot, a gallop, or a canter, but a stampede, and made up of all conceivable gaits. No spurs were necessary. There was a muleteer to every donkey and a dozen volunteers beside, and they banged the donkeys with their goad-sticks, and pricked them with their spikes, and shouted something that sounded like "*Sekki-yah!*" and kept up a din and a racket that was worse than Bedlam itself. These rascals were all on foot; but no matter, they were always up to time—they can outrun and outlast a donkey. Altogether ours was a lively and a picturesque procession, and drew crowded audiences to the balconies wherever we went.

Blucher could do nothing at all with his donkey. The beast scampered zigzag across the road and the others ran into him; he scraped Blucher against carts and the corners of houses; the road was fenced in with high stone walls, and the donkey gave him a polishing first on one side and then on the other, but never once took the middle; he finally came to the house he was born in and darted into the parlour, scraping Blucher off at the doorway. After remounting, Blucher said to the muleteer, " Now, that's enough, you know; you go slow hereafter." But the fellow knew no English, and did not understand, so he simply said, "*Sekki-yah !*" and the donkey was off again like a shot. He turned a corner suddenly, and Blucher went over his head. And, to speak truly, every mule stumbled over the two, and the whole cavalcade was piled up in a heap. No harm done. A fall from one of those donkeys is of little more consequence than rolling off a sofa. The donkeys all stood still after the catastrophe, and waited for their dismembered saddles to be patched up and put on by the noisy muleteers. Blucher was pretty angry, and wanted to swear, but every time he opened his mouth his animal did so also, and let off a series of brays that drowned all other sounds.

It was fun, skurrying around the breezy hills and through the beautiful cañons. There was that rare thing, novelty, about it; it was a fresh, new, exhilarating sensation, this donkey riding, and worth a hundred worn and threadbare home pleasures.

The roads were a wonder, and well they might be. Here was an island with only a handful of people in it—25,000—and yet such fine roads do not exist in the United States outside of Central Park. Everywhere you go, in any direction, you find either a hard, smooth, level thoroughfare, just sprinkled with black lava sand, and bordered with little gutters neatly paved with small smooth pebbles, or compactly paved ones like Broadway. They talk much of the Russ pavement in New York, and call it a new invention—yet here they have been using it in this remote little isle of the sea for two hundred years! Every street in Horta is handsomely paved with the heavy Russ blocks, and the surface is neat and true as a floor —not marred by holes like Broadway. And every road is fenced in by tall, solid lava walls, which will last a thousand years in this land where frost is unknown. They are very thick, and are often plastered and whitewashed, and capped with projecting slabs of cut stone. Trees from gardens above hang their swaying tendrils down, and contrast their bright green with the whitewash or the black lava of the walls, and make them beautiful. The trees and vines stretch across these narrow roadways sometimes, and so shut out the sun that you seem to be riding through a tunnel. The pavements, the roads, and the bridges are all Government work.

The bridges are of a single span—a single arch—of cut stone, without support, and paved on top with flags of lava and ornamental pebble work. Everywhere are walls, walls, walls, and all of them tasteful and handsome and eternally substantial; and everywhere are those marvellous pavements, so neat, so smooth, and so indestructible. And if ever roads and streets, and the outsides of houses were perfectly free from any sign or semblance of dirt, or dust, or mud, or uncleanliness of any kind, it is Horta, it is Fayal. The lower classes of the people, in their persons and their domiciles, are not clean—but there it stops—the town and the island are miracles of cleanliness.

We arrived home finally, after a ten-mile excursion, and the irrepressible muleteers scampered at our heels through the main street, goading the donkeys, shouting the everlasting " *Sekki-yah*," and singing " John Brown's Body " in ruinous English.

When we were dismounted and it came to settling, the shouting and jawing, and swearing and quarrelling among the muleteers and with us, was nearly deafening. One fellow would demand a dollar an hour for

the use of his donkey; another claimed half a dollar
for pricking him up, another a quarter for helping in
that service, and about fourteen guides presented
bills for showing us the way through the town and
its environs; and every vagrant of them was more
vociferous, and more vehement and more frantic in
gesture than his neighbour. We paid one guide,
and paid for one muleteer to each donkey.

The mountains on some of the islands are very high.
We sailed along the shore of the Island of Pico, under
a stately green pyramid that rose up with one un-
broken sweep from our very feet to an altitude of
7613 feet, and thrust its summit above the white
clouds like an island adrift in a fog!

We got plenty of fresh oranges, lemons, figs,
apricots, etc., in these Azores, of course. But I will
desist. I am not here to write Patent-Office reports.

We are on our way to Gibraltar, and shall reach
there five or six days out from the Azores.

CHAPTER VII

A WEEK of buffeting a tempestuous and relentless
sea; a week of sea-sickness and deserted cabins; of
lonely quarter-decks drenched with spray—spray so
ambitious that it even coated the smoke-stacks thick
with a white crust of salt to their very tops; a week
of shivering in the shelter of the life-boats and deck-
houses by day, and blowing suffocating " clouds "
and boisterously performing at dominoes in the
smoking-room at night.

And the last night of the seven was the stormiest
of all. There was no thunder, no noise but the

pounding bows of the ship, the keen whistling of the gale through the cordage, and the rush of the seething waters. But the vessel climbed aloft as if she would climb to heaven—then paused an instant that seemed a century, and plunged headlong down again, as from a precipice. The sheeted sprays drenched the decks like rain. The blackness of darkness was everywhere. At long intervals a flash of lightning clove it with a quivering line of fire that revealed a heaving world of water where was nothing before, kindled the dusky cordage to glittering silver, and lit up the faces of the men with a ghastly lustre!

Fear drove many on deck that were used to avoiding the night-winds and the spray. Some thought the vessel could not live through the night, and it seemed less dreadful to stand out in the midst of the wild tempest and *see* the peril that threatened than to be shut up in the sepulchral cabins, under the dim lamps and imagine the horrors that were abroad on the ocean. And once out—once where they could see the ship struggling in the strong grasp of the storm—once where they could hear the shriek of the winds, and face the driving spray and look out upon the majestic picture the lightnings disclosed, they were prisoners to a fierce fascination they could not resist, and so remained. It was a wild night—and a very, very long one.

Everybody was sent scampering to the deck at seven o'clock this lovely morning of the 30th of June with the glad news that land was in sight! It was a rare thing and a joyful to see *all* the ship's family abroad once more, albeit the happiness that sat upon every countenance could only partly conceal the ravages which that long siege of storms had wrought there. But dull eyes soon sparkled with

pleasure, pallid cheeks flushed again, and frames
weakened by sickness gathered new life from the
quickening influences of the bright, fresh morning.
Yea, and from a still more potent influence; the
worn castaways were to see the blessed land again!—
and to see it was to bring back that mother-land that
was in all their thoughts.

Within the hour we were fairly within the Straits of
Gibraltar, the tall yellow-splotched hills of Africa on
our right, with their bases veiled in a blue haze and
their summits swathed in clouds—the same being
according to Scripture, which says that "cloud and
darkness are over the land." The words were spoken
of this particular portion of Africa, I believe. On
our left were the granite-ribbed domes of Old Spain.
The Strait is only thirteen miles wide in its narrowest
part.

At short intervals, along the Spanish shore, were
quaint-looking old stone towers—Moorish, we thought
—but learned better afterwards. In former times
the Morocco rascals used to coast along the Spanish
Main in their boats till a safe opportunity seemed to
present itself, and then dart in and capture a Spanish
village, and carry off all the pretty women they could
find. It was a pleasant business, and was very
popular. The Spaniards built these watch-towers
on the hills to enable them to keep a sharper look-
out on the Moroccan speculators.

The picture on the other hand was very beautiful
to eyes weary of the changeless sea, and by-and-
by the ship's company grew wonderfully cheerful.
But while we stood admiring the cloud-capped peaks
and the lowlands robed in misty gloom, a finer picture
burst upon us and chained every eye like a magnet
—a stately ship, with canvas piled on canvas till

The Innocents Abroad

she was one towering mass of bellying sail! She came speeding over the sea like a great bird. Africa and Spain were forgotten. All homage was for the beautiful stranger. While everybody gazed, she swept superbly by and flung the Stars and Stripes to the breeze! Quicker than thought, hats and handkerchiefs flashed in the air, and a cheer went up! She was beautiful before—she was radiant now. Many a one on our decks knew then for the first time how tame a sight his country's flag is at home compared to what it is in a foreign land. To see it is to see a vision of home itself and all its idols, and feel a thrill that would stir a very river of sluggish blood!

We were approaching the famed Pillars of Hercules, and already the African one, "Ape's Hill," a grand old mountain with summit streaked with granite ledges, was in sight. The other, the great Rock of Gibraltar, was yet to come. The ancients considered the Pillars of Hercules the head of navigation and the end of the world. The information the ancients didn't have was very voluminous. Even the prophets wrote book after book and epistle after epistle, yet never once hinted at the existence of a great continent on our side of the water; yet they must have known it was there, I should think.

In a few moments a lonely and enormous mass of rock standing seemingly in the centre of the wide strait, and apparently washed on all sides by the sea, swung magnificently into view, and we needed no tedious travelled parrot to tell us it was Gibraltar. There could not be two rocks like that in one kingdom.

The Rock of Gibraltar is about a mile and a half long, I would say, by 1400 to 1500 feet high, and a quarter of a mile wide at its base. One side and one end of it come about as straight up out of the sea as the side of a house, the other end is irregular, and the other side is a steep slant which an army would find very difficult to climb. At the foot of this slant is the walled town of Gibraltar—or rather the town occupies part of the slant. Everywhere—on hillside, in the precipice, by the sea, on the heights—everywhere you choose to look, Gibraltar is clad with masonry and bristling with guns. It makes a striking and lively picture, from whatsoever point you contemplate it. It is pushed out into the sea on the end of a flat, narrow strip of land, and is suggestive of a " gob " of mud on the end of a shingle. A few hundred yards of this flat ground at its base belong to the English, and then, extending across the strip from the Atlantic to the Mediterranean, a distance of a quarter of a mile, comes the " Neutral Ground," a space two or three hundred yards wide, which is free to both parties.

" Are you going through Spain to Paris? " That question was bandied about the ship day and night from Fayal to Gibraltar, and I thought I never could get so tired of hearing any one combination of words again, or more tired of answering, " I don't know." At the last moment six or seven had sufficient decision of character to make up their minds to go, and did go, and I felt a sense of relief at once—it was for ever too late now, and I could make up my mind at my leisure not to go. I must have a prodigious quantity of mind; it takes me as much as a week, sometimes, to make it up.

But behold how annoyances repeat themselves. We had no sooner gotten rid of the Spain distress than the Gibraltar guides started another—a tiresome repetition of a legend that had nothing very astonishing about it, even in the first place: " That high hill yonder is called the Queen's Chair; it is because one of the Queens of Spain placed her chair there when the French and Spanish troops were besieging Gibraltar, and said she would never move from the spot till the English flag was lowered from the fortresses. If the English hadn't been gallant enough to lower the flag for a few hours one day, she'd have had to break her oath or die up there."

We rode on asses and mules up the steep, narrow streets and entered the subterranean galleries the English have blasted out in the rock. These galleries are like spacious railway tunnels, and at short intervals in them great guns frown out upon sea and town through port-holes five or six hundred feet above the ocean. There is a mile or so of this subterranean work, and it must have cost a vast deal of money and labour. The gallery guns command the peninsula and the harbours of both oceans, but they might as well not be there, I should think, for an army could hardly climb the perpendicular wall of the rock, anyhow. Those lofty port-holes afford superb views of the sea, though. At one place, where a jutting crag was hollowed out into a great chamber whose furniture was huge cannon, and whose windows were port-holes, a glimpse was caught of a hill not far away, and a soldier said—

" That high hill yonder is called the Queen's Chair; it is because a Queen of Spain placed her chair there once, when the French and Spanish troops were besieging Gibraltar, and said she would never move from the spot till the English flag was lowered from the fortresses. If the English hadn't been gallant enough to lower the flag for a few hours one day, she'd have had to break her oath or die up there."

The Innocents Abroad

On the topmost pinnacle of Gibraltar we halted a good while, and no doubt the mules were tired. They had a right to be. The military road was good, but rather steep, and there was a good deal of it. The view from the narrow ledge was magnificent; from it vessels seeming like the tiniest little toy boats, were turned into noble ships by the telescopes; and other vessels that were fifty miles away, and even sixty, they said, and invisible to the naked eye, could be clearly distinguished through those same telescopes. Below, on one side, we looked down upon an endless mass of batteries, and on the other straight down to the sea.

While I was resting ever so comfortably on a rampart, and cooling my baking head in the delicious breeze, an officious guide belonging to another party came up and said—

" Senor, that high hill yonder is called the Queen's Chair——"

" Sir, I am a helpless orphan in a foreign land. Have pity on me. Don't—now *don't* inflict that most in-FERNAL old legend on me any more to-day! "

There—I had used strong language, after promising I would never do so again, but the provocation was more than human nature could bear. If you had been bored so, when you had the noble panorama of Spain and Africa and the blue Mediterranean spread abroad at your feet, and wanted to gaze, and enjoy, and surfeit yourself with its beauty in silence, you might have even burst into stronger language than I did.

Gibraltar has stood several protracted sieges, one of them of nearly four years' duration (it failed), and the English only captured it by stratagem. The wonder is that anybody should ever dream of trying so impossible a project as the taking it by assault—and yet it has been tried more than once.

The Moors held the place twelve hundred years ago, and a staunch old castle of theirs of that date still frowns from the middle of the town, with moss-grown battlements and sides well scarred by shots fired in battles and sieges that are forgotten now. A secret chamber, in the rock behind it, was discovered some time ago, which contained a sword of exquisite workmanship, and some quaint old armour of a fashion that antiquaries are not acquainted with, though it is supposed to be Roman. Roman armour and Roman relics, of various kinds, have been found in a cave in the sea extremity of Gibraltar; history says Rome held this part of the country about the Christian era, and these things seem to confirm the statement.

In that cave, also, are found human bones, crusted with a very thick, stony coating, and wise men have ventured to say that those men not only lived before the flood, but as much as ten thousand years before it. It may be true—it looks reasonable enough—but as long as those parties can't vote any more, the matter can be of no great public interest. In this cave, likewise, are found skeletons and fossils of animals that exist in every part of Africa, yet within memory and tradition have never existed in any portion of Spain save this lone peak of Gibraltar! So the theory is that the channel between Gibraltar and Africa was once dry land, and that the low, neutral neck between Gibraltar and the Spanish hills behind it was once ocean, and of course that these African animals, being over at Gibraltar (after rock, perhaps—there is plenty there), got closed out when the great change occurred. The hills in Africa, across the channel, are full of apes, and there are now, and always have been, apes on the rock of Gibraltar —but not elsewhere in Spain! The subject is an interesting one.

There is an English garrison at Gibraltar of 6000 or 7000 men, and so uniforms of flaming red are plenty; and red and blue, and undress costumes of snowy white, and also the queer uniform of the bare-kneed Highlander; and one sees soft-eyed Spanish girls from San Roque, and veiled Moorish beauties (I suppose they are beauties) from Tarifa, and turbaned, sashed, and trowsered Moorish merchants from Fez, and long-robed, bare-legged, ragged Mohammedan vagabonds from Tetouan and Tangier, some brown, some yellow, and some as black as virgin ink—and Jews from all around, in gaberdine, skull-cap, and slippers, just as they are in pictures and theatres, and just as they were three thousand years ago, no doubt. You can easily understand that a tribe (somehow our pilgrims suggest that expression, because they march in a straggling procession through these foreign places with such an Indian-like air of complacency and independence about them) like ours, made up from fifteen or sixteen States of the Union, found enough to stare at in this shifting panorama of fashion to-day.

Speaking of our pilgrims reminds me that we have one or two people among us who are sometimes an annoyance. However, I do not count the Oracle in that list. I will explain that the Oracle is an innocent old ass who eats for four and looks wiser than the whole Academy of France would have any right to look, and never uses a one-syllable word when he can think of a longer one, and never by any possible chance knows the meaning of any long word he uses, or ever gets it in the right place: yet he will serenely venture an opinion on the most abstruse subject, and back it up complacently with quotations from authors who never existed, and finally when cornered will slide to the other side of the question, say he has been there all the time, and come back at you with your own spoken arguments, only with the big words all tangled, and play them in your very teeth as original with himself. He reads a chapter in the guide-books, mixes the facts all up, with his bad memory, and then goes off to inflict the whole mess on somebody as wisdom which has been festering in his brain for years, and which he gathered in college from erudite authors who are dead now, and out of print. This morning at breakfast, he pointed out of the window and said:

"Do you see that there hill out there on that African coast?—It's one of them Pillows of Herkewls, I should say—and there's the ultimate one alongside of it."

"The ultimate one—that is a good word—but the Pillars are not both on the same side of the strait." (I saw he had been deceived by a carelessly written sentence in the Guide Book.)

"Well, it aint for you to say, nor for me. Some authors states it that way, and some states it different. Old Gibbons don't say nothing about it—just shirks it complete—Gibbons always done that when he got stuck—but there is Rolampton, what does *he* say? Why, he says that they was both on the same side, and Trinculian, and Sobaster, and Syraccus, and Langomarganbl——"

"Oh! that will do—that's enough. If you have got your hand in for inventing authors and testimony,

The Innocents Abroad

I have nothing more to say—let them *be* on the same side."

We don't mind the Oracle. We rather like him. We can tolerate the Oracle very easily; but we have a poet and a good-natured enterprising idiot on board, and they *do* distress the company. The one gives copies of his verses to Consuls, commanders, hotel-keepers, Arabs, Dutch—to anybody, in fact, who will submit to a grievous infliction most kindly meant. His poetry is all very well on shipboard, notwithstanding when he wrote an "Ode to the Ocean in a Storm" in one half-hour, and an "Apostrophe to the Rooster in the Waist of the Ship" in the next, the transition was considered to be rather abrupt; but when he sends an invoice of rhymes to the Governor of Fayal and another to the commander-in-chief and other dignitaries in Gibraltar, with the compliments of the Laureate of the Ship, it is not popular with the passengers.

The other personage I have mentioned is young and green, and not bright, not learned, and not wise. He will be, though, some day, if he recollects the answers to all his questions. He is known about the ship as the "Interrogation Point," and this by constant use has become shortened to "Interrogation." He has distinguished himself twice already. In Fayal they pointed out a hill and told him it was eight hundred feet high and eleven hundred feet long. And they told him there was a tunnel two thousand feet long and one thousand feet high running through the hill, from end to end. He believed it. He repeated it to everybody, discussed it, and read it from his notes. Finally, he took a useful hint from this remark which a thoughtful old pilgrim made:

"Well, yes, it *is* a little remarkable—singular

The Innocents Abroad

tunnel altogether—stands up out of the top of the hill about two hundred feet, and one end of it sticks out of the hill about nine hundred!"

Here in Gibraltar he corners these educated British officers, and badgers them with braggadocio about America and the wonders she can perform. He told one of them a couple of our gunboats could come here and knock Gibraltar into the Mediterranean Sea!

At this present moment, half a dozen of us are taking a private pleasure excursion of our own devising. We form rather more than half the list of white passengers on board a small steamer bound for the venerable Moorish town of Tangier, Africa. Nothing could be more absolutely certain than that we are enjoying ourselves. One cannot do otherwise who speeds over these sparkling waters, and breathes the soft atmosphere of this sunny land. Care cannot assail us here. We are out of its jurisdiction.

We even steamed recklessly by the frowning fortress of Malabat (a stronghold of the Emperor of Morocco) without a twinge of fear. The whole garrison turned out under arms, and assumed a threatening attitude—yet still we did not fear. The entire garrison marched and countermarched, within the rampart, in full view—yet notwithstanding even this, we never flinched.

I suppose we really do not know what fear is. I inquired the name of the garrison of the fortress of Malabat, and they said it was Mehemet Ali Ben Sancom. I said it would be a good idea to get some more garrisons to help him; but they said no; he had nothing to do but hold the place, and he was competent to do that; had done it two years already. That was evidence which one could not well refute. There is nothing like reputation.

The Innocents Abroad

Every now and then my glove purchase in Gibraltar last night intrudes itself upon me. Dan and the ship's surgeon and I had been up to the great square, listening to the music of the fine military bands, and contemplating English and Spanish female loveliness and fashion; and at nine o'clock were on our way to the theatre, when we met the General, the Judge, the Commodore, the Colonel, and the Commissioner

"The whole garrison turned out........"

of the United States of America to Europe, Asia, and Africa, who had been to the Club House, to register their several titles and impoverish the bill of fare; and they told us to go over to the little variety store, near the Hall of Justice, and buy some kid gloves. They said they were elegant, and very moderate in price. It seemed a stylish thing to go to the theatre in kid gloves, and we acted upon the hint. A very handsome young lady in the store offered me a pair of blue gloves. I did not want blue, but she said they would look very pretty on a hand like mine. The remark touched me tenderly. I glanced furtively at my hand, and somehow it did seem a rather comely member. I tried a glove on my left, and blushed a little. Manifestly the size was too small for me. But I felt gratified when she said:

" Oh, it is just right! "—yet I knew it was no such thing.

I tugged at it diligently, but it was discouraging work. She said:

" Ah! I see *you* are accustomed to wearing kid gloves—but some gentlemen are *so* awkward about putting them on."

It was the last compliment I had expected. I only understand putting on the buckskin article perfectly. I made another effort, and tore the glove from the base of the thumb into the palm of the hand, and tried to hide the rent. She kept up her compliments, and I kept up my determination to deserve them or die.

" Ah, you have had experience! " [A rip down the back of the hand.] " They are just right for you —your hand is very small—if they tear you need not pay for them." [A rent across the middle.] " I can always tell when a gentleman understands putting on kid gloves. There is a grace about it that only comes with long practice." [The whole after-guard of the glove " fetched away," as the sailors say, the fabric parted across the knuckles, and nothing was left but a melancholy ruin.]

I was too much flattered to make an exposure, and throw the merchandise on the angel's hands. I was hot, vexed, confused, but still happy; but I hated the other boys for taking such an absorbing interest in the proceedings. I wished they were in Jericho. I felt exquisitely mean when I said, cheerfully :

The Innocents Abroad

" This one does very well: it fits elegantly. I like a glove that fits. No, never mind, ma'am, never mind; I'll put the other on in the street. It is warm here."

It *was* warm. It was the warmest place I ever was in. I paid the bill, and as I passed out with a fascinating bow, I thought I detected a light in the woman's eye that was gently ironical; and when I looked back from the street, and she was laughing all to herself about something or other, I said to myself, with withering sarcasm, " Oh, certainly; *you* know how to put on kid gloves, don't you?—a self-complacent ass, ready to be flattered out of your senses by every petticoat that chooses to take the trouble to do it! "

The silence of the boys annoyed me. Finally, Dan said, musingly:

" Some gentlemen don't know how to put on kid gloves at all; but some do."

And the doctor said (to the moon I thought)—

" But it is always easy to tell when a gentleman is used to putting on kid gloves."

Dan soliloquised, after a pause:

" Ah, yes; there is a grace about it that only comes with long, very long practice."

" Yes, indeed, I've noticed that when a man hauls on a kid glove as if he was dragging a cat out of an ash-hole by the tail, *he* understands putting on kid gloves; *he's* had ex——"

" Boys, enough of a thing's enough! You think you are very smart, I suppose, but I don't. And if you go and tell any of those old gossips in the ship about this thing, I'll never forgive you for it; that's all."

They let me alone, for the time being. We always let each other alone in time to prevent ill feeling from spoiling a joke. But they had bought gloves, too, as I did. We threw all the purchases away together this morning. They were coarse, unsubstantial, freckled all over with broad yellow splotches, and could neither stand wear nor public exhibition. We had entertained an angel unawares, but we did not take her in. She did that for us.

Tangier! A tribe of stalwart Moors are wading into the sea to carry us ashore on their backs from the small boats.

CHAPTER VIII

THIS is royal! Let those who went up through Spain make the best of it—these dominions of the Emperor of Morocco suit our little party well enough. We have had enough of Spain at Gibraltar for the present. Tangier is the spot we have been longing for all the time. Elsewhere we have found foreign-looking things and foreign-looking people, but always with things and people intermixed that we were familiar with before, and so the novelty of the situation lost a deal of its force. We wanted something thoroughly and uncompromisingly foreign—foreign from top to bottom—foreign from centre to circumference—foreign inside and outside and all around—nothing anywhere about it to dilute its foreignness—nothing to remind us of any other people or any other land under the sun. And lo! in Tangier we have found it. Here is not the slightest thing that ever we have seen save in pictures—and we always mistrusted the pictures before. We cannot any more. The pictures used to seem exaggerations—they seemed too weird and fanciful for reality. But behold, they were not wild enough—they were not fanciful enough —they have not told half the story. Tangier is a foreign land if ever there was one; and the true spirit of it can never be found in any book save the Arabian Nights. Here are no white men visible, yet swarms of humanity are all about us. Here is a packed and jammed city enclosed in a massive stone wall which is more than a thousand years old. All the houses nearly are one and two-story; made of thick walls of stone; plastered outside; square as a dry-goods box; flat as a floor on top; no cornices; whitewashed all over—a crowded city of snowy tombs! And the doors are arched with the peculiar arch we see in Moorish pictures ; the floors are laid in vari-coloured diamond-flags; in tesselated many-coloured porcelain squares wrought in the furnaces of Fez; in red tiles and broad bricks that time cannot wear; there is no furniture in the rooms (of Jewish dwellings) save divans—what there is in Moorish ones no man may know; within their sacred walls no Christian dog can enter. And the streets are Oriental—some of them three feet wide, some six, but only two that are over a dozen; a man can blockade the most of them by extending his body across them. Isn't it an Oriental picture?

There are stalwart Bedouins of the desert here, and stately Moors, proud of a history that goes back to the night of time; and Jews, whose fathers fled hither centuries upon centuries ago; and swarthy Riffians from the mountains—born cut-throats—and original, genuine negroes, as black as Moses; and howling dervishes, and a hundred breeds of Arabs— all sorts and descriptions of people that are foreign and curious to look upon.

The Innocents Abroad

And their dresses are strange beyond all description.
Here is a bronzed Moor in a prodigious white turban,
curiously embroidered jacket, gold and crimson sash
of many folds, wrapped round and round his waist,
trowsers that only come a little below his knee, and
yet have twenty yards of stuff in them, ornamented
scimetar, bare shins, stockingless feet, yellow slippers,
and gun of preposterous length—a mere soldier!—I
thought he was the Emperor at least. And here are
aged Moors with flowing white beards, and long white
robes with vast cowls; and Bedouins with long,
cowled, striped cloaks, and negroes and Riffians with
heads clean-shaven, except a kinky scalp-lock back
of the ear, or rather up on the after corner of the skull,
and all sorts of barbarians in all sorts of weird costumes, and all more or less ragged. And here are
Moorish women who are enveloped from head to foot
in coarse white robes, and whose sex can only be
determined by the fact that they only leave one eye
visible, and never look at men of their own race, or
are looked at by them in public. Here are five
thousand Jews in blue gaberdines, sashes about their
waists, slippers upon their feet, little skull-caps upon
the backs of their heads, hair combed down on the
forehead, and cut straight across the middle of it
from side to side—the self-same fashion their Tangier
ancestors have worn for I don't know how many
bewildering centuries. Their feet and ankles are
bare. Their noses are all hooked, and hooked alike.
They all resemble each other so much that one could
almost believe they were of one family. Their
women are plump and pretty, and do smile upon
a Christian in a way which is in the last degree
comforting.

What a funny old town it is! It seems like profanation to laugh, and jest, and bandy the frivolous chat of our day amid its hoary relics. Only the stately phraseology and the measured speech of the sons of the Prophet are suited to a venerable antiquity like this. Here is a crumbling wall that was old when Columbus discovered America; was old when Peter the Hermit roused the knightly men of the Middle Ages to arm for the first Crusade; was old when Charlemagne and his paladins beleaguered enchanted castles and battled with giants and genii in the fabled days of the olden times; was old when Christ and his disciples walked the earth; stood where it stands to-day when the lips of Memnon were vocal and men bought and sold in the streets of ancient Thebes!

The Phœnicians, the Carthaginians, the English, Moors, Romans, all have battled for Tangier—all have won it and lost it. Here is a ragged, Oriental-looking negro from some desert place in interior Africa, filling his goat-skin with water from a stained and battered fountain built by the Romans twelve hundred years ago. Yonder is a ruined arch of a bridge built by Julius Cæsar nineteen hundred years ago. Men who had seen the infant Saviour in the Virgin's arms have stood upon it, may be.

Near it are the ruins of a dockyard where Cæsar repaired his ships and loaded them with grain when he invaded Britain, fifty years before the Christian era.

Here, under the quiet stars, these old streets seem thronged with the phantoms of forgotten ages. My eyes are resting upon a spot where stood a monument which was seen and described by Roman historians less than two thousand years ago, whereon was inscribed:

" WE ARE THE CANAANITES. WE ARE THEY THAT

HAVE BEEN DRIVEN OUT OF THE LAND OF CANAAN BY
THE JEWISH ROBBER, JOSHUA."

Joshua drove them out, and they came here. Not
many leagues from here is a tribe of Jews whose
ancestors fled thither after an unsuccessful revolt
against King David, and these their descendants are
still under a ban and keep to themselves.

Tangier has been mentioned in history for three
thousand years. And it was a town, though a queer
one, when Hercules, clad in his lion-skin, landed here,
four thousand years ago. In these streets he met
Anitus, the king of the country, and brained him with
his club, which was the fashion among gentlemen in
those days. The people of Tangier (called Tingis
then) lived in the rudest possible huts, and dressed
in skins and carried clubs, and were as savage as the
wild beasts they were constantly obliged to war with.
But they were a gentlemanly race, and did no work.
They lived on the natural products of the land. Their
king's country residence was at the famous Garden of
Hesperides, seventy miles down the coast from here.
The garden, with its golden apples (oranges) is gone
now—no vestige of it remains. Antiquarians con-
cede that such a personage as Hercules did exist in
ancient times, and agree that he was an enterprising
and energetic man, but decline to believe him a good
bonâ fide god, because that would be unconstitutional.

Down here at Cape Spartel is the celebrated cave
of Hercules, where that hero took refuge when he was
vanquished and driven out of the Tangier country.
It is full of inscriptions in the dead languages, which
fact makes me think Hercules could not have travelled
much, else he would not have kept a journal.

Five days' journey from here—say two hundred
miles—are the ruins of an ancient city, of whose

history there is neither record nor tradition. And yet its arches, its columns, and its statues proclaim it to have been built by an enlightened race.

The general size of a store in Tangier is about that of an ordinary shower-bath in a civilised land. The Mohammedan merchant, tinman, shoemaker, or vendor of trifles, sits cross-legged on the floor, and reaches after any article you may want to buy. You can rent a whole block of these pigeon-holes for fifty dollars a month. The market people crowd the market place with their baskets of figs, dates, melons, apricots, etc., and among them file trains of laden asses, not much larger, if any, that a Newfoundland dog. The scene is lively, is picturesque, and smells like a police court. The Jewish money-changers have their dens close at hand; and all day long are counting bronze coins and transferring them from one bushel basket to another. They don't coin much money now-a-days I think. I saw none but what was dated four or five hundred years back, and was badly worn and battered. These coins are not very valuable. Jack went out to get a Napoleon changed, so as to have money suited to the general cheapness of things, and came back and said he had " swamped the bank; had bought eleven quarts of coin, and the head of the firm had gone on the street to negotiate for the balance of the change.'' I bought nearly half a pint of their money for a shilling myself. I am not proud on account of having so much money, though. I care nothing for wealth.

The Moors have some small silver coins, and also some silver slugs worth a dollar each. The latter are exceedingly scarce—so much so, that when poor ragged Arabs see one they beg to be allowed to kiss it.

They have also a small gold coin worth two dollars. And that reminds me of something. When Morocco is in a state of war, Arab couriers carry letters through the country, and charge a liberal postage. Every now and then they fall into the hands of marauding bands and get robbed. Therefore, warned by experience, as soon as they have collected two dollars' worth of money they exchange it for one of those little gold pieces, and when robbers come upon them, swallow it. The stratagem was good while it was unsuspected, but after that the marauders simply gave the sagacious United States mail an emetic and sat down to wait.

The Emperor of Morocco is a soulless despot, and the great officers under him are despots on a smaller scale. There is no regular system of taxation, but when the Emperor or the Bashaw want money, they levy on some rich man, and he has to furnish the cash or go to prison. Therefore, few men in Morocco dare to be rich. It is too dangerous a luxury. Vanity occasionally leads a man to display wealth, but sooner or later the Emperor trumps up a charge against him —any sort of one will do—and confiscates his property. Of course, there are many rich men in the empire, but their money is buried, and they dress in rags and counterfeit poverty. Every now and then the Emperor imprisons a man who is suspected of the crime of being rich, and makes things so uncomfortable for him that he is forced to discover where he has hidden his money.

Moors and Jews sometimes place themselves under the protection of the foreign consuls, and then they can flout their riches in the Emperor's face with impunity.

The Innocents Abroad

CHAPTER IX

ABOUT the first adventure we had yesterday afternoon
after landing here, came near finishing that heedless
Blucher. We had just mounted some mules and asses
and started out under the guardianship of the stately,
the princely, the magnificent Hadji Mohammed
Lamarty (may his tribe increase!) when we came upon
a fine Moorish mosque, with tall tower, rich with
checker-work of many-coloured porcelain, and every
part and portion of the edifice adorned with the quaint
architecture of the Alhambra, and Blucher started to
ride into the open doorway. A startling " Hi-hi! "
from our camp-followers, and a loud " Halt! " from
an English gentleman in the party, checked the
adventurer, and then we were informed that so dire
a profanation is it for a Christian dog to set foot upon
the sacred threshold of a Moorish mosque, that no
amount of purification can ever make it fit for the
faithful to pray in again. Had Blucher succeeded
in entering the place, he would no doubt have been
chased through the town and stoned; and the time
has been, and not many years ago either, when a
Christian would have been ruthlessly slaughtered, if
captured in a mosque. We caught a glimpse of the
handsome tesselated pavements within, and of the
devotees performing their ablutions at the fountains;
but even that we took that glimpse was a thing not
relished by the Moorish bystanders.

Some years ago the clock in the tower of the mosque
got out of order. The Moors of Tangier have so
degenerated that it has been long since there was an
artificer among them capable of curing so delicate a

patient as a debilitated clock. The great men of the city met in solemn conclave to consider how the difficulty was to be met. They discussed the matter thoroughly, but arrived at no solution. Finally, a patriarch arose and said—

" Oh, children of the Prophet, it is known unto you that a Portuguese dog of a Christian clock-mender pollutes the city of Tangier with his presence. Ye know also that when the mosques are builded, asses bear the stones and the cement, and cross the sacred threshold. Now, therefore, send the Christian dog on all fours, and barefoot, into the holy place to mend the clock, and let him go as an ass! "

And in that way it was done. Therefore, if Blucher ever sees the inside of a mosque, he will have to cast aside his humanity and go in his natural character. We visited the gaol, and found Moorish prisoners making mats and baskets. (This thing of utilising crime savours of civilisation.) Murder is punished with death. A short time ago three murderers were taken beyond the city walls and shot. Moorish guns are not good, and neither are Moorish marksmen. In this instance, they set up the poor criminals at long range, like so many targets, and practised on them— kept them hopping about and dodging bullets for half an hour before they managed to drive the centre.

When a man steals cattle, they cut off his right hand and left leg, and nail them up in the market-place as a warning to everybody. Their surgery is not artistic. They slice round the bone a little, then break off the limb. Sometimes the patient gets well; but as a general thing he don't. However, the Moorish heart is stout. The Moors were always brave. These criminals undergo the fearful operation without a wince, without a tremor of any kind, without a groan! No amount of suffering can bring down the pride of a Moor, or make him shame his dignity with a cry.

Here marriage is contracted by the parents of the parties to it. There are no valentines, no stolen interviews, no riding out, no courting in dim parlours, no lovers' quarrels and reconciliations—no nothing that is proper to approaching matrimony. The young man takes the girl his father selects for him, marries her, and after that she is unveiled, and he sees her for the first time. If after due acquaintance she suits him, he retains her; but if he suspects her purity, he bundles her back to her father; if he finds her diseased, the same; or if, after just and reasonable time is allowed her, she neglects to bear children, back she goes to the home of her childhood.

Mohammedans here, who can afford it, keep a good many wives on hand. They are called wives, though I believe the Koran only allows four genuine wives—the rest are concubines. The Emperor of Morocco don't know how many wives he has, but thinks he has five hundred. However, that is near enough—a dozen or so, one way or the other, don't matter.

Even the Jews in the interior have a plurality of wives.

I have caught a glimpse of the faces of several Moorish women (for they are only human, and will expose their faces for the admiration of a Christian dog when no male Moor is by), and I am full of veneration for the wisdom that leads them to cover up such atrocious ugliness.

They carry their children at their backs, in a sack, like other savages the world over.

Many of the negroes are held in slavery by the Moors. But the moment a female slave becomes her master's concubine her bonds are broken, and as soon as a male slave can read the first chapter of the Koran (which contains the creed) he can no longer be held in bondage.

They have three Sundays a week in Tangier. The Mohammedans' comes on Friday, the Jews' on Saturday, and that of the Christian Consuls on Sunday. The Jews are the most radical. The Moor goes to his mosque about noon on his Sabbath, as on any other day, removes his shoes at the door, performs his ablutions, makes his salaams, pressing his forehead to the pavement time and again, says his prayers, and goes back to his work.

But the Jew shuts up shop; will not touch copper or bronze money at all; soils his fingers with nothing meaner than silver and gold; attends the synagogue devoutly; will not cook or have anything to do with fire; and religiously refrains from embarking on any enterprise.

The Moor who has made a pilgrimage to Mecca is entitled to high distinction. Men call him Hadji, and he is thenceforward a great personage. Hundreds of Moors come to Tangier every year, and embark for Mecca. They go part of the way in English steamers; and the ten or twelve dollars they pay for passage is about all the trip costs. They take with them a quantity of food, and when the commissary department fails, they "skirmish," as Jack terms it in his sinful, slangy way. From the time they leave till they get home again, they never wash, either on land or sea. They are usually gone from five to seven months, and as they do not change their clothes during all that time, they are totally unfit for the drawing-room when they get back.

Many of them have to rake and scrape a long time

to gather together the ten dollars their steamer passage costs; and when one of them gets back he is a bankrupt for ever after. Few Moors can ever build up their fortunes again in one short lifetime, after so reckless an outlay. In order to confine the dignity of Hadji to gentlemen of patrician blood and possessions, the Emperor decreed that no man should make the pilgrimage save bloated aristocrats who were worth a hundred dollars in specie. But behold how iniquity can circumvent the law! For a consideration the Jewish money-changer lends the pilgrim one hundred dollars long enough for him to swear himself through, and then receives it back before the ship sails out of the harbour!

Spain is the only nation the Moors fear. The reason is, that Spain sends her heaviest ships of war and her loudest guns to astonish these Moslems; while America and other nations send only a little contemptible tub of a gun-boat occasionally. The Moors, like other savages, learn by what they see; not what they hear or read. We have great fleets in the Mediterranean, but they seldom touch at African ports. The Moors have a small opinion of England, France, and America, and put their representatives to a deal of red tape circumlocution before they grant them their common rights, let alone a favour. But the moment the Spanish minister makes a demand, it is acceded to at once, whether it be just or not.

Spain chastised the Moors five or six years ago, about a disputed piece of property opposite Gibraltar, and captured the city of Tetouan. She compromised on an augmentation of her territory, twenty million dollars indemnity in money, and peace. And then she gave up the city. But she never gave it up until the Spanish soldiers had eaten up all the cats. They would not compromise as long as the cats held out. Spaniards are very fond of cats. On the contrary, the Moors reverence cats as something sacred. So the Spaniards touched them on a tender point that time. Their unfeline conduct in eating up all the Tetouan cats aroused a hatred toward them in the breasts of the Moors, to which even the driving them out of Spain was tame and passionless. Moors and Spaniards are foes for ever now. France had a minister here once who embittered the nation against him in the most innocent way. He killed a couple of battalions of cats (Tangier is full of them) and made a parlour carpet out of their hides. He made his carpet in circles—first a circle of old grey tom-cats, with their tails all pointing towards the centre; then a circle of yellow cats; next a circle of black cats and a circle of white ones; then a circle of all sorts of cats; and, finally, a centre-piece of assorted kittens. It was very beautiful; but the Moors curse his memory to this day.

When we went to call on our American Consul-General to-day, I noticed that all possible games for parlour amusement seemed to be represented on his centre-tables. I thought that hinted at lonesomeness. The idea was correct. His is the only American family in Tangier. There are many foreign Consuls in this place, but much visiting is not indulged in. Tangier is clear out of the world; and what is the use of visiting when people have nothing on earth to talk about? There is none. So each Consul's family stays at home chiefly, and amuses itself as best it can. Tangier is full of interest for one day, but after that it is a weary prison. The Consul-General has been here five years, and has got enough of it to do him for a century, and is going home shortly. His family seize upon their letters and papers when the mail arrives, read them over and over again for two days or three, talk them over and over again for two or three more, till they wear them out, and after that, for days together, they eat and drink and sleep, and ride out over the same old road, and see the same old tiresome things that even decades of centuries have scarcely changed, and say never a single word! They have literally nothing whatever to talk about. The arrival of an American man-of-war is a godsend to them. "Oh, Solitude! where are the charms which sages have seen in thy face?" It is the completest exile that I can conceive of. I would seriously recommend to the Government of the United States, that when a man commits a crime so heinous that the law provides no adequate punishment for it, they make him Consul-General to Tangier.

I am glad to have seen Tangier—the second oldest town in the world. But I am ready to bid it good-by, I believe.

We shall go hence to Gibraltar this evening or in the morning; and doubtless the *Quaker City* will sail from that port within the next forty-eight hours.

CHAPTER X

WE passed the Fourth of July on board the *Quaker City* in mid-ocean. It was in all respects a characteristic Mediterranean day—faultlessly beautiful. A cloudless sky; a refreshing summer wind; a radiant sunshine that glinted cheerily from dancing wavelets instead of crested mountains of water; a sea beneath us that was so wonderfully blue, so richly, brilliantly blue, that it overcame the dullest sensibilities with the spell of its fascination.

They even have fine sunsets on the Mediterranean— a thing that is certainly rare in most quarters of the globe. The evening we sailed away from Gibraltar, that hard-featured rock was swimming in a creamy mist so rich, so soft, so enchantingly vague and dreamy, that even the Oracle, that serene, that inspired, that overpowering humbug, scorned the dinner-gong and tarried to worship!

He said, " Well, that's gorgis, ain't it! They don't have none of them things in our parts, *do* they? I consider that them effects is on account of the superior refragability, as you may say, of the sun's diramic combination with the lymphatic forces of the perihelion of Jubiter. What should you think? "

" Oh, *go* to bed! " Dan said that, and went away.

" Oh, yes, it's all very well to say go to bed when a man makes an argument which another man can't answer. Dan don't never stand any chance in an argument with me. And he knows it too. What should you say, Jack? "

" Now, doctor, don't you come bothering around me with that dictionary bosh. I don't do you any harm, do I? Then you let *me* alone."

" He's gone too. Well, them fellows have all tackled the old Oracle, as they say, but the old man's most too many for 'em. Maybe the Poet Lariat ain't satisfied with them deductions? "

The poet replied with a barbarous rhyme, and went below.

" 'Pears that *he* can't qualify, neither. Well, I didn't expect nothing out of *him*. I never see one of them poets yet that knowed anything. He'll go down now, and grind out about four reams of the awfullest slush about that old rock, and give it to a consul, or a pilot, or a nigger, or anybody he comes across first which he can impose on. Pity but somebody'd take that poor old lunatic and dig all that poetry rubbage out of him. Why can't a man put his intellect onto things that's some value? Gibbons, and Hippocratus, and Sarcophagus, and all them old ancient philosophers, was down on poets——"

"Doctor," I said, "you are going to invent authorities, now, and I'll leave you too. I always enjoy your conversation, notwithstanding the luxuriance of your syllables, when the philosophy you offer rests on your own responsibility; but when you begin to soar—when you begin to support it with the evidence of authorities who are the creations of your own fancy, I lose confidence."

That was the way to flatter the doctor. He considered it a sort of acknowledgment on my part of a fear to argue with him. He was always persecuting the passengers with abstruse propositions framed in language that no man could understand, and they endured the exquisite torture a minute or two and then abandoned the field. A triumph like this, over half a dozen antagonists, was sufficient for one day; from that time forward he would patrol the decks beaming blandly upon all comers, and so tranquilly, blissfully happy!

But I digress. The thunder of our two brave cannon announced the Fourth of July, at daylight, to all who were awake. But many of us got our information at a later hour, from the almanac. All the flags were sent aloft, except half a dozen that were needed to decorate portions of the ship below, and in a short time the vessel assumed a holiday appearance. During the morning meetings were held and all manner of committees set to work on the celebration ceremonies. In the afternoon the ship's company assembled aft, on deck, under the awnings; the flute, the asthmatic melodeon, and the consumptive clarionet crippled the "Star Spangled Banner," the choir chased it to cover, and George came in with a peculiarly lacerating screech on the final note and slaughtered it. Nobody mourned.

We carried out the corpse on three cheers (that joke was not intentional and I do not indorse it), and then the President, throned behind a cable-locker with a national flag spread over it, announced the "Reader," who rose up and read that same old Declaration of Independence which we have all listened to so often without paying any attention to what it said; and after that the President piped the Orator of the Day to quarters, and he made that same old speech about our national greatness which we so religiously believe and so fervently applaud. Now came the choir into court again, with the complaining instruments, and assaulted "Hail Columbia"; and when victory hung wavering in the scale, George returned with his dreadful wild-goose stop turned on, and the choir won of course. A minister pronounced the benediction, and the patriotic little gathering disbanded. The Fourth of July was safe, as far as the Mediterranean was concerned.

At dinner in the evening, a well-written original poem was recited with spirit by one of the ship's captains, and thirteen regular toasts were washed down with several baskets of champagne. The speeches were bad—execrable, almost without exception. In fact, without *any* exception, but one. Captain Duncan made a good speech; he made the only good speech of the evening. He said—

The Innocents Abroad

" LADIES AND GENTLEMEN,—May we all live to a green old age, and be prosperous and happy. Steward, bring up another basket of champagne."

It was regarded as a very able effort.

The festivities, so to speak, close with another of those miraculous balls on the promenade deck. We were not used to dancing on an even keel, though, and it was only a questionable success. But take it altogether, it was a bright, cheerful, pleasant Fourth.

Towards nightfall the next evening we steamed into the great artificial harbour of this noble city of Marseilles, and saw the dying sunlight gild its clustering spires and ramparts, and flood its leagues of environing verdure with a mellow radiance that touched with an added charm the white villas that flecked the landscape far and near. [Copyright secured according to law.]

There were no stages out, and we could not get on the pier from the ship. It was annoying. We were full of enthusiasm—we wanted to see France! Just at nightfall our party of three contracted with a waterman for the privilege of using his boat as a bridge—its stern was at our companion ladder and its bow touched the pier. We got in and the fellow backed out into the harbour. I told him in French that all we wanted was to walk over his thwarts and step ashore, and asked him what he went away out there for? He said he could not understand me. I repeated. Still he could not understand. He appeared to be very ignorant of French. The doctor tried him, but he could not understand the doctor. I asked this boatman to explain his conduct, which he did; and then I couldn't understand *him*. Dan said—

81

The Innocents Abroad

" Oh, go to the pier, you old fool—that's where we want to go!"

We reasoned calmly with Dan that it was useless to speak to this foreigner in English—that he had better let us conduct this business in the French language and not let the stranger see how uncultivated he was.

" Well, go on, go on," he said, " don't mind me.   I

"He appeared to be very ignorant of French"

don't wish to interfere. Only, if you go on telling him in your kind of French he never will find out where we want to go to. That is what I think about it."

We rebuked him severely for this remark, and said we never knew an ignorant person yet but was prejudiced. The Frenchman spoke again, and the doctor said—

" There now, Dan, he says he is going to *allez* to the *douane*. Means he is going to the hotel. Oh, certainly—*we* don't know the French language."

The Innocents Abroad

This was a crusher, as Jack would say. It silenced further criticism from the disaffected member. We coasted past the sharp bows of a navy of great steamships, and stopped at last at a government building on a stone pier. It was easy to remember then, that the *douane* was the custom-house, and not the hotel. We did not mention it, however. With winning French politeness, the officers merely opened and closed our satchels, declined to examine our passports, and sent us on our way. We stopped at the first *café* we came to, and entered. An old woman seated us at a table and waited for orders. The doctor said—

"Avez-vous du vin?"

The dame looked perplexed. The doctor said again, with elaborate distinctness of articulation—

"Avez-vous du—vin!"

The dame looked more perplexed than before. I said—

"Doctor, there is a flaw in your pronunciation somewhere. Let me try her. Madame, avez-vous du vin? It isn't any use, doctor—take the witness."

"Madame, avez-vous du vin—ou fromage—pain —pickled pigs' feet—beurre—des œfs—du beuf— horse-radish, sourcrout, hog and hominy—anything, *anything* in the world that will stay a Christian stomach!"

She said—

"Bless you! why didn't you speak English before? —I don't know anything about your plagued French!"

The humiliating taunts of the disaffected member spoiled the supper, and we despatched it in angry silence and got away as soon as we could. Here we were in beautiful France — in a vast storehouse of quaint architecture—surrounded by all manner of curiously-worded French signs — stared at by strangelyhabited, bearded French people—everything gradually and surely forcing upon us the coveted consciousness that at last, and beyond all question we *were* in beautiful France, and absorbing its nature to the forgetfulness of everything else, and coming to feel the happy romance of the thing in all its enchanting delightfulness—and to think of this skinny veteran intruding with her vile English, at such a moment, to blow the fair vision to the winds! It was exasperating.

We set out to find the centre of the city, inquiring the direction every now and then. We never did succeed in making anybody understand just exactly what we wanted, and neither did we ever succeed in comprehending just exactly what they said in reply; but then they always pointed—they always did that—and we bowed politely and said " Merci, Monsieur," and so it was a blighted triumph over the disaffected member, any way. He was restive under these victories and often asked—

" What did that pirate say ? "

" Why, he told us which way to go to find the Grand Casino."

" Yes, but what did he *say* ? "

" Oh, it don't matter what he said—*we* understood him. These are educated people — not like that absurd boatman."

" Well, I wish they were educated enough to tell a man a direction that goes *some* where—for we've been going around in a circle for an hour. I've passed this same old drug store seven times."

We said it was a low, disreputable falsehood (but we knew it was not). It was plain that it would not do to pass that drug store again, though—we might go on asking directions, but we must cease from

following finger-pointings if we hoped to check the
suspicions of the disaffected member.

A long walk through smooth, asphaltum-paved
streets bordered by blocks of vast new mercantile
houses of cream-coloured stone—every house and
every block precisely like all the other houses and all
the other blocks for a mile, and all brilliantly lighted—
brought us at last to the principal thoroughfare. On
every hand were bright colours, flashing constellations
of gas-burners, gaily dressed men and women thronging the side-walks—hurry, life, activity, cheerfulness,
conversation, and laughter everywhere! We found
the Grand Hôtel du Louvre et de la Paix, and wrote
down who we were, where we were born, what our
occupations were, the place we came from last,
whether we were married or single, how we liked it,
how old we were, where we were bound for and when
we expected to get there, and a great deal of information of similar importance—all for the benefit of the
landlord and the secret police. We hired a guide
and began the business of sight-seeing immediately.
That first night on French soil was a stirring one. I
cannot think of half the places we went to, or what
we particularly saw; we had no disposition to examine
carefully into anything at all—we only wanted to
glance and go—to move, keep moving! The spirit of
the country was upon us. We sat down finally, at a
late hour, in the great Casino, and called for unstinted
champagne. It is so easy to be bloated aristocrats
where it costs nothing of consequence! There were
about five hundred people in that dazzling place, I
suppose, though the walls being papered entirely with
mirrors, so to speak, one could not really tell but that
there were a hundred thousand. Young, daintily
dressed exquisites, and young, stylishly dressed

women, and also old gentlemen and old ladies, sat in couples and groups about innumerable marble-topped tables, and ate fancy suppers, drank wine, and kept up a chattering din of conversation that was dazing to the senses. There was a stage at the far end, and a large orchestra; and every now and then actors and actresses in preposterous comic dresses came out and sang the most extravagantly funny songs, to judge by their absurd actions; but that audience merely suspended its chatter, stared cynically, and never once smiled, never once applauded! I had always thought that Frenchmen were ready to laugh at anything.

CHAPTER XI

WE are getting foreignised rapidly, and with facility. We are getting reconciled to halls and bed-chambers with unhomelike stone floors and no carpets—floors that ring to the tread of one's heels with a sharpness that is death to sentimental musing. We are getting used to tidy, noiseless waiters, who glide hither and thither, and hover about your back and your elbows like butterflies, quick to comprehend orders, quick to fill them; thankful for a gratuity without regard to the amount; and always polite—never otherwise than polite. That is the strangest curiosity yet—a really polite hotel waiter who isn't an idiot. We are getting used to driving right into the central court of the hotel, in the midst of a fragrant circle of vines and flowers, and in the midst also of parties of gentlemen sitting quietly reading the paper and smoking. We are getting used to ice frozen by artificial process in ordinary bottles—the only kind of ice they have here.

The Innocents Abroad

We are getting used to all these things; but we are *not* getting used to carrying our own soap. We are sufficiently civilised to carry our own combs and tooth-brushes; but this thing of having to ring for soap every time we wash is new to us, and not pleasant at all. We think of it just after we get our heads and faces thoroughly wet or just when we think we have been in the bath-tub long enough, and then of course an annoying delay follows. These Marseillaise make Marseillaise hymns, and Marseilles vests, and Marseilles soap for all the world; but they never sing their hymns, or wear their vests, or wash with their soap themselves.

We have learned to go through the lingering routine of the table d'hôte with patience, with serenity, with satisfaction. We take soup; then wait a few minutes for the fish; a few minutes more and the plates are changed, and the roast beef comes; another change and we take peas; change again and take lentils; change and take snail patties (I prefer grass-hoppers); change and take roast chicken and salad; then strawberry pie and ice cream; then green figs, pears, oranges, green almonds, &c.; finally coffee. Wine with every course, of course, being in France. With such a cargo on board, digestion is a slow process, and we must sit long in the cool chambers and smoke —and read French newspapers, which have a strange fashion of telling a perfectly straight story till you get to the " nub " of it, and then a word drops in that no man can translate, and that story is ruined. An embankment fell on some Frenchmen yesterday, and the papers are full of it to-day; but whether those sufferers were killed, or crippled, or bruised, or only scared, is more than I can possibly make out, and yet I would just give anything to know.

The Innocents Abroad

We were troubled a little at dinner to-day by the conduct of an American, who talked very loudly and coarsely, and laughed boisterously where all others were so quiet and well-behaved. He ordered wine with a royal flourish and said: " I never dine without wine, sir " (which was a pitiful falsehood), and looked around upon the company to bask in the admiration he expected to find in their faces. All these airs in a land where they would as soon expect to leave the soup out of the bill of fare as the wine!—in a land where wine is nearly as common among all ranks as water! This fellow said: " I am a free-born sovereign, sir, an American, sir, and I want everybody to know it! " He did not mention that he was a lineal descendant of Balaam's ass; but everybody knew that without his telling it.

We have driven in the Prado, that superb avenue, bordered with patrician mansions and noble shade-trees; and have visited the Château Boarely and its curious museum. They showed us a miniature cemetery there—a copy of the first graveyard that was ever in Marseilles no doubt. The delicate little skeletons were lying in broken vaults, and had their household gods and kitchen utensils with them. The original of this cemetery was dug up in the principal street of the city a few years ago. It had remained there, only twelve feet underground, for a matter of twenty-five hundred years or thereabouts. Romulus was here before he built Rome, and thought something of founding a city on this spot, but gave up the idea. He may have been personally acquainted with some of these Phœnicians whose skeletons we have been examining.

In the great Zoological Gardens, we found specimens of all the animals the world produces, I think, including a dromedary, a monkey, ornamented with tufts of brilliant blue and carmine hair—a very gorgeous monkey he was—a hippopotamus from the Nile, and a sort of tall, long-legged bird with a beak like a powder-horn, and close-fitting wings like the tails of a dress-coat. This fellow stood up with his eyes shut and his shoulders stooped forward a little, and looked as if he had his hands under his coat tails. Such tranquil stupidity, such supernatural gravity, such self - righteousness, and such ineffable complacency as were in the countenance and attitude of that grey-bodied, dark-winged, bald-headed, and preposterously uncomely bird! He was so ungainly, so pimply about the head, so scaly about the legs, yet so serene, so unspeakably satisfied! He was the most comical looking creature that can be imagined. It was good to hear Dan and the doctor laugh—such natural and such enjoyable laughter had not been heard among our excursionists since our ship sailed away from America. This bird was a godsend to us, and I should be an ingrate if I forgot to make honourable mention of him in these pages. Ours was a pleasure excursion, therefore we stayed with that bird an hour, and made the most of him. We stirred him up occasionally, but he only unclosed an eye and slowly closed it again, abating no jot of his stately piety of demeanour or his tremendous seriousness. He only seemed to say, "Defile not Heaven's anointed with unsanctified hands." We did not know his name, and so we called him "The Pilgrim." Dan said—

"All he wants now is a Plymouth Collection."

The boon companion of the colossal elephant was a common cat! This cat had a fashion of climbing up the elephant's hind legs, and roosting on his back.

She would sit up there, with her paws curved under her breast, and sleep in the sun half the afternoon. It used to annoy the elephant at first, and he would reach up and take her down, but she would go aft and climb up again. She persisted until she finally conquered the elephant's prejudices, and now they are inseparable friends. The cat plays about her comrade's forefeet or his trunk often, until dogs approach, and then she goes aloft out of danger. The elephant has annihilated several dogs lately, that pressed his companion too closely.

We hired a sail-boat and a guide and made an excursion to one of the small islands in the harbour to visit the Castle d'If. This ancient fortress has a melancholy history. It has been used as a prison for political offenders for two or three hundred years, and its dungeon walls are scarred with the rudely carved names of many and many a captive who fretted his life away here, and left no record of himself but these sad epitaphs wrought with his own hands. How thick the names were! And their long-departed owners seemed to throng the gloomy cells and corridors with their phantom shapes. We loitered through dungeon after dungeon, away down into the living rock below the level of the sea, it seemed. Names everywhere! —some plebeian, some noble, some even princely. Plebeian, prince, and noble had one solicitude in common—they would not be forgotten! They could suffer solitude, inactivity, and the horrors of a silence that no sound ever disturbed; but they could not bear the thought of being utterly forgotten by the world. Hence the carved names. In one cell, where a little light penetrated, a man had lived twenty-seven years without seeing the face of a human being—lived in filth and wretchedness, with no companionship but his own thoughts, and they were sorrowful enough, and hopeless enough, no doubt. Whatever his jailers considered he needed was conveyed to his cell by night through a wicket. This man carved the walls of his prison-house from floor to roof with all manner of figures of men and animals, grouped in intricate designs. He had toiled there year after year, at his self-appointed task, while infants grew to boyhood— to vigorous youth—idled through school and college —acquired a profession—claimed man's mature estate —married and looked back to infancy as to a thing of some vague, ancient time almost. But who shall tell how many ages it seemed to this prisoner? With the one, time flew sometimes; with the other, never— it crawled always. To the one, nights spent in dancing had seemed minutes instead of hours: to the other, those self-same nights had been like all other nights of dungeon life, and seemed made of slow, dragging weeks, instead of hours and minutes.

One prisoner of fifteen years had scratched verses upon his walls, and brief prose sentences—brief but full of pathos. These spoke not of himself and his hard estate; but only of the shrine where his spirit fled the prison to worship—of home and the idols that were templed there. He never lived to see them.

The walls of these dungeons are as thick as some bed-chambers at home are wide—fifteen feet. We saw the damp, dismal cells in which two of Dumas' heroes passed their confinement—heroes of " Monte Cristo." It was here that the brave Abbé wrote a book with his own blood; with a pen made of a piece of iron hoop, and by the light of a lamp made out of shreds of cloth soaked in grease obtained from his food; and then dug through the thick wall with some trifling instrument which he wrought himself out of a stray piece of iron or table cutlery, and freed Dantés from his chains. It was a pity that so many weeks of dreary labour should have come to naught at last.

They showed us the noisome cell where the celebrated " Iron Mask "—that ill-starred brother of a hard-hearted king of France—was confined for a season, before he was sent to hide the strange mystery of his life from the curious in the dungeons of St. Marguerite. The place had a far greater interest for us than it could have had if we had known beyond all question who the Iron Mask was, and what his history had been, and why this most unusual punishment had been meted out to him. Mystery! That was the charm. That speechless tongue, those prisoned features, that heart so freighted with unspoken troubles, and that breast so oppressed with its piteous secret, had been here. These dank walls had known the man whose dolorous story is a sealed book for ever! There was fascination in the spot.

CHAPTER XII

WE have come five hundred miles by rail through the heart of France. What a bewitching land it is!—What a garden! Surely the leagues of bright green lawns are swept and brushed and watered every day and their grasses trimmed by the barber. Surely the hedges are shaped and measured and their symmetry preserved by the most architectural of gardeners. Surely the long straight rows of stately poplars that divide the beautiful landscape like the squares of a checker-board are set with line and plummet, and their uniform height determined with a spirit-level.

The Innocents Abroad

Surely the straight, smooth, pure white turnpikes are jack-planed and sand-papered every day. How else are these marvels of symmetry, cleanliness, and order attained? It is wonderful. There are no unsightly stone walls, and never a fence of any kind. There is no dirt, no decay, no rubbish anywhere—nothing that even hints at untidiness — nothing that ever suggests neglect. All is orderly and beautiful—everything is charming to the eye.

We had such glimpses of the Rhone gliding along between its grassy banks; of cosy cottages buried in flowers and shrubbery; of quaint old red-tiled villages with mossy Mediæval cathedrals looming out of their midst; of wooded hills with ivy-grown towers and turrets of feudal castles projecting above the foliage; such glimpses of Paradise, it seemed to us, such visions of fabled fairy-land!

We knew, then, what the poet meant when he sang of—

> " ——thy cornfields green, and sunny vines,
>   O pleasant land of France! "

And it *is* a pleasant land. No word describes it so felicitously as that one. They say there is no word for " home " in the French language. Well, considering that they have the article itself in such an attractive aspect, they ought to manage to get along without the word. Let us not waste too much pity on " homeless " France. I have observed that Frenchmen abroad seldom wholly give up the idea of going back to France some time or other. I am not surprised at it now.

We are not infatuated with these French railway cars, though. We took first - class passage, not because we wished to attract attention by doing a thing which is uncommon in Europe, but because we could make our journey quicker by so doing. It is hard to make railroading pleasant, in any country. It is too tedious. Stage-coaching is infinitely more delightful. Once I crossed the plains and deserts and mountains of the West, in a stage-coach, from the Missouri line to California, and since then all my pleasure trips must be measured to that rare holiday frolic. Two thousand miles of ceaseless rush and rattle and clatter, by night and by day, and never a weary moment, never a lapse of interest! The first seven hundred miles a level continent, its grassy carpet greener and softer and smoother than any sea, and figured with designs fitted to its magnitude—the shadows of the clouds. Here were no scenes but summer scenes, and no disposition inspired by them but to lie at full length on the mail sacks, in the grateful breeze, and dreamily smoke the pipe of peace —what other, where all was repose and contentment? In cool mornings, before the sun was fairly up, it was worth a lifetime of city toiling and moiling, to perch in the foretop with the driver and see the six mustangs scamper under the sharp snapping of a whip that never touched them; to scan the blue distances of a world that knew no lords but us; to cleave the wind with uncovered head and feel the sluggish pulses rousing to the spirit of a speed that pretended to the resistless rush of a typhoon! Then thirteen hundred miles of desert solitudes; of limitless panoramas of bewildering perspective; of mimic cities, of pinnacled cathedrals, of massive fortresses, counterfeited in the eternal rocks and splendid with the crimson and gold of the setting sun; of dizzy altitudes among fog-wreathed peaks and never-melting snows, where thunders and lightnings and tempests warred magnificently at our feet and the storm-clouds above swung their shredded banners in our very faces!

But I forgot. I am in elegant France now, and not skurrying through the great South Pass and the Wind River Mountains, among antelopes and buffaloes, and painted Indians on the war path. It is not meet that I should make too disparaging comparisons between hum-drum travel on a railway and that royal summer flight across a continent in a stage coach. I meant in the beginning to say that railway journeying is tedious and tiresome, and so it is—though at the time I was thinking particularly of a dismal fifty-hour pilgrimage between New York and St. Louis. Of course our trip through France was not really tedious, because all its scenes and experiences were new and strange; but as Dan says, it had its "discrepancies."

The cars are built in compartments that hold eight persons each. Each compartment is partially sub-divided, and so there are two tolerably distinct parties of four in it. Four face the other four. The seats and backs are thickly padded and cushioned and are very comfortable; you can smoke, if you wish; there are no bothersome pedlers; you are saved the inflic-tion of a multitude of disagreeable fellow-passengers. So far, so well. But then the conductor locks you in when the train starts; there is no water to drink in the car; there is no heating apparatus for night travel; if a drunken rowdy should get in, you could not remove a matter of twenty seats from him, or enter another car; but above all, if you are worn out and must sleep, you must sit up and do it in naps, with cramped legs and in a torturing misery that leaves you withered and lifeless the next day—for behold they have not that culmination of all charity and human kind-ness, a sleeping car, in all France. I prefer the

The Innocents Abroad

American system. Is has not so many grievous "discrepancies."

In France, all is clockwork, all is order. They make no mistakes. Every third man wears a uniform, and whether he be a Marshal of the Empire or a brakeman, he is ready and perfectly willing to answer all your questions with tireless politeness, ready to tell you which car to take, yea, and ready to go and put you into it to make sure that you shall not go astray. You cannot pass into the waiting-room of the depôt till you have secured your ticket, and you cannot pass from its only exit till the train is at its threshold to receive you. Once on board, the train will not start till your ticket has been examined—till every passenger's ticket has been inspected. This is chiefly for your own good. If by any possibility you have managed to take the wrong train, you will be handed over to a polite official who will take you whither you belong, and bestow you with many an affable bow. Your ticket will be inspected every now and then along the route, and when it is time to change cars you will know it. You are in the hands of officials who zealously study your welfare and your interest, instead of turning their talents to the invention of new methods of discommoding and snubbing you, as is very often the main employment of that exceedingly self-satisfied monarch, the railroad conductor of America.

But the happiest regulation in French railway government is—thirty minutes to dinner! No five-minute boltings of flabby rolls, muddy coffee, questionable eggs, gutta-percha beef, and pies whose conception and execution are a dark and bloody mystery to all save the cook that created them! No; we sat calmly down—it was in old Dijon, which is so easy to

96

spell and is impossible to pronounce, except when you civilise it and call it Demijohn—and poured out rich Burgundian wines and munched calmly through a long table d'hôte bill of fare, snail-patties, delicious fruits and all, then paid the trifle it cost and stepped happily aboard the train again, without once cursing the railroad company. A rare experience, and one to be treasured for ever.

They say they do not have accidents on these French roads, and I think it must be true. If I remember rightly, we passed high above waggon roads, or through tunnels under them, but never crossed them on their own level.

About every quarter of a mile, it seemed to me, a man came out and held up a club till the train went by, to signify that everything was safe ahead. Switches were changed a mile in advance, by pulling a wire rope that passed along the ground by the rail, from station to station. Signals for the day and signals for the night gave constant and timely notice of the position of switches.

No, they have no railroad accidents to speak of in France. But why? Because when one occurs, *somebody* has to hang for it![1] Not hang, maybe, but be punished at least with such vigour of emphasis as to make negligence a thing to be shuddered at by railroad officials for many a day thereafter. "No blame attached to the officers"—that lying and disaster-breeding verdict so common to our soft-hearted juries, is seldom rendered in France. If the trouble occurred in the conductor's department, that officer must suffer if his subordinate cannot be proven guilty; if in the engineer's depart-

[1] They go on the principle that it is better that one innocent man should suffer than five hundred.

ment, and the case be similar, the engineer must answer.

By Lyons and the Saone (where we saw the lady of Lyons and thought little of her comeliness); by Villa Franca, Tonnere, venerable Sens, Melun, Fontainebleau, and scores of other beautiful cities we swept, always noting the absence of hog-wallows, broken fences, cowlots, unpainted houses and mud, and always noting as well the presence of cleanliness, grace, taste in adorning and beautifying, even to the disposition of a tree or the turning of a hedge, the marvel of roads in perfect repair, void of ruts and guiltless of even an inequality of surface, we bowled along, hour after hour, that brilliant summer day, and as nightfall approached we entered a wilderness of odorous flowers and shrubbery, sped through it, and then excited, delighted, and half persuaded that we were only the sport of a beautiful dream, lo, we stood in magnificent Paris!

What excellent order they kept about that vast depôt! There was no frantic crowding and jostling, no shouting and swearing, and no swaggering intrusion of services by rowdy hackmen. These latter gentry stood outside, stood quietly by their long line of vehicles and said never a word. A kind of hackman-general seemed to have the whole matter of transportation in his hands. He politely received the passengers and ushered them to the kind of conveyance they wanted, and told the driver where to deliver them. There was no " talking back," no dissatisfaction about overcharging, no grumbling about anything. In a little while we were speeding through the streets of Paris, and delightfully recognising certain names and places with which books had long ago made us familiar. It was like meeting

an old friend when we read " *Rue de Rivoli* " on the
street corner; we knew the genuine vast palace of
the Louvre as well as we knew its picture; when
we passed by the Column of July we needed no one
to tell us what it was, or to remind us that on its
site once stood the grim Bastile, that grave of human
hopes and happiness, that dismal prison - house,
within whose dungeons so many young faces put
on the wrinkles of age, so many proud spirits grew
humble, so many brave hearts broke.

We secured rooms at the hotel, or rather we had
three beds put into one room, so that we might be
together, and then we went out to a restaurant, just
after lamp-lighting, and ate a comfortable, satisfactory, lingering dinner. It was a pleasure to eat
where everything was so tidy, the food so well cooked,
the waiters so polite, and the coming and departing
company so moustached, so frisky, so affable, so
fearfully and wonderfully Frenchy! All the surroundings were gay and enlivening. Two hundred
people sat at little tables on the sidewalk, sipping
wine and coffee; the streets were thronged with
light vehicles and with joyous pleasure-seekers;
there was music in the air, life and action all
about us, and a conflagration of gaslight everywhere!

After dinner we felt like seeing such Parisian
specialties as we might see without distressing exertion,
and so we sauntered through the brilliant streets and
looked at the dainty trifles in variety stores and
jewellery shops. Occasionally, merely for the pleasure of being cruel, we put unoffending Frenchmen
on the rack with questions framed in the incomprehensible jargon of their native language, and while
they writhed, we impaled them, we peppered them,

we sacrificed them, with their own vile verbs and participles.

We noticed that in the jewellery stores they had some of the articles marked " gold," and some labelled " imitation." We wondered at this extravagance of honesty, and inquired into the matter. We were informed that inasmuch as most people are not able to tell false gold from the genuine article, the Government compels jewellers to have their gold work assayed and stamped officially according to its fineness, and their imitation work duly labelled with the sign of its falsity. They told us the jewellers would not dare to violate this law, and that whatever a stranger bought in one of their stores might be depended upon as being strictly what it was represented to be. Verily, a wonderful land is France!

Then we hunted for a barber-shop. From earliest infancy it had been a cherished ambition of mine to be shaved some day in a palatial barber-shop of Paris. I wished to recline at full length in a cushioned invalid chair, with pictures about me, and sumptuous furniture; with frescoed walls and gilded arches above me, and vistas of Corinthian columns stretching far before me; with perfumes of Araby to intoxicate my senses, and the slumbrous drone of distant noises to soothe me to sleep. At the end of an hour I would wake up regretfully and find my face as smooth and soft as an infant's. Departing, I would lift my hands above that barber's head and say, " Heaven bless you, my son! "

So we searched high and low, for a matter of two hours, but never a barber-shop could we see. We saw only wig-making establishments, with shocks of dead and repulsive hair bound upon the heads of painted waxen brigands who stared out from glass

The Innocents Abroad

boxes upon the passer-by, with their stony eyes, and scared him with the ghostly white of their countenances. We shunned these signs for a time, but finally we concluded that the wig-makers must of necessity be the barbers as well, since we could find no single legitimate representative of the fraternity. We entered and asked, and found that it was even so.

I said I wanted to be shaved. The barber inquired where my room was. I said, never mind where my room was, I wanted to be shaved—there, on the spot. The doctor said he would be shaved also. Then there was an excitement among those two barbers! There was a wild consultation, and afterwards a hurrying to and fro, and a feverish gathering up of razors from obscure places, and a ransacking for soap. Next they took us into a little mean, shabby back room; they got two ordinary sitting-room chairs and placed us in them, with our coats on. My old, old dream of bliss vanished into thin air!

I sat bolt upright, silent, sad, and solemn. One of the wig-making villains lathered my face for ten terrible minutes, and finished by plastering a mass of suds into my mouth. I expelled the nasty stuff with a strong English expletive and said, "Foreigner, beware!" Then this outlaw strapped his razor on his boot, hovered over me ominously for six fearful seconds, and then swooped down upon me like the genius of destruction. The first rake of his razor loosened the very hide from my face, and lifted me out of the chair. I stormed and raved, and the other boys enjoyed it. Their beards are not strong and thick. Let us draw the curtain over this harrowing scene. Suffice it that I submitted, and went through with the cruel infliction of a shave by a French barber; tears of exquisite agony coursed down my cheeks now and then, but I survived. Then the incipient assassin held a basin of water under my chin and slopped its contents over my face, and into my bosom, and down the back of my neck, with a mean pretence of washing away the soap and blood. He dried my features with a towel, and was going to comb my hair; but I asked to be excused. I said, with withering irony, that it was sufficient to be skinned—I declined to be scalped.

I went away from there with my handkerchief about my face, and never, never, never desired to dream of palatial Parisian barber-shops any more. The truth is, as I believe I have since found out, that they have no barber-shops worthy of the name in Paris—and no barbers either, for that matter. The impostor who does duty as a barber, brings his pans and napkins and implements of torture to your residence, and deliberately skins you in your private apartments. Ah, I have suffered, suffered, suffered here in Paris, but never mind, the time is coming when I shall have a dark and bloody revenge. Some day a Parisian barber will come to my room to skin me, and from that day forth that barber will never be heard of more.

At eleven o'clock we alighted upon a sign which manifestly referred to billiards. Joy! We had played billiards in the Azores with balls that were not round, and on an ancient table that was very little smoother than a brick pavement—one of those wretched old things with dead cushions, and with patches in the faded cloth and invisible obstructions that made the balls describe the most astonishing and unsuspected angles, and perform feats in the way of unlooked-for and almost impossible " scratches," that were perfectly bewildering. We had played at Gibraltar with balls the size of a walnut, on a table like a public square; and in both instances we

The Innocents Abroad

achieved far more aggravation than amusement. We expected to fare better here, but we were mistaken. The cushions were a good deal higher than the balls, and as the balls had a fashion of always stopping under the cushions, we accomplished very little in the way of caroms. The cushions were hard and unelastic, and the cues were so crooked that in making a shot you had to allow for the curve, or you would infallibly put the " English " on the wrong side of the ball. Dan was to mark while the doctor and I played. At the end of an hour neither of us had made a count, and so Dan was tired of keeping tally with nothing to tally, and we were heated and angry and disgusted. We paid the heavy bill—about six cents—and said we would call around some time when we had a week to spend, and finish the game.

We adjourned to one of those pretty *cafés* and took supper and tested the wines of the country, as we had been instructed to do, and found them harmless and unexciting. They might have been exciting, however, if we had chosen to drink a sufficiency of them.

To close our first day in Paris cheerfully and pleasantly, we now sought our grand room in the Grand Hôtel du Louvre and climbed into our sumptuous bed, to read and smoke—but alas!

> It was pitiful
> In a whole city-full,
> Gas we had none.

No gas to read by—nothing but dismal candles. It was a shame. We tried to map out excursions for the morrow; we puzzled over French " Guides to Paris "; we talked disjointedly in a vain endeavour to make head or tail of the wild chaos of the day's sights and experiences; we subsided to indolent

103

smoking; we gaped and yawned and stretched—then feebly wondered if we were really and truly in renowned Paris, and drifted drowsily away into that vast mysterious void which men call sleep.

CHAPTER XIII

THE next morning we were up and dressed at ten o'clock. We went to the *commissionaire* of the hotel —I don't know what a *commissionaire* is, but that is the man we went to—and told him we wanted a guide. He said the great International Exposition had drawn such multitudes of Englishmen and Americans to Paris that it would be next to impossible to find a good guide unemployed. He said he usually kept a dozen or two on hand, but he only had three now. He called them. One looked so like a very pirate that we let him go at once. The next one spoke with a simpering precision of pronunciation that was irritating, and said—

"If ze zhentlemans will to me make ze grande honneur to me rattain in hees serveece, I shall show to him every sing zat is magnifique to look upon in ze beautiful Parree. I speaky ze Angleesh pair-faitemaw."

He would have done well to have stopped there, because he had that much by heart and said it right off without making a mistake. But his self-complacency seduced him into attempting a flight into regions of unexplored English, and the experiment was his ruin. Within ten seconds he was so tangled up in a maze of mutilated verbs and torn and bleeding forms of speech that no human ingenuity could ever have gotten him out of it with credit. It was plain

The Innocents Abroad

enough that he could not "speaky" the English quite as "pairfaitemaw" as he had pretended he could.

The third man captured us. He was plainly dressed, but he had a noticeable air of neatness about him. He wore a high silk hat which was a little old, but had been carefully brushed. He wore second-hand kid gloves, in good repair, and carried a small rattan cane with a curved handle—a female leg, of ivory. He stepped as gently and as daintily as a cat crossing a muddy street; and oh! he was urbanity; he was quiet, unobtrusive self-possession; he was deference itself! He spoke softly and guardedly; and when he was about to make a statement on his sole responsibility, or offer a suggestion, he weighed it by drachms and scruples first, with the crook of his little stick placed meditatively to his teeth. His opening speech was perfect. It was perfect in construction, in phraseology, in grammar, in emphasis, in pronunciation—everything. He spoke little and guardedly, after that. We were charmed. We were more than charmed—we were overjoyed. We hired him at once. We never even asked him his price. This man—our lackey, our servant, our unquestioning slave though he was, was still a gentleman—we could see that—while of the other two one was coarse and awkward, and the other was a born pirate. We asked our man Friday's name. He drew from his pocket-book a snowy little card, and passed it to us with a profound bow:

A. BILLFINGER,
Guide to Paris, France, Germany,
Spain, &c., &c.,
Grand Hôtel du Louvre.

The Innocents Abroad

"BILLFINGER! Oh, carry me home to die!"

That was an "aside" from Dan. The atrocious name grated harshly on my ear too. The most of us can learn to forgive, and even to like, a countenance that strikes us unpleasantly at first; but few of us, I fancy, become reconciled to a jarring name so easily. I was almost sorry we had hired this man, his name was so unbearable. However, no matter. We were impatient to start. Billfinger stepped to the door to call a carriage, and then the doctor said—

"Well, the guide goes with the barber-shop, with the billiard-table, with the gasless room, and maybe with many another pretty romance of Paris. I expected to have a guide named Henri de Montmorency, or Armand de la Chartreuse, or something that would sound grand in letters to the villagers at home; but to think of a Frenchman by the name of Billfinger! Oh! this is absurd, you know. This will never do. We can't say Billfinger; it is nauseating. Name him over again: what had we better call him? Alexis du Caulaincourt?"

"Alphonse Henri Gustave de Hauteville," I suggested.

"Call him Ferguson," said Dan.

That was practical, unromantic good sense. Without debate, we expunged Billfinger *as* Billfinger, and called him Ferguson.

The carriage — an open barouche — was ready. Ferguson mounted beside the driver, and we whirled away to breakfast. As was proper, Mr. Ferguson stood by to transmit our orders and answer questions. By-and-by, he mentioned casually—the artful adventurer—that he would go and get his breakfast as soon as we had finished ours. He knew we could not get along without him, and that we would not want to loiter about and wait for him. We asked him to sit down and eat with us. He begged, with many a bow, to be excused. It was not proper, he said; he would sit at another table. We ordered him peremptorily to sit down with us.

Here endeth the first lesson. It was a mistake.

As long as we had that fellow after that, he was always hungry; he was always thirsty. He came early; he stayed late; he could not pass a restaurant; he looked with a lecherous eye upon every wine-shop. Suggestions to stop, excuses to eat and to drink, were forever on his lips. We tried all we could to fill him so full that he would have no room to spare for a fortnight; but it was a failure. He did not hold enough to smother the cravings of his superhuman appetite.

He had another "discrepancy" about him. He was always wanting us to buy things. On the shallowest pretences he would inveigle us into shirt stores, boot stores, tailor shops, glove shops—anywhere under the broad sweep of the heavens that there seemed a chance of our buying anything. Any one could have guessed that the shopkeepers paid him a per centage on the sales; but in our blessed innocence we didn't, until this feature of his conduct grew unbearably prominent. One day Dan happened to mention that he thought of buying three or four silk dress patterns for presents. Ferguson's hungry eye was upon him in an instant. In the course of twenty minutes the carriage stopped.

"What's this?"

"Zis is ze finest silk magazin in Paris—ze most celebrate."

"What did you come here for? We told you to take us to the palace of the Louvre."

" I suppose ze gentleman say he wish to buy some silk."

" You are not required to ' suppose ' things for the party, Ferguson. We do not wish to tax your energies too much. We will bear some of the burden and heat of the day ourselves. We will endeavour to do such ' supposing ' as is really necessary to be done. Drive on." So spake the doctor.

Within fifteen minutes the carriage halted again, and before another silk store. The doctor said—

" Ah! the palace of the Louvre: beautiful, beautiful edifice! Does the Emperor Napoleon live here now, Ferguson? "

" Ah, doctor! you do jest; zis is not ze palace; we come there directly. But since we pass right by zis store, where is such beautiful silk——"

" Ah! I see, I see. I meant to have told you that we did not wish to purchase any silks to-day; but in my absent-mindedness I forgot it. I also meant to tell you we wished to go directly to the Louvre; but I forgot that also. However, we will go there now. Pardon my seeming carelessness, Ferguson. Drive on."

Within the half hour, we stopped again—in front of another silk store. We were angry; but the doctor was always serene, always smooth-voiced. He said—

" At last! How imposing the Louvre is, and yet how small! how exquisitely fashioned! how charmingly situated!—Venerable, venerable pile——"

" Pairdon, doctor, zis is not ze Louvre—it is——"

" *What* is it? "

" I have ze idea—it comes to me in a moment—zat ze silk in zis magazin——"

" Ferguson, how heedless I am. I fully intended to tell you that we did not wish to buy any silks to-day, and I also intended to tell you that we yearned to go immediately to the palace of the Louvre, but enjoying the happiness of seeing you devour four breakfasts this morning has so filled me with pleasurable emotions that I neglect the commonest interests of the time. However, we will proceed now to the Louvre Ferguson."

"But doctor" (excitedly) "it will take not a minute—not but one small minute! Ze gentleman need not to buy if he not wish to—but only *look* at ze silk—*look* at ze beautiful fabric." [Then pleadingly.] "*Sair*—just only one *leetle* moment!"

Dan said, "Confound the idiot! I don't want to see any silks to-day, and I *won't* look at them. Drive on."

And the doctor, "We need no silks now, Ferguson. Our hearts long for the Louvre. Let us journey on—let us journey on."

"But *doctor!* it is only one moment—one leetle moment. And ze time will be save—entirely save! Because zere is nothing to see now—it is too late. It want ten minute to four, and ze Louvre close at four—*only* one leetle moment, doctor!"

The treacherous miscreant! After four breakfasts and a gallon of champagne, to serve us such a scurvy trick. We got no sight of the countless treasures of art in the Louvre galleries that day, and our only poor little satisfaction was in the reflection that Ferguson sold not a solitary silk dress pattern.

I am writing this chapter partly for the satisfaction of abusing that accomplished knave, Billfinger, and partly to show whosoever shall read this how Americans fare at the hands of the Paris guides, and what sort of people Paris guides are. It need not be supposed that we were a stupider or an easier prey than our countrymen generally are, for we were not. The guides deceive and defraud every American who goes to Paris for the first time and sees its sights alone or in company with others as little experienced as himself. I shall visit Paris again some day, and then let the guides beware! I shall go in my war-paint— I shall carry my tomahawk along.

I think we have lost but little time in Paris. We have gone to bed every night tired out. Of course we visited the renowned International Exposition. All the world did that. We went there on our third day in Paris—and we stayed there *nearly two hours*. That was our first and last visit. To tell the truth, we saw at a glance that one would have to spend weeks —yea, even months—in that monstrous establishment, to get an intelligible idea of it. It was a wonderful show, but the moving masses of people of all nations we saw there were a still more wonderful show. I discovered that if I were to stay there a month, I should still find myself looking at the people instead of the inanimate objects on exhibition. I got a little interested in some curious old tapestries of the thirteenth century, but a party of Arabs came by, and their dusky faces and quaint costumes called my attention away at once. I watched a silver swan which had a living grace about his movements, and a living intelligence in his eyes—watched him swimming about as comfortably and as unconcernedly as if he had been born in a morass instead of a jeweller's shop—watched him seize a silver fish from under the water and hold up his head and go through all the customary and elaborate motions of swallowing it—but the moment it disappeared down his throat some tattooed South Sea Islanders approached and I yielded to their attractions. Presently I found a revolving pistol several hundred years old which looked strangely like a modern Colt, but just then I heard that the Empress of the French was in another part of the building, and hastened away to see what she might look like. We heard martial music—we saw an unusual number of soldiers walking hurriedly about—there was a general movement among the people. We inquired what it was all about, and learned that the Emperor of the French and the Sultan of Turkey were about to review twenty-five thousand troops at the *Arc de l'Etoile*. We immediately departed. I had a greater anxiety to see these men than I could have had to see twenty Expositions.

We drove away and took up a position in an open space opposite the American Minister's house. A speculator bridged a couple of barrels with a board and we hired standing-places on it. Presently there was a sound of distant music; in another minute a pillar of dust came moving slowly towards us; a moment more, and then, with colours flying and a grand crash of military music, a gallant array of cavalrymen emerged from the dust and came down the street on a gentle trot. After them came a long line of artillery; then more cavalry, in splendid uniforms; and then their Imperial Majesties Napoleon III. and Abdul-Aziz. The vast concourse of people swung their hats and shouted—the windows and house-tops in the wide vicinity burst into a snow-storm of waving handkerchiefs, and the wavers of the same mingled their cheers with those of the masses below. It was a stirring spectacle.

But the two central figures claimed all our attention. Was ever such a contrast set up before a multitude till then? Napoleon, in military uniform—a long-bodied, short-legged man, fiercely moustached, old, wrinkled, with eyes half closed, and *such* a deep, crafty, scheming expression about them!—Napoleon, bowing ever so gently to the loud plaudits, and watching everything and everybody with his cat-eyes from under his depressed hat-brim, as if to discover any sign that those cheers were not heartfelt and cordial.

Abdul-Aziz, absolute lord of the Ottoman Empire—clad in dark green European clothes, almost without ornament or insignia of rank; a red Turkish fez on his head—a short, stout, dark man, black-bearded, black-eyed, stupid, unprepossessing—a man whose whole appearance somehow suggested that if he only had a cleaver in his hand and a white apron on, one would not be at all surprised to hear him say: " A mutton-roast to-day, or will you have a nice porter-house steak ? "

Napoleon III., the representative of the highest modern civilisation, progress, and refinement; Abdul-Aziz, the representative of a people by nature and training filthy, brutish, ignorant, unprogressive, superstitious—and a government whose Three Graces are Tyranny, Rapacity, Blood. Here in brilliant Paris, under this majestic Arch of Triumph, the First Century greets the Nineteenth!

Napoleon III., Emperor of France! Surrounded by shouting thousands, by military pomp, by the splendours of his capital city, and companioned by kings and princes—this is the man who was sneered at, and reviled, and called Bastard—yet who was dreaming of a crown and an empire all the while; who was driven into exile—but carried his dreams with him; who associated with the common herd in America, and ran foot-races for a wager—but still sat upon a throne, in fancy; who braved every danger to go to his dying mother—and grieved that she could not be spared to see him cast aside his plebeian vestments for the purple of royalty; who kept his faithful watch and walked his weary beat a common policeman of London—but dreamed the while of a coming night when he should tread the long-drawn corridors of the Tuileries; who made the miserable *fiasco* of Strasbourg; saw his poor, shabby eagle, forgetful of its lesson, refuse to perch upon his shoulder; delivered his carefully-prepared, sententious burst of eloquence into unsympathetic ears; found himself a prisoner, the butt of small wits, a mark for the pitiless ridicule of all the world—yet went on dreaming of coronations and splendid pageants, as before; who lay a forgotten captive in the dungeons of Ham—and still schemed and planned and pondered over future glory and future power; President of France at last! A *coup d'état*, and surrounded by applauding armies, welcomed by the thunders of cannon, he mounts a throne and waves before an astounded world the sceptre of a mighty empire! Who talks of the marvels of fiction? Who speaks of the wonders of romance? Who prates of the tame achievements of Aladdin and the Magii of Arabia?

Abdul-Aziz, Sultan of Turkey, Lord of the Ottoman Empire! Born to a throne; weak, stupid, ignorant almost as his meanest slave; chief of a vast royalty, yet the puppet of his Premier and the obedient child of a tyrannical mother; a man who sits upon a throne—the beck of whose finger moves navies and armies—who holds in his hands the power of life and death over millions—yet who sleeps, sleeps, eats, eats, idles with his eight hundred concubines, and when he

is surfeited with eating and sleeping and idling, and
would rouse up and take the reins of government and
threaten to *be* a Sultan, is charmed from his purpose
by wary Fuad Pacha with a pretty plan for a new
palace or a new ship—charmed away with a new toy,
like any other restless child; a man who sees his
people robbed and oppressed by soulless tax-gatherers,
but speaks no word to save them; who believes in
gnomes, and genii, and the wild fables of the Arabian
Nights, but has small regard for the mighty magicians
of to-day, and is nervous in the presence of their
mysterious railroads and steamboats and telegraphs;
who would see undone in Egypt all that great Mehemet
Ali achieved, and would prefer rather to forget than
emulate him; a man who found his great Empire
a blot upon the earth—a degraded, poverty-stricken,
miserable, infamous agglomeration of ignorance,
crime, and brutality, and will idle away the allotted
days of his trivial life, and then pass to the dust and
the worms and leave it so!

Napoleon has augmented the commercial prosperity
of France, in ten years, to such a degree that figures
can hardly compute it. He has rebuilt Paris, and has
partly rebuilt every city in the State. He condemns
a whole street at a time, assesses the damages, pays
them, and rebuilds superbly. Then speculators buy
up the ground and sell, but the original owner is
given the first choice by the government at a stated
price before the speculator is permitted to purchase.
But above all things, he has taken the sole control of
the Empire of France into his hands, and made it a
tolerably free land—for people who will not attempt
to go too far in meddling with government affairs.
No country offers greater security to life and property
than France, and one has all the freedom he wants,

but no licence—no licence to interfere with anybody, or make any one uncomfortable.

As for the Sultan, one could set a trap anywhere and catch a dozen abler men in a night.

The bands struck up, and the brilliant adventurer, Napoleon III., the genius of Energy, Persistence, Enterprise; and the feeble Abdul-Aziz, the genius of Ignorance, Bigotry, and Indolence, prepared for the Forward—March!

We saw the splendid review, we saw the white-moustached old Crimean soldier Canrobert, Marshal of France, we saw—well, we saw everything, and then we went home satisfied.

CHAPTER XIV

WE went to see the Cathedral of Notre Dame.—We had heard of it before. It surprises me sometimes to think how much we *do* know, and how intelligent we are. We recognised the brown old Gothic pile in a moment; it was like the pictures. We stood at a little distance and changed from one point of observation to another, and gazed long at its lofty square towers and its rich front, clustered thick with stony, mutilated saints who had been looking calmly down from their perches for ages. The Patriarch of Jerusalem stood under them in the old days of chivalry and romance, and preached the third Crusade, more than six hundred years ago; and since that day they have stood there and looked quietly down upon the most thrilling scenes, the grandest pageants, the most extraordinary spectacles that have grieved or delighted Paris. These battered and broken-nosed old fellows saw many and many a cavalcade of mail-clad knights come marching home from Holy Land; they heard the bells above them toll the signal for the St. Bartholomew's Massacre, and they saw the slaughter that followed; later, they saw the Reign of Terror, the carnage of the Revolution, the overthrow of a king, the coronation of two Napoleons, the christening of the young prince that lords it over a regiment of servants in the Tuileries to-day—and they may possibly continue to stand there until they see the Napoleon dynasty swept away and the banners of a great Republic floating above its ruins. I wish these old parties could speak. They could tell a tale worth the listening to.

They say that a pagan temple stood where Notre Dame now stands, in the old Roman days, eighteen or twenty centuries ago—remains of it are still preserved in Paris; and that a Christian church took its place about A.D. 300; another took the place of that in A.D. 500; and that the foundations of the present Cathedral were laid about A.D. 1100. The ground ought to be measurably sacred by this time, one would think. One portion of this noble old edifice is suggestive of the quaint fashions of ancient times. It was built by Jean Sans-Peur, Duke of Burgundy, to set his conscience at rest—he had assassinated the Duke of Orleans. Alas! those good old times are gone, when a murderer could wipe the stain from his name and soothe his troubles to sleep simply by getting out his bricks and mortar and building an addition to a church.

The portals of the great western front are bisected by square pillars. They took the central one away in 1852, on the occasion of thanksgivings for the re-institution of the Presidential power—but precious soon they had occasion to reconsider that motion and put it back again! And they did.

We loitered through the grand aisles for an hour or two, staring up at the rich stained-glass windows embellished with blue and yellow and crimson saints and martyrs, and trying to admire the numberless great pictures in the chapels, and then we were admitted to the sacristy and shown the magnificent robes which the Pope wore when he crowned Napoleon I.; a waggon-load of solid gold and silver utensils used in the great public processions and ceremonies of the church; some nails of the true cross, a fragment of the cross itself, a part of the crown of thorns. We had already seen a large piece of the true cross in a church in the Azores, but no nails. They showed us likewise the bloody robe which that Archbishop of Paris wore who exposed his sacred person and braved the wrath of the insurgents of 1848, to mount the barricades and hold aloft the olive branch of peace in the hope of stopping the slaughter. His noble effort cost him his life. He was shot dead. They showed us a cast of his face, taken after death, the bullet that killed him, and the two vertebræ in which it lodged. These people have a somewhat singular taste in the matter of relics. Ferguson told us that the silver cross which the good Archbishop wore at his girdle was seized and thrown into the Seine, where it lay embedded in the mud for fifteen years, and then an angel appeared to a priest and told him where to dive for it; he *did* dive for it and got it, and now it is there on exhibition at Notre Dame, to be inspected by anybody who feels an interest in inanimate objects of miraculous intervention.

Next we went to visit the Morgue, that horrible receptacle for the dead who die mysteriously and leave the manner of their taking off a dismal secret. We stood before a grating and looked through into a room which was hung all about with the clothing of dead men; coarse blouses, water-soaked; the delicate garments of women and children; patrician vestments, hacked and stabbed and stained with red; a hat that was crushed and bloody. On a slanting stone lay a drowned man, naked, swollen, purple; clasping the fragment of a broken bush with a grip which death had so petrified that human strength could not unloose it—mute witness of the last despairing effort to save the life that was doomed beyond all help. A stream of water trickled ceaselessly over the hideous face. We knew that the body and the clothing were there for identification by friends, but still we wondered if anybody could love that repulsive object or grieve for its loss. We grew meditative and wondered if, some forty years ago, when the mother of that ghastly thing was dandling it upon her knee, and kissing it, and petting it, and displaying it with satisfied pride to the passers-by, a prophetic vision of this dread ending ever flitted through her brain. I half feared that the mother, or the wife, or a brother of the dead man might come while we stood there, but nothing of the kind occurred. Men and women came, and some looked eagerly in, and pressed their faces against the bars; others glanced carelessly at the body, and turned away with a disappointed look —people, I thought, who live upon strong excitements, and who attend the exhibitions of the Morgue regularly, just as other people go to see theatrical spectacles every night. When one of these looked in and passed on, I could not help thinking—

"Now this don't afford you any satisfaction— a party with his head shot off is what *you* need."

The Innocents Abroad

One night we went to the celebrated *Jardin Mabille*, but only stayed a little while. We wanted to see some of this kind of Paris life, however, and therefore, the next night, we went to a similar place of entertainment in a great garden in the suburb of Asnières. We went to the railroad depôt, towards evening, and Ferguson got tickets for a second-class carriage. Such a perfect jam of people I have not often seen—but there was no noise, no disorder, no rowdyism. Some of the women and young girls that entered the train we knew to be of the *demi-monde*, but others we were not at all sure about.

The girls and women in our carriage behaved themselves modestly and becomingly, all the way out, except that they smoked. When we arrived at the garden in Asnières, we paid a franc or two admission, and entered a place which had flower-beds in it, and grass plats, and long, curving rows of ornamental shrubbery, with here and there a secluded bower convenient for eating ice-cream in. We moved along the sinuous gravel walks, with the great concourse of girls and young men, and suddenly a domed and filigreed white temple, starred over and over and over again with brilliant gas jets, burst upon us like a fallen sun. Near by was a large, handsome house with its ample front illuminated in the same way, and above its roof floated the Star Spangled banner of America.

" Well! " I said. " How is this? " It nearly took my breath away.

Ferguson said an American—a New Yorker—kept the place, and was carrying on quite a stirring opposition to the *Jardin Mabille*.

Crowds, composed of both sexes and nearly all ages, were frisking about the garden or sitting in the open air in front of the flag-staff and the temple, drinking wine and coffee, or smoking. The dancing had not begun yet. Ferguson said there was to be an exhibition. The famous Blondin was going to perform on a tight-rope in another part of the garden. We went thither. Here the light was dim, and the masses of people were pretty closely packed together. And now I made a mistake which any donkey might make, but a sensible man never. I committed an error which I find myself repeating every day of my life.—Standing right before a young lady, I said—

"Dan, just look at this girl, how beautiful she is!"

"I thank you more for the evident sincerity of the compliment, sir, than for the extraordinary publicity you have given to it!" This in good, pure English.

We took a walk, but my spirits were very, very sadly dampened. I did not feel right comfortable for some time afterwards. Why *will* people be so stupid as to suppose themselves the only foreigners among a crowd of ten thousand persons?

But Blondin came out shortly. He appeared on a stretched cable, far away above the sea of tossing hats and handkerchiefs, and in the glare of the hundreds of rockets that whizzed heavenwards by him he looked like a wee insect. He balanced his pole and walked the length of his rope—two or three hundred feet; he came back and got a man and carried him across; he returned to the centre and danced a jig; next he performed some gymnastic and balancing feats too perilous to afford a pleasant spectacle; and he finished by fastening to his person a thousand Roman candles, Catherine wheels, serpents, and rockets of all manner of brilliant colours, setting them on fire all at once and walking and waltzing across his rope again in a blinding blaze of glory that lit up the garden and the people's faces like a great conflagration at midnight.

The dance had begun, and we adjourned to the temple. Within it was a drinking saloon; and all around it was a broad circular platform for the dancers. I backed up against the wall of the temple, and waited. Twenty sets formed, the music struck up, and then—I placed my hands before my face for shame. But I looked through my fingers. They were dancing the renowned "*Can-can*." A handsome girl in the set before me tripped forward lightly to meet the opposition gentleman—tripped back again, grasped her dresses vigorously on both sides with her hands, raised them pretty high, danced an extraordinary jig that had more activity and exposure about it than any jig I ever saw before, and then, drawing her clothes still higher, she advanced gaily to the centre and launched a vicious kick full at her *vis-à-vis* that must infallibly have removed his nose if he had been seven feet high. It was a mercy he was only six.

That is the *can-can*. The idea of it is to dance as wildly, as noisily, as furiously as you can; expose yourself as much as possible if you are a woman; and kick as high as you can, no matter which sex you belong to. There is no word of exaggeration in this. Any of the staid, respectable, aged people who were there that night can testify to the truth of the statement. There were a good many such people present. I suppose French morality is not of that straitlaced description which is shocked at trifles.

I moved aside and took a general view of the *can-can*. Shouts, laughter, furious music, a bewildering chaos of darting and intermingling forms, stormy jerking and snatching of gay dresses, bobbing heads,

"*But I looked through my fingers.*"

flying arms, lightning-flashes of white stockinged calves and dainty slippers in the air, and then a grand final rush, riot, a terrific hubbub and a wild stampede! Heavens! Nothing like it has been seen on earth since trembling Tam O'Shanter saw the devil and the witches at their orgies that stormy night in " Alloway's auld haunted kirk."

We visited the Louvre, at a time when we had no silk purchases in view, and looked at its miles of paintings by the old masters. Some of them were beautiful, but at the same time they carried such evidences about them of the cringing spirit of those great men that we found small pleasure in examining them. Their nauseous adulation of princely patrons was more prominent to me and chained my attention more surely than the charms of colour and expression which are claimed to be in the pictures. Gratitude for kindnesses is well, but it seems to me that some of those artists carried it so far that it ceased to be gratitude, and became worship. If there is a plausible excuse for the worship of men, then by all means let us forgive Rubens and his brethren.

But I will drop the subject, lest I say something about the old masters that might as well be left unsaid.

Of course we drove in the *Bois de Boulogne*, that limitless park, with its forests, its lakes, its cascades, and its broad avenues. There were thousands upon thousands of vehicles abroad, and the scene was full of life and gaiety. There were very common hacks, with father and mother and all the children in them; conspicuous little open carriages with celebrated ladies of questionable reputation in them; there were dukes and duchesses abroad, with gorgeous footmen perched behind, and equally gorgeous outriders perched on each of the six horses; there were blue and silver, and green and gold, and pink and black, and all sorts and descriptions of stunning and startling liveries out, and I almost yearned to be a flunkey myself, for the sake of the fine clothes.

But presently the Emperor came along and he out-shone them all. He was preceded by a bodyguard of gentlemen on horseback in showy uniforms, his carriage-horses (there appeared to be somewhere in the remote neighbourhood of a thousand of them) were bestridden by gallant-looking fellows, also in stylish uniforms, and after the carriage followed another detachment of body guards. Everybody got out of the way; everybody bowed to the Emperor and his friend the Sultan, and they went by on a swinging trot and disappeared.

I will not describe the *Bois de Boulogne*. I cannot do it. It is simply a beautiful, cultivated, endless, wonderful wilderness. It is an enchanting place. It is in Paris now, one may say, but a crumbling old cross in one portion of it reminds one that it was not always so. The cross marks the spot where a celebrated troubadour was waylaid and murdered in the fourteenth century. It was in this park that the fellow with an unpronounceable name made the attempt upon the Russian Czar's life last spring with a pistol. The bullet struck a tree. Ferguson showed us the place. Now in America that interesting tree would be chopped down or forgotten within the next five years, but it will be treasured here. The guides will point it out to visitors for the next 800 years, and when it decays and falls down they will put up another there and go on with the same old story just the same.

The Innocents Abroad

CHAPTER XV

ONE of our pleasantest visits was to Père la Chaise, the national burying-ground of France, the honoured resting-place of some of her greatest and best children, the last home of scores of illustrious men and women who were born to no titles, but achieved fame by their own energy and their own genius. It is a solemn city of winding streets, and of miniature marble temples and mansions of the dead gleaming white from out a wilderness of foliage and fresh flowers. Not every city is so well peopled as this, or has so ample an area within its walls. Few palaces exist in any city that are so exquisite in design, so rich in art, so costly in material, so graceful, so beautiful.

We had stood in the ancient church of St. Denis, where the marble effigies of thirty generations of kings and queens lay stretched at length upon the tombs, and the sensations invoked were startling and novel; the curious armour, the obsolete costumes, the placid faces, the hands placed palm to palm in eloquent supplication—it was a vision of grey antiquity. It seemed curious enough to be standing face to face, as it were, with old Dagobert I., and Clovis, and Charlemagne, those vague, colossal heroes, those shadows, those myths of a thousand years ago! I touched their dust-covered faces with my fingers, but Dagobert was deader than the sixteen centuries that have passed over him, Clovis slept well after his labour for Christ, and old Charlemagne went on dreaming of his paladins, of bloody Roncesvalles, and gave no heed to me.

The Innocents Abroad

The great names of Père la Chaise impress one too, but differently. There the suggestion brought constantly to his mind is, that this place is sacred to a nobler royalty—the royalty of heart and brain. Every faculty of mind, every noble trait of human nature, every high occupation which men engage in, seems represented by a famous name. The effect is a curious medley. Davoust and Massena, who wrought in many a battle-tragedy, are here, and so also is Rachel, of equal renown in mimic tragedy on the stage. The Abbé Sicard sleeps here—the first great teacher of the deaf and dumb—a man whose heart went out to every unfortunate, and whose life was given to kindly offices in their service; and not far off, in repose and peace at last, lies Marshal Ney, whose stormy spirit knew no music like the bugle call to arms. The man who originated public gas-lighting, and that other benefactor who introduced the cultivation of the potato, and thus blessed millions of his starving countrymen, lie with the Prince of Masserano, and with exiled queens and princes of Further India. Gay-Lussac the chemist, Laplace the astronomer, Larrey the surgeon, de Séze the advocate, are here, and with them are Talma, Bellini, Rubini; de Balzac, Beaumarchais, Béranger; Molière, and Lafontaine, and scores of other men whose names and whose worthy labours are as familiar in the remote by-places of civilisation as are the historic deeds of the kings and princes that sleep in the marble vaults of St. Denis.

But among the thousands and thousands of tombs in Père la Chaise, there is one that no man, no woman, no youth of either sex, ever passes by without stopping to examine. Every visitor has a sort of indistinct idea of the history of its dead, and compre-

hends that homage is due there, but not one in twenty
thousand clearly remembers the story of that tomb
and its romantic occupants. This is the grave of
Abelard and Heloise—a grave which has been more
revered, more widely known, more written and sung
about and wept over, for seven hundred years, than
any other in Christendom, save only that of the
Saviour. All visitors linger pensively about it; all
young people capture and carry away keepsakes and
mementoes of it; all Parisian youths and maidens
who are disappointed in love come there to bail out
when they are full of tears; yea, many stricken lovers
make pilgrimages to this shrine from distant provinces to weep and wail and " grit " their teeth over
their heavy sorrows, and to purchase the sympathies
of the chastened spirits of that tomb with offerings
of immortelles and budding flowers.

Go when you will, you find somebody snuffing
over that tomb. Go when you will, you find it
furnished with those bouquets and immortelles. Go
when you will, you find a gravel-train from Marseilles
arriving to supply the deficiencies caused by memento-
cabbaging Vandals whose affections have miscarried.

In Paris we often saw in shop windows the sign,
" English Spoken Here," just as one sees in the windows at home the sign, " Ici on parle français." We
always invaded these places at once, and invariably
received the information, framed in faultless French,
that the clerk who did the English for the establishment had just gone to dinner, and would be back
in an hour, would Monsieur buy something? We
wondered why those parties happened to take their
dinners at such erratic and extraordinary hours, for
we never called at a time when an exemplary Christian
would be in the least likely to be abroad on such an

errand. The truth was, it was a base fraud—a snare to trap the unwary—chaff to catch fledgelings with. They had no English-murdering clerk. They trusted to the sign to inveigle foreigners into their lairs, and trusted to their own blandishments to keep them there till they bought something.

We ferreted out another French imposition—a frequent sign to this effect:—" ALL MANNER OF AMERICAN DRINKS ARTISTICALLY PREPARED HERE." We procured the services of a gentlemen experienced in the nomenclature of the American bar, and moved upon the works of one of these impostors. A bowing, aproned Frenchman skipped forward and said—

" Que voulez les messieurs? " I do not know what " Que voulez les messieurs " means, but such was his remark.

Our General said, " We will take a whisky-straight."

[A stare from the Frenchman.]

" Well, if you don't know what that is, give us a champagne cock-tail."

[A stare and a shrug.]

" Well, then, give us a sherry cobbler."

The Frenchman was checkmated. This was all Greek to him.

" Give us a brandy smash! "

The Frenchman began to back away, suspicious of the ominous vigour of the last order—began to back away, shrugging his shoulders and spreading his hands apologetically.

The General followed him up and gained a complete victory. The uneducated foreigner could not even furnish a Santa Cruz Punch, an Eye-Opener, a Stone-Fence, or an Earthquake. It was plain that he was a wicked impostor.

An acquaintance of mine said the other day, that

he was doubtless the only American visitor to the Exposition who had had the high honour of being escorted by the Emperor's body guard. I said with unobtrusive frankness that I was astonished that such a long-legged, lantern-jawed, unprepossessing looking spectre as he should be singled out for a distinction like that, and asked how it came about. He said he had attended a great military review in the *Champ de Mars*, some time ago, and while the multitude about him was growing thicker and thicker every moment, he observed an open space inside the railing. He left his carriage and went into it. He was the only person there, and so he had plenty of room, and the situation being central, he could see all the preparations going on about the field. By-and-by there was a sound of music, and soon the Emperor of the French and the Emperor of Austria, escorted by the famous *Cent Gardes*, entered the inclosure. They seemed not to observe him, but directly, in response to a sign from the commander of the Guard, a young lieutenant came toward him with a file of his men following, halted, raised his hand and gave the military salute, and then said in a low voice that he was sorry to have to disturb a stranger and a gentleman, but the place was sacred to royalty. Then this New Jersey phantom rose up and bowed and begged pardon, then with the officer beside him, the file of men marching behind him, and with every mark of respect, he was escorted to his carriage by the imperial *Cent Gardes!* The officer saluted again and fell back, the New Jersey sprite bowed in return and had presence of mind enough to pretend that he had simply called on a matter of private business with those emperors, and so waved them an adieu, and drove from the field!

The Innocents Abroad

Imagine a poor Frenchman ignorantly intruding upon a public rostrum sacred to some sixpenny dignitary in America. The police would scare him to death, first with a storm of their elegant blasphemy, and then pull him to pieces getting him away from there. We are measurably superior to the French in some things, but they are immeasurably our betters in others.

Enough of Paris for the present. We have done our whole duty by it. We have seen the Tuileries, the Napoleon Column, the Madeleine, that wonder of wonders the tomb of Napoleon, all the great churches and museums, libraries, imperial palaces, and sculpture and picture galleries, the Pantheon, *Jardin des Plantes*, the opera, the circus, the Legislative Body, the billiard-rooms, the barbers, the *grisettes*—

Ah, the *grisettes*! I had almost forgotten. They are another romantic fraud. They were (if you let the books of travel tell it) always so beautiful—so neat and trim, so graceful—so naive and trusting—so gentle, so winning—so faithful to their shop duties, so irresistible to buyers in their prattling importunity—so devoted to their poverty-stricken students of the Latin Quarter—so light-hearted and happy on their Sunday picnics in the suburbs—and oh, so charmingly, so delightfully immoral!

Stuff! For three or four days I was constantly saying:

" Quick, Ferguson! is that a *grisette* ? "

And he always said " No."

He comprehended at last that I wanted to see a grisette. Then he showed me dozens of them. They were like nearly all the Frenchwomen I ever saw— homely. They had large hands, large feet, large mouths; they had pug noses as a general thing, and

moustaches that not even good breeding could over-
look; they combed their hair straight back without
parting; they were ill-shaped, they were not winning,
they were not graceful; I knew by their looks that
they ate garlic and onions; and lastly and finally,
to my thinking, it would be base flattery to call them
immoral.

Aroint thee, wench! I sorrow for the vagabond
student of the Latin Quarter now even more than
formerly I envied him. Thus topples to earth another
idol of my infancy.

We have seen everything, and to-morrow we go to
Versailles. We shall see Paris only for a little while
as we come back to take up our line of march for the
ship, and so I may as well bid the beautiful city a
regretful farewell. We shall travel many thousands
of miles after we leave here, and visit many great
cities, but we shall find none so enchanting as this.

Some of our party have gone to England, intending
to take a roundabout course and rejoin the vessel
at Leghorn or Naples, several weeks hence. We
came near going to Geneva, but have concluded to
return to Marseilles, and go up through Italy from
Genoa.

I will conclude this chapter with a remark that I
am sincerely proud to be able to make, and glad as
well that my comrades cordially indorse it—to wit,
by far the handsomest women we have seen in France
were born and reared in America.

. I feel now like a man who has redeemed a failing
reputation, and shed lustre upon a dimmed escutcheon
by a single just deed done at the eleventh hour.

Let the curtain fall to slow music.

The Innocents Abroad

CHAPTER XVI

VERSAILLES! It is wonderfully beautiful! You gaze, and stare, and try to understand that it is real, that it is on the earth, that it is not the Garden of Eden— but your brain grows giddy, stupefied by the world of beauty around you, and you half believe you are the dupe of an exquisite dream. The scene thrills one like military music! A noble palace stretching its ornamented front block upon block away, till it seemed that it would never end; a grand promenade before it, whereon the armies of an empire might parade; all about it rainbows of flowers, and colossal statues that were almost numberless, and yet seemed only scattered over the ample space; broad flights of stone steps leading down from the promenade to lower grounds of the park—stairways that whole regiments might stand to arms upon and have room to spare; vast fountains whose bronze effigies discharged rivers of sparkling water into the air and mingled a hundred curving jets together in forms of matchless beauty; wide grass-carpeted avenues that branched hither and thither in every direction and wandered to seemingly interminable distances, walled all the way on either side with compact ranks of leafy trees whose branches met above and formed arches as faultless and as symmetrical as ever were carved in stone; and here and there were glimpses of sylvan lakes with miniature ships glassed in their surfaces. And everywhere—on the palace steps, and the great promenade, around the fountains, among the trees, and far under the arches of the endless avenues, hundreds and hundreds of people in gay costumes walked or ran or danced, and gave to the fairy picture the life and animation which was all of perfection it could have lacked.

It was worth a pilgrimage to see. Everything is on so gigantic a scale. Nothing is small—nothing is cheap. The statues are all large; the palace is grand; the park covers a fair-sized county; the avenues are interminable. All the distances and all the dimensions about Versailles are vast. I used to think the pictures exaggerated these distances and these dimensions beyond all reason, and that they made Versailles more beautiful than it was possible for any place in the world to be. I know now that the pictures never came up to the subject in any respect, and that no painter could represent Versailles on canvas as beautiful as it is in reality. I used to abuse Louis XIV. for spending two hundred millions of dollars in creating this marvellous park, when bread was so scarce with some of his subjects; but I have forgiven him now. He took a tract of land sixty miles in circumference and set to work to make this park and build this palace and a road to it from Paris. He kept 36,000 men employed daily on it, and the labour was so unhealthy that they used to die and be hauled off by cart-loads every night. The wife of a nobleman of the time speaks of this as an " *inconvenience*," but naively remarks that " it does not seem worthy of attention in the happy state of tranquillity we now enjoy."

I always thought ill of people at home, who trimmed their shrubbery into pyramids, and squares, and spires, and all manner of unnatural shapes, and when I saw the same thing being practised in this great park I began to feel dissatisfied. But I soon saw the idea of the thing and the wisdom of it. They seek the *general* effect. We distort a dozen sickly trees into unaccustomed shapes in a little yard no bigger than a dining-room, and then surely they look absurd enough. But here they take two hundred thousand tall forest trees and set them in a double row; allow no sign of leaf or branch to grow on the trunk lower down than six feet above the ground; from that point the boughs begin to project, and very gradually they extend outward further and further till they meet overhead, and a faultless tunnel of foliage is formed. The arch is mathematically precise. The effect is then very fine. They make the trees take fifty different shapes, and so these quaint effects are infinitely varied and picturesque. The trees in no two avenues are shaped alike, and consequently the eye is not fatigued with anything in the nature of monotonous uniformity. I will drop this subject now, leaving it to others to determine how these people manage to make endless ranks of lofty trees grow to just a certain thickness of trunk (say a foot and two-thirds); how they make them spring to precisely the same height for miles; how they make them grow so close together; how they compel one huge limb to spring from the same identical spot on each tree and form the main sweep of the arch; and how all these things are kept exactly in the same condition, and in the same exquisite shapeliness and symmetry month after month and year after year—for I have tried to reason out the problem, and have failed.

We walked through the great hall of sculpture and the one hundred and fifty galleries of paintings in the palace of Versailles, and felt that to be in such a place was useless unless one had a whole year at his disposal. These pictures are all battle-scenes, and only one solitary little canvas among them all treats of anything but great French victories. We wandered, also, through the Grand Trianon and the Petit Trianon, those monuments of royal prodigality, and with histories so mournful—filled, as it is, with souvenirs of Napoleon the First, and three dead Kings and as many Queens. In one sumptuous bed they had all slept in succession, but no one occupies it now. In a large dining-room stood the table at which Louis XIV. and his mistress, Madame Maintenon, and after them Louis XV., and Pompadour, had sat at their meals naked and unattended—for the table stood upon a trap door which descended with it to regions below when it was necessary to replenish its dishes. In a room of the Petit Trianon stood the furniture, just as poor Marie Antoinette left it when the mob came and dragged her and the King to Paris, never to return. Near at hand, in the stables, were prodigious carriages that showed no colour but gold— carriages used by former Kings of France on state occasions, and never used now save when a kingly head is to be crowned, or an imperial infant christened. And with them were some curious sleighs, whose bodies were shaped like lions, swans, tigers, etc.— vehicles that had once been handsome with pictured designs and fine workmanship, but were dusty and decaying now. They had their history. When Louis XIV. had finished the Grand Trianon, he told Maintenon he had created a Paradise for her, and asked if she could think of anything now to wish for. He said he wished the Trianon to be perfection—nothing less. She said she could think of but one thing— it was summer, and it was balmy France—yet she would like well to sleigh-ride in the leafy avenues of Versailles! The next morning found miles and miles of grassy avenues spread thick with snowy salt and sugar, and a procession of those quaint sleighs waiting to receive the chief concubine of the gayest and most unprincipled court that France has ever seen!

From sumptuous Versailles, with its palaces, its statues, its gardens and its fountains, we journeyed back to Paris and sought its antipodes—the Faubourg St. Antoine. Little narrow streets; dirty children blockading them; greasy, slovenly women capturing and spanking them; filthy dens on first floors, with rag stores in them (the heaviest business in the Faubourg is the chiffonier's); other filthy dens where whole suits of second and third-hand clothing are sold at prices that would ruin any proprietor who did not steal his stock; still other filthy dens where they sold groceries—sold them by the half-pennyworth— five dollars would buy the man out, goodwill and all. Up these little crooked streets they will murder a man for seven dollars and dump the body in the Seine. And up some other of these streets—most of them, I should say—live lorettes.

All through this Faubourg St. Antoine, misery, poverty, vice and crime go hand in hand, and the evidences of it stare one in the face from every side. Here the people live who begin the revolutions. Whenever there is anything of that kind to be done, they are always ready. They take as much genuine pleasure in building a barricade as they do in cutting a throat or shoving a friend into the Seine. It is these savage-looking ruffians who storm the splendid halls of the Tuileries, occasionally, and swarm into Versailles when a King is to be called to account.

But they will build no more barricades, they will break no more soldiers' heads with paving-stones. Louis Napoleon has taken care of all that. He is annihilating the crooked streets, and building in their

stead noble boulevards as straight as an arrow—
avenues which a cannon ball could traverse from end
to end without meeting an obstruction more irresistible
than the flesh and bones of men—boulevards whose
stately edifices will never afford refuges and plotting-
places for starving, discontented revolution-breeders.
Five of these great thoroughfares radiate from one
ample centre—a centre which is exceedingly well
adapted to the accommodation of heavy artillery.
The mobs used to riot there, but they must seek
another rallying-place in future. And this ingenious
Napoleon paves the streets of his great cities with a
smooth, compact composition of asphaltum and sand.
No more barricades of flag-stones—no more assaulting
his Majesty's troops with cobbles. I cannot feel
friendly toward my quondam fellow-American, Napoleon III., especially at this time,[1] when I see his
credulous victim, Maximilian, lying stark and stiff
in Mexico, and his maniac widow watching eagerly
from her French asylum for the form that will never
come—but I do admire his nerve, his calm self-
reliance, his shrewd good sense.

CHAPTER XVII

WE had a pleasant journey of it seaward again. We
found that for the three past nights our ship had been
in a state of war. The first night the sailors of a
British ship, being happy with grog, came down on
the pier and challenged our sailors to a free fight.
They accepted with alacrity, repaired to the pier
and gained—their share of a drawn battle. Several

[1] July 1867.

bruised and bloody members of both parties were carried off by the police, and imprisoned until the following morning. The next night the British boys came again to renew the fight, but our men had had strict orders to remain on board and out of sight. They did so, and the besieging party grew noisy, and more and more abusive as the fact became apparent (to them) that our men were afraid to come out. They went away, finally, with a closing burst of ridicule and offensive epithets. The third night they came again, and were more obstreperous than ever. They swaggered up and down the almost deserted pier, and hurled curses, obscenity and stinging sarcasms at our crew. It was more than human nature could bear. The executive officer ordered our men ashore—with instructions not to fight. They charged the British and gained a brilliant victory. I probably would not have mentioned this war had it ended differently. But I travel to learn, and I still remember that they picture no French defeats in the battle-galleries of Versailles.

It was like home to us to step on board the comfortable ship again, and smoke and lounge about her breezy decks. And yet it was not altogether like home, either, because so many members of the family were away. We missed some pleasant faces which we would rather have found at dinner, and at night there were gaps in the euchre-parties which could not be satisfactorily filled. "Moult." was in England, Jack in Switzerland, Charley in Spain. Blucher was gone, none could tell where. But we were at sea again, and we had the stars and the ocean to look at, and plenty of room to meditate in.

In due time the shores of Italy were sighted, and as we stood gazing from the decks early in the bright summer morning, the stately city of Genoa rose up out of the sea and flung back the sunlight from her hundred palaces.

Here we rest for the present—or rather, here we have been trying to rest, for some little time, but we run about too much to accomplish a great deal in that line

I would like to remain here. I had rather not go any further. There may be prettier women in Europe, but I doubt it. The population of Genoa is 120,000; two-thirds of these are women, I think, and at least two-thirds of the women are beautiful. They are as dressy, and as tasteful, and as graceful as they could possibly be without being angels. However, angels are not very dressy, I believe. At least the angels in pictures are not—they wear nothing but wings. But these Genoese women do look so charming. Most of the young demoiselles are robed in a cloud of white from head to foot, though many trick themselves out more elaborately. Nine-tenths of them wear nothing on their heads but a filmy sort of veil, which falls down their backs like a white mist. They are very fair, and many of them have blue eyes, but black and dreamy dark brown ones are met with oftenest.

The ladies and gentlemen of Genoa have a pleasant fashion of promenading in a large park on the top of a hill in the centre of the city, from six till nine in the evening, and then eating ices in a neighbouring garden an hour or two longer. We went to the park on Sunday evening. Two thousand persons were present, chiefly young ladies and gentlemen. The gentlemen were dressed in the very latest Paris fashions, and the robes of the ladies glinted among the trees like so many snow-flakes. The multitude

The Innocents Abroad

moved round and round the park in a great procession.
The bands played, and so did the fountains; the moon
and the gas-lamps lit up the scene, and altogether it
was a brilliant and an animated picture. I scanned
every female face that passed, and it seemed to me
that all were handsome. I never saw such a freshet
of loveliness before. I do not see how a man of only
ordinary decision of character could marry here,
because before he could get his mind made up he
would fall in love with somebody else.

Never smoke any Italian tobacco. Never do it on
any account. It makes me shudder to think what it
must be made of. You cannot throw an old cigar
" stub " down anywhere, but some vagabond will
pounce upon it on the instant. I like to smoke a good
deal, but it wounds my sensibilities to see one of
these stub-hunters watching me out of the corners
of his hungry eyes and calculating how long my cigar
will be likely to last. It reminded me too painfully
of that San Francisco undertaker who used to go to
sick-beds with his watch in his hand and time the
corpse. One of these stub-hunters followed us all
over the park last night, and we never had a smoke
that was worth anything. We were always moved
to appease him with the stub before the cigar was
half gone, because he looked so viciously anxious.
He regarded us as his own legitimate prey, by right
of discovery, I think, because he drove off several
other professionals who wanted to take stock in us.

Now, they surely must grind up those old stubs,
and dry and sell them for smoking-tobacco. Therefore, give your custom to other than Italian brands
of the article.

" The Superb " and the " City of Palaces " are
names which Genoa has held for centuries. She is full

of palaces, certainly, and the palaces are sumptuous inside, but they are very rusty without, and make no pretensions to architectural magnificence. " Genoa, the Superb," would be a felicitous title if it referred to the women.

We have visited several of the palaces—immense thick-walled piles, with great stone staircases, tesselated marble pavements on the floors (sometimes they make a mosaic work, of intricate designs, wrought in pebbles, or little fragments of marble laid in cement), and grand *salons* hung with pictures by Rubens, Guido, Titian, Paul Veronese, and so on, and portraits of heads of the family, in plumed helmets and gallant coats of mail, and patrician ladies, in stunning costumes of centuries ago. But, of course, the folks were all out in the country for the summer, and might not have known enough to ask us to dinner if they had been at home, and so all the grand empty *salons*, with their resounding pavements, their grim pictures of dead ancestors, and tattered banners with the dust of bygone centuries upon them, seemed to brood solemnly of death and the grave, and our spirits ebbed away, and our cheerfulness passed from us. We never went up to the eleventh story. We always began to suspect ghosts. There was always an undertaker-looking servant along too, who handed us a programme, pointed to the picture that began the list of the *salon* he was in, and then stood stiff and stark and unsmiling in his petrified livery till we were ready to move on to the next chamber, whereupon he marched sadly ahead and took up another malignantly respectful position as before. I wasted so much time praying that the roof would fall in on these dispirited flunkeys that I had but little left to bestow upon palace and pictures.

The Innocents Abroad

And besides, as in Paris, we had a guide. Perdition catch all the guides! This one said he was the most gifted linguist in Genoa, as far as English was concerned, and that only two persons in the city beside himself could talk the language at all. He showed us the birthplace of Christopher Columbus, and after we had reflected in silent awe before it for fifteen minutes, he said it was not the birthplace of Columbus, but of Columbus's grandmother! When we demanded an explanation of his conduct he only shrugged his shoulders and answered in barbarous Italian. I shall speak further of this guide in a future chapter. All the information we got out of him we shall be able to carry along with us, I think.

I have not been to church so often in a long time as I have in the last few weeks. The people in these old lands seem to make churches their specialty. Especially does this seem to be the case with the citizens of Genoa. I think there is a church every three or four hundred yards all over town. The streets are sprinkled from end to end with shovel-hatted, long-robed, well-fed priests, and the church bells by dozens are pealing all the day long, nearly. Every now and then one comes across a friar of orders grey, with shaven head, long coarse robe, rope girdle and beads, and with feet cased in sandals or entirely bare. These worthies suffer in the flesh, and do penance all their lives, I suppose, but they look like consummate famine-breeders. They are all fat and serene.

The old Cathedral of San Lorenzo is about as notable a building as we have found in Genoa. It is vast, and has colonnades of noble pillars, and a great organ, and the customary pomp of gilded mouldings, pictures, frescoed ceilings, and so forth. I cannot describe it, of course—it would require a good many pages to do that. But it is a curious place. They said that half of it—from the front door half way down to the altar—was a Jewish Synagogue before the Saviour was born, and that no alteration had been made in it since that time. We doubted the statement, but did it reluctantly. We would much rather have believed it. The place looked in too perfect repair to be so ancient.

The main point of interest about the Cathedral is the little Chapel of St. John the Baptist. They only allow women to enter it on one day in the year, on account of the animosity they still cherish against the sex because of the murder of the Saint to gratify a caprice of Herodias. In this Chapel is a marble chest, in which, they told us, were the ashes of St. John; and around it was wound a chain, which, they said, had confined him when he was in prison. We did not desire to disbelieve these statements, and yet we could not feel certain that they were correct— partly because we could have broken that chain, and so could St. John, and partly because we had seen St. John's ashes before, in another Church. We could not bring ourselves to think St. John had two sets of ashes.

They also showed us a portrait of the Madonna which was painted by St. Luke, and it did not look half as old and smoky as some of the pictures by Rubens. We could not help admiring the Apostle's modesty in never once mentioning in his writings that he could paint.

But isn't this relic matter a little overdone? We find a piece of the true cross in every old church we go into, and some of the nails that held it together. I would not like to be positive, but I think we have seen as much as a keg of these nails. Then there is the crown of thorns; they have part of one in Sainte Chapelle, in Paris, and part of one, also, in Notre Dame. And as for bones of St. Denis, I feel certain we have seen enough of them to duplicate him, if necessary.

I only meant to write about the churches, but I keep wandering from the subject. I could say that the Church of the Annunciation is a wilderness of beautiful columns, of statues, gilded mouldings, and pictures almost countless, but that would give no one an entirely perfect idea of the thing, and so where is the use? One family built the whole edifice, and have got money left. There is where the mystery lies. We had an idea at first that only a mint could have survived the expense.

These people here live in the heaviest, highest, broadest, darkest, solidest houses one can imagine. Each one might " laugh a siege to scorn." A hundred feet front and a hundred high is about the style, and you go up three flights of stairs before you begin to come upon signs of occupancy. Everything is stone, and stone of the heaviest—floors, stairways, mantels, benches — everything. The walls are four to five feet thick. The streets generally are four or five to eight feet wide, and as crooked as a corkscrew. You go along one of these gloomy cracks, and look up and behold the sky like a mere ribbon of light, far above your head, where the tops of the tall houses on either side of the street bend almost together. You feel as if you were at the bottom of some tremendous abyss, with all the world far above you. You wind in and out, and here and there, in the most mysterious way, and have no more idea of the points of the compass than if you were a blind man. You can never persuade yourself that these are actually streets, and the frowning, dingy, monstrous houses dwellings, till you see one of these beautiful, prettily-dressed women emerge from them—see her emerge from a dark, dreary-looking den that looks dungeon all over, from the ground away half-way up to heaven. And then you wonder that such a charming moth could come from such a forbidding shell as that. The streets are wisely made narrow and the houses heavy and thick and stony, in order that the people may be cool in this roasting climate. And they are cool, and stay so. And while I think of it—the men wear hats and have very dark complexions, but the women wear no head-gear but a flimsy veil like a gossamer's web, and yet are exceedingly fair as a general thing. Singular, isn't it?

The huge palaces of Genoa are each supposed to be occupied by one family, but they could accommodate a hundred, I should think. They are relics of the grandeur of Genoa's palmy days—the days when she was a great commercial and maritime power several centuries ago. These houses, solid marble palaces though they be, are in many cases of a dull pinkish colour outside, and from pavement to eaves are pictured with Genoese battle-scenes, with monstrous Jupiters and Cupids, and with familiar illustrations from Grecian mythology. Where the paint has yielded to age and exposure, and is peeling off in flakes and patches, the effect is not happy. A noseless Cupid, or a Jupiter with an eye out, or a Venus with a fly-blister on her breast, are not attractive features in a picture. Some of these painted walls reminded me somewhat of the tall van, plastered with fanciful bills and posters, that follows the bandwaggon of a circus about a country village. I have not read or heard that the outsides of the houses of any other European city are frescoed in this way.

I cannot conceive of such a thing as Genoa in ruins. Such massive arches, such ponderous substructions as support these towering broad-winged edifices, we have seldom seen before; and surely the great blocks of stone of which these edifices are built can never decay; walls that are as thick as an ordinary American doorway is high, cannot crumble.

The Republics of Genoa and Pisa were very powerful in the middle ages. Their ships filled the Mediterranean, and they carried on an extensive commerce with Constantinople and Syria. Their warehouses were the great distributing depôts from whence the costly merchandise of the East was sent abroad over Europe. They were warlike little nations, and defied, in those days, governments that overshadow them now as mountains overshadow molehills. The Saracens captured and pillaged Genoa nine hundred years ago, but during the following century Genoa and Pisa entered into an offensive and defensive alliance and besieged the Saracen colonies in Sardinia and the Balearic Isles with an obstinacy that maintained its pristine vigour, and held to its purpose for forty long years. They were victorious at last, and divided their conquests equably among their great patrician families. Descendants of some of those proud families still inhabit the palaces of Genoa, and trace in their own features a resemblance to the grim knights whose portraits hang in their stately halls, and to pictured beauties with pouting lips and merry eyes whose originals have been dust and ashes for many a dead and forgotten century.

The hotel we live in belonged to one of those great orders of knights of the Cross in the times of the

The Innocents Abroad

Crusades, and its mailed sentinels once kept watch and ward in its massive turrets and woke the echoes of these halls and corridors with their iron heels.

But Genoa's greatness has degenerated into an unostentatious commerce in velvets and silver filigree work. They say that each European town has its specialty. These filigree things are Genoa's specialty. Her smiths take silver ingots and work them up into all manner of graceful and beautiful forms. They make bunches of flowers, from flakes and wires of silver, that counterfeit the delicate creations the frost weaves upon a window pane; and we were shown a miniature silver temple whose fluted columns, whose Corinthian capitals and rich entablatures, whose spire, statues, bells, and ornate lavishness of sculpture were wrought in polished silver, and with such matchless art that every detail was a fascinating study, and the finished edifice a wonder of beauty.

We are ready to move again, though we are not really tired yet of the narrow passages of this old marble cave. Cave is a good word, when speaking of Genoa under the stars. When we have been prowling at midnight through the gloomy crevices they call streets, where no footfalls but ours were echoing, where only ourselves were abroad, and lights appeared only at long intervals and at a distance, and mysteriously disappeared again, and the houses at our elbows seemed to stretch upward farther than ever toward the heavens, the memory of a cave I used to know at home was always in my mind, with its lofty passages, its silence and solitude, its shrouding gloom, its sepulchral echoes, its flitting lights, and more than all, its sudden revelations of branching crevices and corridors where we least expected them.

The Innocents Abroad

We are not tired of the endless processions of cheerful, chattering gossipers that throng these courts and streets all day long, either; nor of the coarse-robed monks; nor of the " Asti " wines, which that old doctor (whom we call the Oracle), with customary felicity in the matter of getting everything wrong, misterms " nasty." But we must go, nevertheless.

Our last sight was the cemetery (a burial-place intended to accommodate 60,000 bodies), and we shall continue to remember it after we shall have forgotten the palaces. It is a vast marble colonnaded corridor extending around a great unoccupied square of ground; its broad floor is marble, and on every slab is an inscription—for every slab covers a corpse. On either side, as one walks down the middle of the passage, are monuments, tombs, and sculptured figures that are exquisitely wrought and are full of grace and beauty. They are new and snowy; every outline is perfect, every feature guiltless of mutilation, flaw, or blemish; and therefore, to us these far-reaching ranks of bewitching forms are a hundredfold more lovely than the damaged and dingy statuary they have saved from the wreck of ancient art, and set up in the galleries of Paris for the worship of the world.

Well provided with cigars and other necessaries of life, we are now ready to take the cars for Milan.

The Innocents Abroad

CHAPTER XVIII

ALL day long we sped through a mountainous country whose peaks were bright with sunshine, whose hillsides were dotted with pretty villas sitting in the midst of gardens and shrubbery, and whose deep ravines were cool and shady, and looked ever so inviting from where we and the birds were winging our flight through the sultry upper air.

We had plenty of chilly tunnels wherein to check our perspiration, though. We timed one of them. We were twenty minutes passing through it, going at the rate of thirty to thirty-five miles an hour.

Beyond Alessandria we passed the battle-field of Marengo.

Towards dusk we drew near Milan, and caught glimpses of the city and the blue mountain-peaks beyond. But we were not caring for these things— they did not interest us in the least. We were in a fever of impatience; we were dying to see the renowned Cathedral! We watched—in this direction and that —all around—everywhere. We needed no one to point it out—we did not wish any one to point it out —we would recognise it, even in the desert of the great Sahara.

At last, a forest of graceful needles, shimmering in the amber sunlight, rose slowly above the pigmy house-tops, as one sometimes sees in the far horizon a gilded and pinnacled mass of cloud lift itself above the waste of waves at sea—the Cathedral! We knew it in a moment.

Half of that night and all of the next day this architectural autocrat was our sole object of interest.

The Innocents Abroad

What a wonder it is! So grand, so solemn, so vast! And yet so delicate, so airy, so graceful! A very world of solid weight, and yet it seems in the soft moonlight only a fairy delusion of frost-work that might vanish with a breath! How sharply its pinnacled angles and its wilderness of spires were cut against the sky, and how richly their shadows fell upon its snowy roof! It was a vision—a miracle!—an anthem sung in stone, a poem wrought in marble!

Howsoever you look at the great Cathedral, it is noble, it is beautiful! Wherever you stand in Milan, or within seven miles of Milan, it is visible—and when it is visible, no other object can claim your whole attention. Leave your eyes unfettered by your will but a single instant and they will surely turn to seek it. It is the first thing you look for when you rise in the morning, and the last your lingering gaze rests upon at night. Surely, it must be the princeliest creation that ever brain of man conceived.

At nine o'clock in the morning we went and stood before this marble colossus. The central one of its five great doors is bordered with a bas-relief of birds and fruits and beasts and insects, which have been so ingeniously carved out of the marble that they seem like living creatures—and the figures are so numerous and the design so complex, that one might study it a week without exhausting its interest. On the great steeple—surmounting the myriad of spires—inside the spires—over the doors, the windows—in nooks and corners—everywhere that a niche or a perch can be found about the enormous building, from summit to base, there is a marble statue, and every statue is a study in itself! Raphael, Angelo, Canova—giants like these gave birth to the designs, and their own pupils carved them. Every face is eloquent with expression, and every attitude is full of grace. Away above, on the lofty roof, rank on rank of carved and fretted spires spring high in the air, and through their rich tracery one sees the sky beyond. In their midst the central steeple towers proudly up like the mainmast of some great Indiaman among a fleet of coasters.

We wished to go aloft. The sacristan showed us a marble stairway (of course it was marble, and of the purest and whitest—there is no other stone, no brick, no wood, among its building materials) and told us to go up one hundred and eighty-two steps and stop till he came. It was not necessary to say stop; we should have done that anyhow. We were tired by the time we got there. This was the roof. Here, springing from its broad marble flagstones, were the long files of spires, looking very tall close at hand, but diminishing in the distance like the pipes of an organ. We could see now that the statue on the top of each was the size of a large man, though they all looked like dolls from the street. We could see also that from the inside of each and every one of these hollow spires, from sixteen to thirty-one marble statues looked out upon the world below.

From the eaves to the comb of the roof stretched in endless succession great curved marble beams like the fore-and-aft braces of a steamboat, and along each beam from end to end stood up a row of richly-carved flowers and fruits, each separate and distinct in kind, and over 15,000 species represented. At a little distance these rows seem to close together, like the ties of a railroad track, and then the mingling together of the buds and blossoms of this marble garden forms a picture that is very charming to the eye.

The Innocents Abroad

We descended and entered. Within the church long rows of fluted columns, like huge monuments, divided the building into broad aisles, and on the figured pavement fell many a soft blush from the painted windows above. I knew the church was very large, but I could not fully appreciate its great size until I noticed that the men standing far down by the altar looked like boys, and seemed to glide rather than walk. We loitered about, gazing aloft at the monster windows all aglow with brilliantly coloured scenes in the lives of the Saviour and his followers. Some of these pictures are mosaics, and so artistically are their thousand particles of tinted glass or stone put together, that the work has all the smoothness and finish of a painting. We counted sixty panes of glass in one window, and each pane was adorned with one of these master achievements of genius and patience.

The guide showed us a coffee-coloured piece of sculpture which he said was considered to have come from the hand of Phidias, since it was not possible that any other artist, of any epoch, could have copied nature with such faultless accuracy. The figure was that of a man without a skin; with every vein, artery, muscle, every fibre and tendon and tissue of the human frame, represented in minute detail. It looked natural, because somehow it looked as if it were in pain. A skinned man would be likely to look that way, unless his attention was occupied with some other matter. It was a hideous thing, and yet there was a fascination about it somewhere. I am very sorry I saw it, because I shall always see it now. I shall dream of it sometimes. I shall dream that it is resting its corded arms on the bed's head and looking down on me with its dead eyes; I shall dream that it is stretched between the sheets with me and touching me with its exposed muscles and its stringy cold legs.

It is hard to forget repulsive things. I remember yet how I ran off from school once, when I was a boy, and then, pretty late at night, concluded to climb into the window of my father's office and sleep on a lounge, because I had a delicacy about going home and getting thrashed. As I lay on the lounge and my eyes grew accustomed to the darkness, I fancied I could see a long, dusky, shapeless thing stretched upon the floor. A shiver went through me. I turned my face to the wall. That did not answer. I was afraid that the thing would creep over and seize me in the dark. I turned back and stared at it for minutes and minutes — they seemed hours. It appeared to me that the lagging moonlight never, never would get to it. I turned to the wall and counted twenty, to pass the feverish time away. I looked— the pale square was nearer. I turned again and counted fifty — it was almost touching it. With desperate will I turned again and counted one hundred and faced about, all in a tremble. A white human hand lay in the moonlight! Such an awful sinking at the heart—such a sudden gasp for breath! I felt, —I cannot tell *what* I felt. When I recovered strength enough, I faced the wall again. But no boy could have remained so with that mysterious hand behind him. I counted again, and looked — the most of a naked arm was exposed. I put my hands over my eyes and counted till I could stand it no longer, and then—the pallid face of a man was there, with the corners of the mouth drawn down, and the eyes fixed and glassy in death. I raised to a sitting posture and glowered on that corpse till the light crept down the bare breast—line by line—inch by inch—past the nipple—and then it disclosed a ghastly stab!

I went away from there. I did not say that I went away in any sort of a hurry, but I simply went, that is sufficient. I went out at the window, and I carried the sash along with me. I did not need the sash, but it was handier to take it than it was to leave it, and so I took it. I was not scared, but I was considerably agitated.

When I reached home they whipped me, but I enjoyed it. It seemed perfectly delightful. That man had been stabbed near the office that afternoon, and they carried him in there to doctor him, but he only lived an hour. I have slept in the same room with him often, since then—in my dreams.

Now we will descend into the crypt, under the grand altar of Milan Cathedral, and receive an impressive sermon from lips that have been silent, and hands that have been gestureless for three hundred years.

The priest stopped in a small dungeon and held up his candle. This was the last resting-place of a good man, a warm-hearted, unselfish man; a man whose whole life was given to succouring the poor, encouraging the faint-hearted, visiting the sick, in relieving distress whenever and wherever he found it. His heart, his hand, and his purse were always open. With his story in one's mind we can almost see his benignant countenance moving calmly among the haggard faces of Milan in the days when the plague swept the city, brave where all others were cowards, full of compassion where pity had been crushed out of all other breasts by the instinct of self-preservation gone mad with terror, cheering all, praying with all, helping all with hand and brain and purse, at a time when parents forsook their children, the friend deserted the friend, and the brother turned away from the sister while her pleadings were still wailing in his ears.

This was good St. Charles Borroméo, Bishop of Milan. The people idolised him; princes lavished uncounted treasures upon him. We stood in his tomb. Near by was the sarcophagus, lighted by the dripping candles. The walls were faced with bas-reliefs representing scenes in his life done in massive silver. The priest put on a short white lace garment over his black robe, crossed himself, bowed reverently, and began to turn a windlass slowly. The sarco-phagus separated in two parts lengthwise, and the lower part sank down and disclosed a coffin of rock crystal as clear as the atmosphere. Within lay the body, robed in costly habiliments covered with gold embroidery and starred with scintillating gems. The decaying head was black with age, the dry skin was drawn tight to the bones, the eyes were gone, there was a hole in the temple and another in the cheek, and the skinny lips were parted as in a grisly smile! Over this dreadful face, its dust and decay, and its mocking grin, hung a crown sown thick with flashing brilliants; and upon the breast lay crosses and croziers of gold that were splendid with emeralds and diamonds.

How poor, and cheap, and trivial these gew-gaws seemed in presence of the solemnity, the grandeur, the awful majesty of Death! Think of Milton, Shakspeare, Washington, standing before a reverent world tricked out in the glass beads, the brass ear-rings and tin trumpery of the savages of the plains!

Dead Bartoloméo preached his pregnant sermon, and its burden was: You that worship the vanities

The Innocents Abroad

of earth—you that long for worldly honour, worldly wealth, worldly fame—behold their worth!

To us it seemed that so good a man, so kind a heart, so simple a nature, deserved rest and peace in a grave sacred from the intrusion of prying eyes, and believed that he himself would have preferred to have it so, but peradventure our wisdom was at fault in this regard.

As we came out upon the floor of the church again, another priest volunteered to show us the treasures of the church. What, more? The furniture of the narrow chamber of death we had just visited weighed six millions of francs in ounces and carats alone, without a penny thrown into the account for the costly workmanship bestowed upon them! But we followed into a large room filled with tall wooden presses like wardrobes. He threw them open, and behold the cargoes of " crude bullion " of the assay offices of Nevada faded out of my memory. There were Virgins and bishops there above their natural size, made of solid silver, each worth by weight from eight hundred thousand to two millions of francs, and bearing gemmed books in their hands worth eighty thousand; there were bas-reliefs that weighed six hundred pounds, carved in solid silver; croziers and crosses, and candlesticks six and eight feet high, all of virgin gold, and brilliant with precious stones; and beside these were all manner of cups and vases, and such things, rich in proportion. It was an Aladdin's palace. The treasures here, by simple weight, without counting workmanship, were valued at fifty millions of francs! If I could get the custody of them for a while, I fear me the market price of silver bishops would advance shortly on account of their exceeding scarcity in the Cathedral of Milan.

The Innocents Abroad

The priests showed us two of St. Paul's fingers, and one of St. Peter's; a bone of Judas Iscariot (it was black), and also bones of all the other disciples; a handkerchief in which the Saviour had left the impression of his face. Among the most precious of the relics were a stone from the Holy Sepulchre, part of the crown of thorns (they have a whole one at Notre Dame), a fragment of the purple robe worn by the Saviour, a nail from the Cross, and a picture of the Virgin and Child painted by the veritable hand of St. Luke. This is the second of St. Luke's Virgins we have seen. Once a year all these holy relics are carried in procession through the streets of Milan.

I like to revel in the dryest details of the great cathedral. The building is five hundred feet long by one hundred and eighty wide, and the principal steeple is in the neighbourhood of four hundred feet high. It has seven thousand one hundred and forty-eight marble statues, and will have upwards of three thousand more when it is finished. In addition, it has one thousand five hundred bas-reliefs. It has one hundred and thirty-six spires—twenty-one more are to be added. Each spire is surmounted by a statue six and a half feet high. Everything about the church is marble, and all from the same quarry; it was bequeathed to the Archbishopric for this purpose centuries ago. So nothing but the mere workmanship costs; still that is expensive—the bill foots up six hundred and eighty-four millions of dollars—and it is estimated that it will take a hundred and twenty years yet to finish the cathedral. It looks complete, but it is far from being so. We saw a new statue put up in its niche yesterday, alongside of one which had been standing these four hundred years, they said. There are four staircases leading up to the main steeple, each of which cost a hundred thousand dollars, with the four hundred and eight statues which adorn them. Marco Compioni was the architect who designed the wonderful structure more than five hundred years ago, and it took him forty-six years to work out the plan and get it ready to hand over to the builders. He is dead now. The building was begun a little less than five hundred years ago, and the third generation hence will not see it completed.

The building looks best by moonlight, because the older portions of it, being stained with age, contrast unpleasantly with the newer and whiter portions. It seems somewhat too broad for its height, but maybe familiarity with it might dissipate this impression.

They say that the Cathedral of Milan is second only to St. Peter's at Rome. I cannot understand how it can be second to anything made by human hands.

We bid it good-by, now—possibly for all time. How surely, in some future day, when the memory of it shall have lost its vividness, shall we half believe we have seen it in a wonderful dream, but never with waking eyes!

CHAPTER XIX

" Do you wis zo haut can be? "

That was what the guide asked, when we were looking up at the bronze horses on the Arch of Peace. It meant, do you wish to go up there? I give it as a specimen of guide-English. These are the people that make life a burthen to the tourist. Their tongues are never still. They talk for ever and for ever, and that is the kind of Billingsgate they use.

The Innocents Abroad

Inspiration itself could hardly comprehend them. If they would only show you a masterpiece of art, or a venerable tomb, or a prison-house, or a battle-field, hallowed by touching memories or historical reminiscences or grand traditions, and then step aside and hold still for ten minutes and let you think, it would not be so bad. But they interrupt every dream, every pleasant train of thought, with their tiresome cackling. Sometimes, when I have been standing before some cherished old idol of mine that I remembered years and years ago in pictures in the geography at school, I have thought I would give a whole world if the human parrot at my side would suddenly perish where he stood and leave me to gaze, and ponder, and worship.

No, we did not " wis zo haut can be." We wished to go to La Scala, the largest theatre in the world, I think they call it. We did so. It was a large place. Seven separate and distinct masses of humanity—six great circles and a monster parquette.

We wished to go to the Ambrosian Library, and we did that also. We saw a manuscript of Virgil, with annotations in the handwriting of Petrarch, the gentleman who loved another man's Laura, and lavished upon her all through life a love which was a clear waste of the raw material. It was sound sentiment, but bad judgment. It brought both parties fame, and created a fountain of commiseration for them in sentimental breasts that is running yet. But who says a word in behalf of poor Mr. Laura? (I do not know his other name.) Who glorifies him? Who bedews him with tears? Who writes poetry about him? Nobody. How do you suppose *he* liked the state of things that has given the world so much pleasure? How did he enjoy having another man following his wife everywhere and making her name a familiar word in every gaelic-exterminating mouth in Italy with his sonnets to her pre-empted eyebrows? *They* got fame and sympathy—he got neither. This is a peculiarly felicitous instance of what is called poetical justice. It is all very fine; but it does not chime with my notions of right. It is too one-sided—too ungenerous. Let the world go on fretting about Laura and Petrarch if it will; but as for me, my tears and my lamentations shall be lavished upon the unsung defendant.

We saw also an autograph letter of Lucrezia Borgia, a lady for whom I have always entertained the highest respect, on account of her rare histrionic capabilities, her opulence in solid gold goblets made of gilded wood, her high distinction as an operatic screamer, and the facility with which she could order a sextuple funeral and get the corpses ready for it. We saw one single coarse yellow hair from Lucrezia's head likewise. It awakes emotions, but we still live. In this same library we saw some drawings by Michael Angelo (these Italians call him Mickel Angelo) and Leonardo da Vinci. (They spell it Vinci and pronounce it Vinchy; foreigners always spell better than they pronounce.) We reserve our opinion of these sketches.

In another building they showed us a fresco representing some lions and other beasts drawing chariots; and they seemed to project so far from the wall that we took them to be sculptures. The artist had shrewdly heightened the delusion by painting dust on the creatures' backs, as if it had fallen there naturally and properly. Smart fellow—if it be smart to deceive strangers.

Elsewhere we saw a huge Roman amphitheatre, with its stone seats still in good preservation. Modernised, it is now the scene of more peaceful recreations than the exhibition of a party of wild beasts with Christians for dinner. Part of the time, the Milanese use it for a race track, and at other seasons they flood it with water and have spirited yachting regattas there. The guide told us these things, and he would hardly try so hazardous an experiment as the telling of a falsehood, when it is all he can do to speak the truth in English without getting the lock-jaw.

In another place we were shown a sort of summer arbour, with a fence before it. We said that was nothing. We looked again, and saw, through the arbour, an endless stretch of garden, and shrubbery, and grassy lawn. We were perfectly willing to go in there and rest, but it could not be done. It was only another delusion—a painting by some ingenious artist with little charity in his heart for tired folk. The deception was perfect. No one could have imagined the park was not real. We even thought we smelled the flowers at first.

We got a carriage at twilight and drove in the shaded avenues with the other nobility, and after dinner we took wine and ices in a fine garden with the great public. The music was excellent, the flowers and shrubbery were pleasant to the eye, the scene was vivacious, everybody was genteel and well-behaved, and the ladies were slightly moustached, and handsomely dressed, but very homely.

We adjourned to a *café* and played billiards an hour, and I made six or seven points by the doctor pocketing his ball, and he made as many by my pocketing my ball. We came near making a carom sometimes, but not the one we were trying to make. The table was of the usual European style—cushions dead and twice as high as the balls; the cues in bad repair. The natives play only a sort of pool on them. We have never seen anybody playing the French three ball game yet, and I doubt if there is any such game known in France, or that there lives any man mad enough to try to play it on one of these European tables. We had to stop playing, finally, because Dan got to sleeping fifteen minutes between the counts and paying no attention to his marking.

Afterward we walked up and down one of the most popular streets for some time, enjoying other people's comfort and wishing we could export some of it to our restless, driving, vitality-consuming marts at home. Just in this one matter lies the main charm of life in Europe—comfort. In America, we hurry —which is well; but when the day's work is done, we go on thinking of losses and gains, we plan for the morrow, we even carry our business cares to bed with us, and toss and worry over them when we ought to be restoring our racked bodies and brains with sleep. We burn up our energies with these excitements, and either die early or drop into a lean and mean old age at a time of life which they call a man's prime in Europe. When an acre of ground has produced long and well, we let it lie fallow and rest for a season; we take no man clear across the continent in the same coach he started in—the coach is stabled somewhere on the plains and its heated machinery allowed to cool for a few days; when a razor has seen long service and refuses to hold an edge, the barber lays it away for a few weeks, and the edge comes back of its own accord. We bestow thoughtful care upon inanimate objects, but none upon ourselves. What a robust people, what a nation of thinkers we might be, if we would only lay ourselves on the shelf occasionally and renew our edges!

The Innocents Abroad

I do envy these Europeans the comfort they take. When the work of the day is done, they forget it. Some of them go, with wife and children, to a beer hall, and sit quietly and genteelly drinking a mug or two of ale and listening to music; others walk the streets, others drive in the avenues; others assemble in the great ornamental squares in the early evening to enjoy the sight and the fragrance of flowers, to hear the military bands play—no European city being without its fine military music at eventide; and yet others of the populace sit in the open air in front of the refreshment houses and eat ices and drink mild beverages that could not harm a child. They go to bed moderately early, and sleep well. They are always quiet, always orderly, always cheerful, comfortable, and appreciative of life and its manifold blessings. One never sees a drunken man among them. The change that has come over our little party is surprising. Day by day we lose some of our restlessness and absorb some of the spirit of quietude and ease that is in the tranquil atmosphere about us and in the demeanour of the people. We grow wise apace. We begin to comprehend what life is for.

We have had a bath in Milan, in a public bath-house. They were going to put all three of us in one bath-tub, but we objected. Each of us had an Italian farm on his back. We could have felt affluent if we had been officially surveyed and fenced in. We chose to have three bath-tubs, and large ones—tubs suited to the dignity of aristocrats who had real estate, and brought it with them. After we were stripped and had taken the first chilly dash, we discovered that haunting atrocity that has embittered our lives in so many cities and villages of Italy and France—there was no soap. I called. A woman answered, and I barely had time to throw myself against the door—she would have been in, in another second. I said:

" Beware, woman! Go away from here—go away, now, or it will be the worse for you. I am an unprotected male, but I will preserve my honour at the peril of my life! "

These words must have frightened her, for she skurried away very fast.

Dan's voice rose on the air—

" Oh, bring some soap, why don't you! "

The reply was Italian. Dan resumed—

" Soap, you know—soap. That is what I want—soap. S-o-a-p, soap; s-o-p-e, soap; s-o-u-p, soap. Hurry up! I don't know how you Irish spell it, but I want it. Spell it to suit yourself, but fetch it. I'm freezing."

I heard the doctor say, impressively—

" Dan, how often have we told you that these foreigners cannot understand English? Why will you not depend upon us? Why will you not tell *us* what you want, and let us ask for it in the language of the country? It would save us a great deal of the humiliation your reprehensible ignorance causes us. I will address this person in his mother tongue: ' Here, cospetto! corpo di Bacco! Sacramento! Solferino!— Soap, you son of a gun! ' Dan, if you would let *us* talk for you, you would never expose your ignorant vulgarity."

Even this fluent discharge of Italian did not bring the soap at once, but there was a good reason for it. There was not such an article about the establishment. It is my belief that there never had been. They had to send far up town, and to several different places before they finally got it, so they said. We had to wait twenty or thirty minutes. The same thing had occurred the evening before, at the hotel. I think I have divined the reason for this state of things at last. The English know how to travel comfortably, and they carry soap with them; other foreigners do not use the article.

At every hotel we stop at we always have to send out for soap, at the last moment, when we are grooming ourselves for dinner, and they put it in the bill along with the candles and other nonsense. In Marseilles they make half the fancy toilet soap we consume in America, but the Marseillaise only have a vague theoretical idea of its use, which they have obtained from books of travel, just as they have acquired an uncertain notion of clean shirts, and the peculiarities of the gorilla, and other curious matters. This reminds me of poor Blucher's note to the landlord in Paris:—

"PARIS, le 7 Juillet.

"*Monsieur le Landlord*—Sir: *Pourquoi* don't you *mettez* some *savon* in your bed-chambers? *Est-ce que vous pensez* I will steal it? *La nuit passée* you charged me *pour deux chandelles* when I only had one; *hier vous avez* charged me *avec glace* when I had none at all; *tout les jours* you are coming some fresh game or other on me, *mais vous ne pouvez pas* play this *savon* dodge on me twice. *Savon* is a necessary *de la vie* to anybody but a Frenchman, *et je l'aurai hors de cet hôtel* or make trouble. You hear *me*. *Allons*.

BLUCHER."

I remonstrated against the sending of this note, because it was so mixed up that the landlord would never be able to make head or tail of it; but Blucher said he guessed the old man could read the French of it and average the rest.

The Innocents Abroad

Blucher's French is bad enough, but it is not much worse than the English one finds in advertisements all over Italy every day. For instance, observe the printed card of the hotel we shall probably stop at on the shores of Lake Como:—

> ## "NOTISH."
>
> "This hotel which the best it is in Italy and most superb, is handsome locate on the best situation of the lake, with the most splendid view near the Villas Melzy, to the King of Belgian, and Serbelloni. This hotel have recently enlarge, do offer all commodities on moderate price, at the strangers gentlemen who whish spend the seasons on the Lake Come."

How is that for a specimen? In the hotel is a handsome little chapel where an English clergyman is employed to preach to such of the guests of the house as hail from England and America, and this fact is also set forth in barbarous English in the same advertisement. Wouldn't you have supposed that the adventurous linguist who framed the card would have known enough to submit it to that clergyman before he sent it to the printer?

Here in Milan, in an ancient tumbledown ruin of a church, is the mournful wreck of the most celebrated painting in the world—"The Last Supper," by Leonardo da Vinci. We are not infallible judges of pictures, but of course we went there to see this wonderful painting, once so beautiful, always so worshipped by masters in art, and forever to be famous in song and story. And the first thing that occurred was the infliction on us of a placard fairly reeking with wretched English. Take a morsel of it—

"Bartholomew (that is the first figure on the left-hand side of the spectator), uncertain and doubtful about what he thinks to have heard, and upon which he wants to be assured by himself at Christ and by no others."

Good, isn't it? And then Peter is described as " argumenting in a threatening and angrily condition at Judas Iscariot."

This paragraph recalls the picture. " The Last Supper " is painted on the dilapidated wall of what was a little chapel attached to the main church in ancient times, I suppose. It is battered and scarred in every direction, and stained and discoloured by time, and Napoleon's horses kicked the legs off most the disciples when they (the horses, not the disciples) were stabled there more than half a century ago.

I recognised the old picture in a moment—the Saviour with bowed head seated at the centre of a long, rough table with scattering fruits and dishes upon it, and six disciples on either side in their long robes, talking to each other—the picture from which all engravings and all copies have been made for three centuries. Perhaps no living man has ever known an attempt to paint the Lord's Supper differently. The world seems to have become settled in the belief long ago, that it is not possible for human genius to outdo this creation of Da Vinci's. I suppose painters will go on copying it as long as any of the original is left visible to the eye. There were a dozen easels in the room, and as many artists transferring the great picture to their canvases. Fifty proofs of steel engravings and lithographs were scattered around too. And, as usual, I could not help noticing how superior the copies were to the original, that is, to my inexperienced eye. Wherever you find a Raphael, a Rubens, a Michael Angelo, a Caracci, or a Da

The Innocents Abroad

Vinci (and we see them every day), you find artists copying them, and the copies are always the handsomest. Maybe the originals were handsome when they were new, but they are not now.

This picture is about thirty feet long, and ten or twelve high, I should think, and the figures are at least life size. It is one of the largest paintings in Europe.

The colours are dimmed with age; the countenances are scaled and marred, and nearly all expression is gone from them; the hair is a dead blur upon the wall, and there is no life in the eyes. Only the attitudes are certain.

People come here from all parts of the world, and glorify this masterpiece. They stand entranced before it with bated breath and parted lips, and when they speak, it is only in the catchy ejaculations of rapture—

" O, wonderful! "
" Such expression! "
" Such grace of attitude! "
" Such dignity! "
" Such faultless drawing! "
" Such matchless colouring ! "
" Such feeling! "
" What delicacy of touch! "
" What sublimity of conception! "
" A vision! a vision! "

I only envy these people; I envy them their honest admiration, if it be honest—their delight, if they feel delight. I harbour no animosity toward any of them. But at the same time the thought *will* intrude itself upon me, How can they see what is not visible? What would you think of a man who looked at some decayed, blind, toothless, pock-marked Cleopatra,

and said, " What matchless beauty! What soul!
What expression! " What would you think of a
man who gazed upon a dingy, foggy sunset, and said—
" What sublimity! what feeling! what richness of
colouring! " What would you think of a man who
stared in ecstasy upon a desert of stumps and said—
" Oh, my soul, my beating heart, what a noble forest
is here! "

You would think that those men had an astonishing
talent for seeing things that had already passed away.
It was what I thought when I stood before the
" Last Supper " and heard men apostrophising
wonders, and beauties, and perfections which had
faded out of the picture and gone, a hundred years
before they were born. We can imagine the beauty
that was once in an aged face; we can imagine the
forest if we see the stumps; but we cannot absolutely
see these things when they are not there. I am willing
to believe that the eye of the practised artist can rest
upon the " Last Supper" and renew a lustre where only
a hint of it is left, supply a tint that has faded away,
restore an expression that is gone; patch, and colour,
and add to the dull canvas until at last its figures
shall stand before him aglow with the life, the feeling,
the freshness, yea, with all the noble beauty that was
theirs when first they came from the hand of the
master. But *I* cannot work this miracle. Can
those other uninspired visitors do it, or do they only
happily imagine they do?

After reading so much about it, I am satisfied that
the " Last Supper " was a very miracle of art once.
But it was three hundred years ago.

It vexes me to hear people talk so glibly of " feeling," " expression," " tone," and those other easily
acquired and inexpensive technicalities of art that

The Innocents Abroad

make such a fine show in conversations concerning pictures. There is not one man in seventy-five hundred that can tell *what* a pictured face is intended to express. There is not one man in five hundred that can go into a court-room and be sure that he will not mistake some harmless innocent of a juryman for the black-hearted assassin on trial. Yet such people talk of "character" and presume to interpret "expression" in pictures. There is an old story that Mathews, the actor, was once lauding the ability of the human face to express the passions and emotions hidden in the breast. He said the countenance could disclose what was passing in the heart plainer than the tongue could.

"Now," he said, "observe my face—what does it express?"

"Despair!"

"Bah, it expresses peaceful resignation! What does *this* express?"

"Rage!"

"Stuff! it means terror! *This!*"

"Imbecility!"

"Fool! it is smothered ferocity! Now *this!*"

"Joy!"

"Oh, perdition! *Any* ass can see it means insanity!"

Expression! People coolly pretend to read it who would think themselves presumptuous if they pretended to interpret the hieroglyphics on the obelisks of Luxor—yet they are fully as competent to do the one thing as the other. I have heard two very intelligent critics speak of Murillo's Immaculate Conception (now in the museum at Seville) within the past few days. One said—

"Oh, the Virgin's face is full of the ecstasy of a

joy that is complete—that leaves nothing more to be desired on earth!"

The other said—

"Ah, that wonderful face is so humble, so pleading —it says as plainly as words could say it—'I fear; I tremble; I am unworthy. But Thy will be done; sustain Thou Thy servant!'"

The reader can see the picture in any drawing-room; it can be easily recognised: the Virgin (the only young and really beautiful Virgin that was ever painted by one of the old masters, some of us think) stands in the crescent of the new moon, with a multitude of cherubs hovering about her, and more coming; her hands are crossed upon her breast, and upon her uplifted countenance falls a glory out of the heavens. The reader may amuse himself, if he chooses, in trying to determine which of these gentlemen read the Virgin's "expression" aright, or if either of them did it.

Any one who is acquainted with the old masters will comprehend how much the "Last Supper" is damaged when I say that the spectator cannot really tell now whether the disciples are Hebrews or Italians. These ancient painters never succeeded in de-nationalising themselves. The Italian artists painted Italian Virgins, the Dutch painted Dutch Virgins, the Virgins of the French painters were French-women—none of them ever put into the face of the Madonna that indescribable something which pro-claims the Jewess, whether you find her in New York, in Constantinople, in Paris, Jerusalem, or in the Empire of Morocco. I saw in the Sandwich Islands once a picture, copied by a talented German artist from an engraving in one of the American illustrated papers. It was an allegory, representing Mr. Davis in the act of signing a secession act or some such document. Over him hovered the ghost of Washington in warning attitude, and in the background a troop of shadowy soldiers in Continental uniform were limping with shoeless, bandaged feet through a driving snow-storm. Valley Forge was suggested, of course. The copy seemed accurate, and yet there was a discrepancy somewhere. After a long examination I discovered what it was—the shadowy soldiers were all Germans! Jeff. Davis was a German! even the hovering ghost was a German ghost! The artist had unconsciously worked his nationality into the picture. To tell the truth, I am getting a little perplexed about John the Baptist and his portraits. In France I finally grew reconciled to him as a Frenchman; here he is unquestionably an Italian. What next? Can it be possible that the painters make John the Baptist a Spaniard in Madrid and an Irishman in Dublin?

We took an open barouche and drove two miles out of Milan to "see ze echo," as the guide expressed it. The road was smooth, it was bordered by trees, fields, and grassy meadows, and the soft air was filled with the odour of flowers. Troops of picturesque peasant girls, coming from work, hooted at us, shouted at us, made all manner of game of us, and entirely delighted me. My long-cherished judgment was confirmed. I always did think those frowsy, romantic, unwashed peasant girls I had read so much about in poetry were a glaring fraud.

We enjoyed our jaunt. It was an exhilarating relief from tiresome sight-seeing.

We distressed ourselves very little about the astonishing echo the guide talked so much about. We were growing accustomed to encomiums on wonders that too often proved no wonders at all.

The Innocents Abroad

And so we were most happily disappointed to find in the sequel that the guide had even failed to rise to the magnitude of his subject.

We arrived at a tumbledown old rookery called the Palazzo Simonetti—a massive hewn-stone affair, occupied by a family of ragged Italians. A good-looking young girl conducted us to a window on the second floor which looked out on a court walled on three sides by tall buildings. She put her head out at the window and shouted. The echo answered more times than we could count. She took a speaking trumpet and through it she shouted, sharp and quick, a single

" Ha! " The echo answered —

" Ha!———ha!——ha!—ha!—ha!-ha! ha! h-a-a-a-a-a! " and finally went off into a rollicking convulsion of the jolliest laughter that could be imagined. It was so joyful—so long continued—so perfectly cordial and hearty, that everybody was forced to join in. There was no resisting it.

Then the girl took a gun and fired it. We stood ready to count the astonishing clatter of reverberations. We could not say one, two, three, fast enough, but we could dot our note-books with our pencil points almost rapidly enough to take down a sort of short-hand report of the result. I could not keep up, but I did as well as I could.

I set down fifty-two distinct repetitions, and then the echo got the advantage of me. The doctor set down sixty-four, and thenceforth the echo moved too fast for him also. After the separate concussions could no longer be noted, the reverberations dwindled to a wild, long-sustained clatter of sounds such as a watchman's rattle produces. It is likely that this is the most remarkable echo in the world.

The Innocents Abroad

The doctor, in jest, offered to kiss the young girl, and was taken a little aback when she said he might for a franc! The commonest gallantry compelled him to stand by his offer, and so he paid the franc and took the kiss. She was a philosopher. She said a franc was a good thing to have, and she did not care anything for one paltry kiss, because she had a million left. Then our comrade, always a shrewd business man, offered to take the whole cargo at thirty days, but that little financial scheme was a failure.

CHAPTER XX

WE left Milan by rail. The Cathedral six or seven miles behind us—vast, dreamy, blueish snow-clad mountains twenty miles in front of us—these were the accented points in the scenery. The more immediate scenery consisted of fields and farm-houses outside the car, and a monster-headed dwarf and a moustached woman inside it. These latter were not show-people. Alas! deformity and female beards are too common in Italy to attract attention.

We passed through a range of wild, picturesque hills, steep, wooded, cone-shaped, with rugged crags projecting here and there, and with dwellings and ruinous castles perched away up toward the drifting clouds. We lunched at the curious old town of Como, at the foot of the lake, and then took the small steamer and had an afternoon's pleasure excursion to this place—Bellaggio.

When we walked ashore, a party of policemen (people whose cocked hats and showy uniforms would shame the finest uniform in the military service of the United States) put us into a little stone cell and locked us in. We had the whole passenger list for company, but their room would have been preferable, for there was no light, there were no windows, no ventilation. It was close and hot. We were much crowded. It was the Black Hole of Calcutta on a small scale. Presently a smoke rose about our feet —a smoke that smelt of all the dead things of earth, of all the putrefaction and corruption imaginable.

We were there five minutes, and when we got out it was hard to tell which of us carried the vilest fragrance.

These miserable outcasts called that " fumigating " us, and the term was a tame one indeed. They fumigated us to guard themselves against the cholera, though we hailed from no infected port. We had left the cholera far behind us all the time. However, they must keep epidemics away somehow or other, and fumigation is cheaper than soap. They must either wash themselves or fumigate other people. Some of the lower classes had rather die than wash, but the fumigation of strangers causes them no pangs. They need no fumigation themselves. Their habits make it unnecessary. They carry their preventive with them; they sweat and fumigate all the day long. I trust I am a humble and a consistent Christian. I try to do what is right. I know it is my duty to " pray for them that despitefully use me; " and therefore, hard as it is, I shall still try to pray for these fumigating, maccaroni-stuffing organ-grinders.

Our hotel sits at the water's edge—at least, its front garden does—and we walk among the shrubbery and smoke at twilight; we look afar off at Switzerland and the Alps, and feel an indolent willingness to look

no closer; we go down the steps and swim in the lake;
we take a shapely little boat and sail abroad among
the reflections of the stars; lie on the thwarts and
listen to the distant laughter, the singing, the soft
melody of flutes and guitars that comes floating across
the water from pleasuring gondolas; we close the
evening with exasperating billiards on one of those
same old execrable tables. A midnight luncheon in
our ample bedchamber; a final smoke in its contracted verandah facing the water, the gardens, and
the mountains; a summing up of the day's events.
Then to bed, with drowsy brains harassed with a
mad panorama that mixes up pictures of France, of
Italy, of the ship, of the ocean, of home, in grotesque
and bewildering disorder. Then a melting away of
familiar faces, of cities and of tossing waves, into a
great calm of forgetfulness and peace.

After which, the nightmare.

Breakfast in the morning, and then the Lake.

I did not like it yesterday. I thought Lake Tahoe
was *much* finer. I have to confess now, however, that
my judgment erred somewhat, though not extravagantly. I always had an idea that Como was a vast
basin of water, like Tahoe, shut in by great mountains.
Well, the border of huge mountains is here, but the
lake itself is not a basin. It is as crooked as any
brook, and only from one-quarter to two-thirds as
wide as the Mississippi river. There is not a yard of
low ground on either side of it—nothing but endless
chains of mountains that spring abruptly from the
water's edge, and tower to altitudes varying from a
thousand to two thousand feet. Their craggy sides
are clothed with vegetation, and white specks of
houses peep out from the luxuriant foliage everywhere; they are even perched upon jutting and

picturesque pinnacles a thousand feet above your head.

Again, for miles along the shores handsome country seats, surrounded by gardens and groves, sit fairly in the water, sometimes in nooks carved by Nature out of the vine-hung precipices, and with no ingress or egress save by boats. Some have great broad stone staircases leading down to the water, with heavy stone balustrades ornamented with statuary, and fancifully adorned with creeping vines and bright-coloured flowers—for all the world like a drop-curtain in a theatre, and lacking nothing but long-waisted, high-heeled women and plumed gallants in silken tights coming down to go serenading in the splendid gondola in waiting.

A great feature of Como's attractiveness is the multitude of pretty houses and gardens that cluster upon its shores and on its mountain sides. They look so snug and so homelike, and at eventide when everything seems to slumber, and the music of the vesper bells comes stealing over the water, one almost believes that nowhere else than on the Lake of Como can there be found such a paradise of tranquil repose.

From my window here in Bellaggio, I have a view of the other side of the lake now, which is as beautiful as a picture. A scarred and wrinkled precipice rises to a height of eighteen hundred feet; on a tiny bench half way up its vast wall, sits a little snow-flake of a church, no bigger than a martin-box apparently; skirting the base of the cliff are a hundred orange groves and gardens, flecked with glimpses of the white dwellings that are buried in them; in front, three or four gondolas lie idle upon the water—and in the burnished mirror of the lake, mountain, chapel, houses, groves, and boats are counterfeited so brightly and so clearly, that one scarce knows where the reality leaves off and the reflection begins!

The surroundings of this picture are fine. A mile away a grove-plumed promontory juts far into the lake and glasses its palace in the blue depths; in midstream a boat is cutting the shining surface and leaving a long track behind, like a ray of light; the mountains beyond are veiled in a dreamy purple haze; far in the opposite direction a tumbled mass of domes and verdant slopes and valleys bars the lake, and here indeed does distance lend enchantment to the view—for on this broad canvas, sun and clouds and the richest of atmospheres have blended a thousand tints together, and over its surface the filmy lights and shadows drift, hour after hour, and glorify it with a beauty that seems reflected out of Heaven itself. Beyond all question, this is the most voluptuous scene we have yet looked upon.

Last night the scenery was striking and picturesque. On the other side crags and trees and snowy houses were reflected in the lake with a wonderful distinctness, and streams of light from many a distant window shot far abroad over the still waters. On this side, near at hand, great mansions, white with moonlight, glared out from the midst of masses of foliage that lay black and shapeless in the shadows that fell from the cliff above—and down in the margin of the lake every feature of the weird vision was faithfully repeated.

To-day we have idled through a wonder of a garden attached to a ducal estate—but enough of description is enough, I judge.

I suspect that this was the same place the gardener's son deceived the Lady of Lyons with, but

I do not know. You may have heard of the passage somewhere—

> " A deep vale,
> Shut out by Alpine hills from the rude world,
> Near a clear lake margined by fruits of gold
> And whispering myrtles:
> Glassing softest skies, cloudless,
> Save with rare and roseate shadows;
> A palace, lifting to eternal heaven its marbled walls,
> From out a glossy bower of coolest foliage musical with birds."

That is all very well, except the " clear " part of the lake. It certainly is clearer than a great many lakes, but how dull its waters are compared with the wonderful transparence of Lake Tahoe! I speak of the north shore of Tahoe, where one can count the scales on a trout at a depth of a hundred and eighty feet. I have tried to get this statement off at par here, but with no success; so I have been obliged to negotiate it at fifty per cent. discount. At this rate I find some takers; perhaps the reader will receive it on the same terms—ninety feet instead of one hundred and eighty. But let it be remembered that those are forced terms—Sheriff's sale prices. As far as I am privately concerned, I abate not a jot of the original assertion that in those strangely magnifying waters one may count the scales on a trout (a trout of the large kind) at a depth of a hundred and eighty feet— may see every pebble on the bottom—might even count a paper of dray-pins. People talk of the transparent waters of the Mexican Bay of Acapulco, but in my own experience I know they cannot compare with those I am speaking of. I have fished for trout in Tahoe, and at a measured depth of eighty-four feet I have seen them put their noses to the bait, and I could see their gills open and shut. I could hardly have seen the trout themselves at that distance in the open air.

As I go back in spirit and recall that noble sea, reposing among the snow-peaks six thousand feet above the ocean, the conviction comes strong upon me again that Como would only seem a bedizened little courtier in that august presence.

Sorrow and misfortune overtake the Legislature that still from year to year permits Tahoe to retain its unmusical cognomen! Tahoe! It suggests no crystal waters, no picturesque shores, no sublimity. Tahoe for a sea in the clouds—a sea that has character, and asserts it in solemn calms at times, at times in savage storms; a sea whose royal seclusion is guarded by a cordon of sentinel peaks that lift their frosty fronts nine thousand feet above the level world; a sea whose every aspect is impressive, whose belongings are all beautiful, whose lonely majesty types the Deity!

Tahoe means grasshoppers. It means grasshopper soup. It is Indian, and suggestive of Indians. They say it is Pi-ute—possibly it is Digger. I feel satisfied it was named by the Diggers—those degraded savages who roast their dead relatives, then mix the human grease and ashes of bones with tar, and " gaum " it thick all over their heads, and foreheads, and ears, and go caterwauling about the hills and call it *mourning*. *These* are the gentry that named the lake.

People say that Tahoe means " Silver Lake "— " Limpid Water " — " Falling Leaf." Bosh. It means grasshopper soup, the favourite dish of the Digger tribe—and of the Pi-utes as well. It isn't worth while, in these practical times, for people to talk about Indian poetry—there never was any in them— except in the Fennimore Cooper Indians. But *they* are an extinct tribe that never existed. I know the

Noble Red Man. I have camped with the Indians; I have been on the war-path with them, taken part in the chase with them—for grasshoppers; helped them steal cattle; I have roamed with them, scalped them, had them for breakfast. I would gladly eat the whole race if I had a chance.

But I am growing unreliable. I will return to my comparison of the Lakes. Como is a little deeper than Tahoe, if people here tell the truth. They say it is eighteen hundred feet deep at this point, but it does not look a dead enough blue for that. Tahoe is one thousand five hundred and twenty-five feet deep in the centre, by the State Geologist's measurement. They say the great peak opposite this town is five thousand feet high; but I feel sure that three thousand feet of that statement is a good honest lie. The lake is a mile wide here, and maintains about that width from this point to its northern extremity, which is distant sixteen miles; from here to its southern extremity—say fifteen miles—it is not over half a mile wide in any place, I should think. Its snow-clad mountains one hears so much about are only seen occasionally, and then in the distance, the Alps. Tahoe is from ten to eighteen miles wide, and its mountains shut it in like a wall. Their summits are never free from snow the year round. One thing about it is very strange—it never has even a skim of ice upon its surface, although lakes in the same range of mountains, lying in a lower and warmer temperature, freeze over in winter.

It is cheerful to meet a shipmate in these out-of-the-way places and compare notes with him. We have found one of ours here—an old soldier of the war, who is seeking bloodless adventures and rest from his campaigns in these sunny lands.

The Innocents Abroad

CHAPTER XXI

WE voyaged by steamer down the Lago di Lecco, through wild mountain scenery, and by hamlets and villas, and disembarked at the town of Lecco. They said it was two hours by carriage to the ancient city of Bergamo, and that we would arrive there in good season for the railway train. We got an open barouche and a wild, boisterous driver, and set out. It was delightful. We had a fast team and a perfectly smooth road. There were towering cliffs on our left, and the pretty Lago di Lecco on our right, and every now and then it rained on us. Just before starting the driver picked up in the street a stump of a cigar an inch long, and put it in his mouth. When he had carried it thus about an hour, I thought it would be only Christian charity to give him a light. I handed him my cigar, which I had just lit, and he put it in his mouth and returned his stump to his pocket! I never saw a more sociable man. At least, I never saw a man who was more sociable on a short acquaintance.

We saw interior Italy now. The houses were of solid stone, and not often in good repair. The peasants and their children were idle, as a general thing, and the donkeys and chickens made themselves at home in drawing-room and bedchamber and were not molested. The drivers of each and every one of the slow-moving market-carts we met were stretched in the sun upon their merchandise, sound asleep. Every three or four hundred yards it seemed to me we came upon the shrine of some saint or other—a rude picture of him built into a huge cross or a stone pillar by the roadside. Some of the pictures of the Saviour were curiosities in their way. They represented him stretched upon the Cross, his countenance distorted with agony. From the wounds of the crown of thorns, from the pierced side, from the mutilated hands and feet, from the scourged body, from every hand-breadth of his person streams of blood were flowing! Such a gory, ghastly spectacle would frighten the children out of their senses, I should think. There were some unique auxiliaries to the painting which added to its spirited effect. These were genuine wooden and iron implements, and were prominently disposed round about the figure: a bundle of nails; the hammer to drive them; the sponge; the reed that supported it; the cup of vinegar; the ladder for the ascent of the Cross; the spear that pierced the Saviour's side. The crown of thorns was made of real thorns, and was nailed to the sacred head. In some Italian church-paintings, even by the older masters, the Saviour and the Virgin wear silver or gilded crowns that are fastened to the pictured head with nails. The effect is as grotesque as it is incongruous.

Here and there, on the fronts of roadside inns, we found huge, coarse frescoes of suffering martyrs like those in the shrines. It could not have diminished their sufferings any to be so uncouthly represented. We were in the heart and home of priestcraft—of a happy, cheerful, contented ignorance, superstition, degradation, poverty, indolence, and everlasting unaspiring worthlessness. And we said fervently, It suits these people precisely; let them enjoy it, along with the other animals, and Heaven forbid that they be molested. *We* feel no malice toward these fumigators.

The Innocents Abroad

We passed through the strangest, funniest, un-dreamt-of old towns, wedded to the customs and steeped in the dreams of the elder ages, and perfectly unaware that the world turns round! And perfectly indifferent, too, as to whether it turns around or stands still. *They* have nothing to do but eat and sleep, and sleep and eat, and toil a little when they can get a friend to stand by and keep them awake. *They* are not paid for thinking—*they* are not paid to fret about the world's concerns. They were not respectable people—they were not worthy people—they were not learned and wise, and brilliant people —but in their breasts, all their stupid lives long, resteth a peace that passeth understanding! How can men, calling themselves men, consent to be so degraded and happy.

We whisked by many a grey old mediæval castle, clad thick with ivy, that swung its green banners down from towers and turrets, where once some old Crusader's flag had floated. The driver pointed to one of these ancient fortresses and said (I translate):—

"Do you see that great iron hook that projects from the wall just under the highest window in the ruined tower?"

We said we could not see it at such a distance, but had no doubt it was there.

"Well," he said, "there is a legend connected with that iron hook. Nearly seven hundred years ago that castle was the property of the noble Count Luigi Gennaro Guido Alphonso di Genova——"

"What was his other name?" said Dan.

"He had no other name. The name I have spoken was all the name he had. He was the son of——"

"Poor but honest parents—that is all right—never mind the particulars—go on with the legend."

The Innocents Abroad

THE LEGEND

Well, then, all the world at that time was in a wild excitement about the Holy Sepulchre. All the great feudal lords in Europe were pledging their lands and pawning their plate to fit out men-at-arms, so that they might join the grand armies of Christendom and win renown in the Holy Wars. The Count Luigi raised money, like the rest, and one mild September morning, armed with battle-axe, port-cullis, and thundering culverin, he rode through the greaves and bucklers of his donjon-keep with as gallant a troop of Christian bandits as ever stepped in Italy. He had his sword, Excalibur, with him. His beautiful countess and her young daughter waved him a tearful adieu from the battering-rams and buttresses of the fortress, and he galloped away with a happy heart.

He made a raid on a neighbouring baron, and completed his outfit with the booty secured. He then razed the castle to the ground, massacred the family, and moved on. They were hardy fellows in the grand old days of chivalry. Alas! those days will never come again.

Count Luigi grew high in fame in Holy Land. He plunged into the carnage of a hundred battles, but his good Excalibur always brought him out alive, albeit often sorely wounded. His face became browned by exposure to the Syrian sun in long marches; he suffered hunger and thirst; he pined in prisons; he languished in loathsome plague-hospitals. And many and many a time he thought of his loved ones at home, and wondered if all was well with them. But his heart said: Peace, is not thy brother watching over thy household?

The Innocents Abroad

Forty-two years waxed and waned; the good fight was won; Godfrey reigned in Jerusalem; the Christian hosts reared the banner of the Cross above the Holy Sepulchre!

Twilight was approaching. Fifty harlequins, in flowing robes, approached this castle wearily, for they were on foot, and the dust upon their garments betokened that they had travelled far. They overtook a peasant, and asked him if it were likely they could get food and a hospitable bed there, for love of Christian charity, and if perchance a moral parlour entertainment might meet with generous countenance; "for," said they, "this exhibition hath no feature that could offend the most fastidious taste."

"Marry," quoth the peasant, "an' it please your worships, ye had better journey many a good rood hence with your juggling circus than trust your bones in yonder castle."

"How now, sirrah!" exclaimed the chief monk, "explain thy ribald speech, or by'r Lady it shall go hard with thee."

"Peace, good mountebank, I did but utter the truth that was in my heart. San Paolo be my witness that did ye but find the stout Count Leonardo in his cups, sheer from the castle's topmost battlements would he hurl ye all! Alack-a-day, the good Lord Luigi reigns not here in these sad times."

"The good Lord Luigi?"

"Ah, none other, please your worship. In his day the poor rejoiced in plenty, and the rich he did oppress; taxes were not known, the fathers of the church waxed fat upon his bounty; travellers went and came, with none to interfere; and whosoever would might tarry in his halls in cordial welcome, and eat his bread and drink his wine withal. But woe is me! some two and forty years agone the good count rode hence to fight for Holy Cross, and many a year hath flown since word or token have we had of him. Men say his bones lie bleaching in the fields of Palestine."

" And now? "

" *Now!* God 'a mercy, the cruel Leonardo lords it in the castle. He wrings taxes from the poor; he robs all travellers that journey by his gates; he spends his days in feuds and murders, and his nights in revel and debauch; he roasts the fathers of the church upon his kitchen spits, and enjoyeth the same, calling it pastime. These thirty years Luigi's countess hath not been seen by any he in all this land, and many whisper that she pines in the dungeons of the castle for that she will not wed with Leonardo, saying her dear lord still liveth, and that she will die ere she prove false to him. They whisper likewise that her daughter is a prisoner as well. Nay, good jugglers, seek ye refreshment other wheres. 'Twere better that ye perished in a Christian way than that ye plunged from off yon dizzy tower. Give ye good-day."

" God keep ye, gentle knave—farewell."

But heedless of the peasant's warning, the players moved straightway toward the castle.

Word was brought to Count Leonardo that a company of mountebanks besought his hospitality.

" 'Tis well. Dispose of them in the customary manner. Yet stay! I have need of them. Let them come hither. Later, cast them from the battlements —or—how many priests have ye on hand? "

" The day's results are meagre, good my lord. An abbot and a dozen beggarly friars is all we have."

The Innocents Abroad

"Hell and furies! Is the estate going to seed? Send hither the mountebanks. Afterward, broil them with the priests."

The robed and close-cowled harlequins entered. The grim Leonardo sat in state at the head of his council board. Ranged up and down the hall on either hand stood near a hundred men-at-arms.

"Ha, villains!" quoth the count, "what can ye do to earn the hospitality ye crave?"

"Dread lord and mighty, crowded audiences have greeted our humble efforts with rapturous applause. Among our body count we the versatile and talented Ugolino; the justly celebrated Rodolpho; the gifted and accomplished Roderigo; the management have spared neither pains nor expense——"

"'Sdeath! what can ye *do*! Curb thy prating tongue."

"Good my lord, in acrobatic feats, in practice with the dumb-bells, in balancing and ground and lofty tumbling are we versed—and sith your highness asketh me, I venture here to publish that the truly marvellous and entertaining Zampillaerostation——"

"Gag him! throttle him! Body of Bacchus! am I a dog that I am to be assailed with polysyllabled blasphemy like to this? But hold! Lucretia, Isabel, stand forth! Sirrah, behold this dame, this weeping wench. The first I marry, within the hour; the other shall dry her tears or feed the vultures. Thou and thy vagabonds shall crown the wedding with thy merry-makings. Fetch hither the priest!"

The dame sprang toward the chief player.

"O, save me!" she cried; "save me from a fate far worse than death! Behold these sad eyes, these sunken cheeks, this withered frame! See thou the wreck this fiend hath made, and let thy heart be moved with pity! Look upon this damosel; note her wasted form, her halting step, her bloomless cheeks where youth should blush and happiness exult in smiles! Hear us and have compassion. This monster was my husband's brother. He who should have been our shield against all harm hath kept us shut within the noisome caverns of his donjon-keep for, lo, these thirty years. And for what crime? None other than that I would not belie my troth, root out my strong love for him who marches with the legions of the cross in Holy Land (for O, he is not dead!) and wed with him! Save us, O, save thy persecuted suppliants!"

She flung herself at his feet and clasped his knees.

"Ha!-ha!-ha!" shouted the brutal Leonardo. "Priest, to thy work;" and he dragged the weeping dame from her refuge. "Say, once for all, *will* you be mine?—for by my halidome, that breath that uttereth thy refusal shall be thy last on earth!"

"NE-VER!"

"Then die!" and the sword leaped from its scabbard.

Quicker than thought, quicker than the lightning's flash, fifty monkish habits disappeared, and fifty knights in splendid armour stood revealed! fifty falchions gleamed in air above the men-at-arms, and brighter, fiercer than them all, flamed Excalibur aloft, and cleaving downward struck the brutal Leonardo's weapon from his grasp.

"A Luigi to the rescue! Whoop!"

"A Leonardo! tare an ouns!"

"Oh God, Oh God, my husband!"

"Oh God, Oh God, my wife!"

"My father!"

"My precious!" [Tableau.]

The Innocents Abroad

Count Luigi bound his usurping brother hand and foot. The practised knights from Palestine made holiday sport of carving the awkward men-at-arms into chops and steaks. The victory was complete. Happiness reigned. The knights all married the daughter. Joy! wassail! finis! "

"But what did they do with the wicked brother?"

"Oh nothing—only hanged him on that iron hook I was speaking of. By the chin."

"As how?"

"Passed it up through his gills into his mouth."

"Leave him there?"

"Couple of years."

"Ah!—is—is he dead?"

"Six hundred and fifty years ago, or such a matter."

"Splendid legend—splendid lie—drive on."

We reached the quaint old fortified city of Bergamo, the renowned in history, some three-quarters of an hour before the train was ready to start. The place has thirty or forty thousand inhabitants, and is remarkable for being the birthplace of harlequin. When we discovered that, that legend of our driver took to itself a new interest in our eyes.

Rested and refreshed, we took the rail happy and contended. I shall not tarry to speak of the handsome Lago di Gardi; its stately castle that holds in its stony bosom the secrets of an age so remote that even tradition goeth not back to it; the imposing mountain scenery that ennobles the landscape thereabouts; nor yet of ancient Padua or haughty Verona; nor of their Montagues and Capulets, their famous balconies and tombs of Juliet and Romeo *et al.*, but hurry straight to the ancient city of the sea, the widowed bride of the Adriatic. It was a long, long ride. But toward evening, as we sat silent and hardly conscious of where we were—subdued into that meditative calm that comes so surely after a conversational storm—some one shouted—

" VENICE! "

And sure enough, afloat on the placid sea a league away, lay a great city, with its towers and domes and steeples drowsing in a golden mist of sunset.

CHAPTER XXII

THIS Venice, which was a haughty, invincible, magnificent Republic for nearly fourteen hundred years; whose armies compelled the world's applause whenever and wherever they battled; whose navies well-nigh held dominion of the seas, and whose merchant fleets whitened the remotest oceans with their sails and loaded these piers with the products of every clime, is fallen a prey to poverty, neglect, and melancholy decay. Six hundred years ago, Venice was the Autocrat of Commerce; her mart was the great commercial centre, the distributing-house from whence the enormous trade of the Orient was spread abroad over the Western world. To-day her piers are deserted, her warehouses are empty, her merchant fleets are vanished, her armies and her navies are but memories. Her glory is departed, and with her crumbling grandeur of wharves and palaces about her she sits among her stagnant lagoons, forlorn and beggared, forgotten of the world. She that in her palmy days commanded the commerce of a hemisphere and made the weal or woe of nations with a beck of her puissant finger, is become the humblest among the peoples of the earth—a pedler of glass beads for women, and trifling toys and trinkets for schoolgirls and children.

The venerable Mother of the Republics is scarce a fit subject for flippant speech or the idle gossiping of tourists. It seems a sort of sacrilege to disturb the glamour of old romance that pictures her to us softly from afar off as through a tinted mist, and curtains her ruin and her desolation from our view. One ought, indeed, to turn away from her rags, her poverty, and her humiliation, and think of her only as she was when she sunk the fleets of Charlemagne, when she humbled Frederick Barbarossa, or waved her victorious banners above the battlements of Constantinople.

We reached Venice at eight in the evening, and entered a hearse belonging to the Grand Hôtel d'Europe. At any rate, it was more like a hearse than anything else, though to speak by the card, it was a gondola. And this was the storied gondola of Venice!—the fairy boat in which the princely cavaliers of the olden time were wont to cleave the waters of the moonlit canals and look the eloquence of love into the soft eyes of patrician beauties, while the gay gondolier in silken doublet touched his guitar and sang as only gondoliers can sing! This the famed gondola and this the gorgeous gondolier!—the one an inky, rusty old canoe, with a sable hearse-body clapped on to the middle of it, and the other a mangy, barefooted gutter-snipe, with a portion of his raiment on exhibition which should have been sacred from public scrutiny. Presently, as he turned a corner and shot his hearse into a dismal ditch between two long rows of towering, untenanted buildings, the gay gondolier began to sing, true to the traditions of his race. I stood it a little while. Then I said—

The Innocents Abroad

" Now, here, Roderigo Gonzales Michael Angelo, I'm a pilgrim, and I'm a stranger, but I am not going to have my feelings lacerated by any such caterwauling as that. If that goes on, one of us has got to take water. It is enough that my cherished dreams of Venice have been blighted for ever as to the romantic gondola and the gorgeous gondolier; this system of destruction shall go no farther; I will accept the hearse, under protest, and you may fly your flag of truce in peace, but here I register a dark and bloody oath that you shan't sing. Another yelp, and overboard you go."

I began to feel that the old Venice of song and story had departed for ever. But I was too hasty. In a few minutes we swept gracefully out into the Grand Canal, and under the mellow moonlight the Venice of poetry and romance stood revealed. Right from the water's edge rose long lines of stately palaces of marble; gondolas were gliding swiftly hither and thither and disappearing suddenly through unsuspected gates and alleys; ponderous stone bridges threw their shadows athwart the glittering waves. There was life and motion everywhere, and yet everywhere there was a hush, a stealthy sort of stillness that was suggestive of secret enterprises of bravoes and of lovers; and clad half in moonbeams and half in mysterious shadows, the grim old mansions of the Republic seemed to have an expression about them of having an eye out for just such enterprises as these at that same moment. Music came floating over the waters—Venice was complete.

It was a beautiful picture—very soft and dreamy and beautiful. But what was this Venice to compare with the Venice of midnight? Nothing. There was a fête—a grand fête in honour of some saint

The Innocents Abroad

who had been instrumental in checking the cholera three hundred years ago, and all Venice was abroad on the water. It was no common affair, for the Venetians did not know how soon they might need the saint's services again, now that the cholera was spreading everywhere. So in one vast space—say a third of a mile wide and two miles long—were collected two thousand gondolas, and every one of them had from two to ten, twenty, and even thirty coloured lanterns suspended about it, and from four to a dozen occupants. Just as far as the eye could reach, these painted lights were massed together—like a vast garden of many-coloured flowers, except that these blossoms were never still; they were ceaselessly gliding in and out, and mingling together, and seducing you into bewildering attempts to follow their mazy evolutions. Here and there a strong red, green, or blue glare from a rocket that was struggling to get away, splendidly illuminated all the boats around it. Every gondola that swam by us, with its crescents and pyramids and circles of coloured lamps hung aloft, and lighting up the faces of the young and the sweet-scented and lovely below, was a picture; and the reflections of those lights, so long, so slender, so numberless, so many-coloured and so distorted and wrinkled by the waves, was a picture likewise, and one that was enchantingly beautiful. Many and many a party of young ladies and gentlemen had their state gondolas handsomely decorated, and ate supper on board, bringing their swallow-tailed, white cravatted varlets to wait upon them, and having their tables tricked out as if for a bridal supper. They had brought along the costly globe lamps from their drawing-rooms, and the lace and silken curtains from the same places, I suppose. And they had also

194

The Innocents Abroad

brought pianos and guitars, and they played and sang operas, while the plebeian paper-lanterned gondolas from the suburbs and the back alleys crowded around to stare and listen.

There was music everywhere — choruses, string bands, brass bands, flutes, everything. I was so surrounded, walled in with music, magnificence, and loveliness, that I became inspired with the spirit of

"I became inspired...... and sang.........myself."

the scene, and sang one tune myself. However, when I observed that the other gondolas had sailed away, and my gondolier was preparing to go overboard, I stopped.

The fête was magnificent. They kept it up the whole night long, and I never enjoyed myself better than I did while it lasted.

What a funny old city this Queen of the Adriatic is! Narrow streets, vast, gloomy marble palaces, black with the corroding damps of centuries, and all partly submerged; no dry land visible anywhere, and no side-walks worth mentioning; if you want to go to church, to the theatre, or to the restaurant, you must call a gondola. It must be a paradise for cripples, for verily a man has no use for legs here.

For a day or two the place looked so like an over-flowed Arkansas town, because of its currentless waters laving the very doorsteps of all the houses, and the cluster of boats made fast under the windows, or skimming in and out of the alleys and by-ways, that I could not get rid of the impression that there was nothing the matter here but a spring freshet, and that the river would fall in a few weeks and leave a dirty high-water mark on the houses, and the streets full of mud and rubbish.

In the glare of day, there is little poetry about Venice, but under the charitable moon her stained palaces are white again, their battered sculptures are hidden in shadows, and the old city seems crowned once more with the grandeur that was hers five hundred years ago. It is easy, then, in fancy, to people these silent canals with plumed gallants and fair ladies—with Shylocks in gaberdine and sandals, venturing loans upon the rich argosies of Venetian commerce—with Othellos and Desdemonas, with Iagos and Roderigos—with noble fleets and victorious legions returning from the wars. In the treacherous sunlight we see Venice decayed, forlorn, poverty-stricken and commerceless—forgotten and utterly insignificant. But in the moonlight, her fourteen centuries of greatness fling their glories about her, and once more is she the princeliest among the nations of the earth.

" There is a glorious city in the sea;
    The sea is in the broad, the narrow streets,
    Ebbing and flowing; and the salt-sea weed

Clings to the marble of her palaces.
No track of men, no footsteps to and fro,
Lead to her gates! The path lies o'er the sea,
Invisible: and from the land we went,
As to a floating city—steering in,
And gliding up her streets, as in a dream,
So smoothly, silently—by many a dome,
Mosque-like, and many a stately portico,
The statues ranged along an azure sky;
By many a pile, in more than Eastern pride,
Of old the residence of merchant kings;
The fronts of some, tho' time had shatter'd them,
Still glowing with the richest hues of art,
As tho' the wealth within them had run o'er."

What would one naturally wish to see first in Venice? The Bridge of Sighs, of course—and next the Church and the Great Square of St. Mark, the Bronze Horses, and the famous Lion of St. Mark.

We intended to go to the Bridge of Sighs, but happened into the Ducal Palace first — a building which necessarily figures largely in Venetian poetry and tradition. In the Senate Chamber of the ancient Republic we wearied our eyes with staring at acres of historical paintings by Tintoretto and Paul Veronese, but nothing struck us forcibly except the one thing that strikes *all* strangers forcibly—a black square in the midst of a gallery of portraits. In one long row, around the great hall, were painted the portraits of the Doges of Venice (venerable fellows, with flowing white beards, for of the three hundred Senators eligible to the office, the oldest was usually chosen Doge) and each had its complimentary inscription attached—till you came to the place that should have had Marino Faliero's picture in it, and that was blank and black—blank, except that it bore a terse inscription, saying that the conspirator had died for his crime. It seemed cruel to keep that pitiless inscription still staring from the walls after the

The Innocents Abroad

unhappy wretch had been in his grave five hundred years.

At the head of the Giant's Staircase, where Marino Faliero was beheaded, and where the Doges were crowned in ancient times, two small slits in the stone wall were pointed out—two harmless, insignificant orifices that would never attract a stranger's attention —yet these were the terrible Lions' Mouths! The heads were gone (knocked off by the French during their occupation of Venice) but these were the throats down which went the anonymous accusation, thrust in secretly at dead of night by an enemy, that doomed many an innocent man to walk the Bridge of Sighs and descend into the dungeon which none entered and hoped to see the sun again. This was in the old days when the Patricians alone governed Venice— the common herd had no vote and no voice. There were one thousand five hundred Patricians; from these, three hundred Senators were chosen; from the Senators a Doge and a Council of Ten were selected, and by secret ballot the Ten chose from their own number a Council of Three. All these were Government spies, then, and every spy was under surveillance himself—men spoke in whispers in Venice, and no man trusted his neighbour—not always his own brother. No man knew who the Council of Three were—not even the Senate, not even the Doge; the members of that dread tribunal met at night in a chamber to themselves, masked, and robed from head to foot in scarlet cloaks, and did not even know each other, unless by voice. It was their duty to judge heinous political crimes, and from their sentence there was no appeal. A nod to the executioner was sufficient. The doomed man was marched down a hall and out at a doorway into the covered Bridge of Sighs, through it and into the dungeon and unto his death. At no time in his transit was he visible to any save his conductor. If a man had an enemy in those old days, the cleverest thing he could do was to slip a note for the Council of Three into the Lion's mouth, saying " This man is plotting against the Government." If the awful Three found no proof, ten to one they would drown him anyhow, because he was a deep rascal, since his plots were unsolvable. Masked judges and masked executioners, with un-limited power, and no appeal from their judg-ments, in that hard, cruel age, were not likely to be lenient with men they suspected yet could not convict.

We walked through the hall of the Council of Ten, and presently entered the infernal den of the Council of Three.

The table around which they had sat was there still, and likewise the stations where the masked inquisitors and executioners formerly stood, frozen, upright and silent, till they received a bloody order, and then without a word, moved off, like the inexorable machines they were, to carry it out. The frescoes on the walls were startlingly suited to the place. In all the other saloons, the halls, the great state cham-bers of the palace, the walls and ceilings were bright with gilding, rich with elaborate carving, and re-splendent with gallant pictures of Venetian victories in war, and Venetian display in foreign courts, and hallowed with portraits of the Virgin, the Saviour of men, and the Holy Saints that preached the Gospel of Peace upon earth—but here, in dismal contrast, were none but pictures of death and dreadful suffer-ing!—not a living figure but was writhing in torture, not a dead one but was smeared with blood, gashed with wounds, and distorted with the agonies that had taken away its life!

From the palace to the gloomy prison is but a step —one might almost jump across the narrow canal that intervenes. The ponderous stone Bridge of Sighs crosses it at the second story—a bridge that is a covered tunnel—you cannot be seen when you walk in it. It is partitioned lengthwise, and through one compartment walked such as bore light sentences in ancient times, and through the other marched sadly the wretches whom the Three had doomed to lingering misery and utter oblivion in the dungeons, or to sudden and mysterious death. Down below the level of the water, by the light of smoking torches, we were shown the damp, thick-walled cells where many a proud patrician's life was eaten away by the long-drawn miseries of solitary imprisonment—without light, air, books; naked, unshaven, uncombed, covered with vermin; his useless tongue forgetting its office, with none to speak to; the days and nights of his life no longer marked, but merged into one eternal eventless night; far away from all cheerful sounds, buried in the silence of a tomb; forgotten by his helpless friends, and his fate a dark mystery to them for ever; losing his own memory at last; and knowing no more who he was or how he came there; devouring the loaf of bread and drinking the water that were thrust into the cell by unseen hands, and troubling his worn spirit no more with hopes and fears and doubts and longings to be free; ceasing to scratch vain prayers and complaints on walls where none, not even himself, could see them, and resigning himself to hopeless apathy, drivelling childishness, lunacy? Many and many a sorrowful story like this these stone walls could tell if they could but speak.

The Innocents Abroad

In a little narrow corridor near by, they showed us where many a prisoner, after lying in the dungeons until he was forgotten by all save his persecutors, was brought by masked executioners and garrotted, or sewed up in a sack, passed through a little window to a boat, at dead of night, and taken to some remote spot and drowned.

They used to show to visitors the implements of torture wherewith the Three were wont to worm secrets out of the accused—villanous machines for crushing thumbs; the stocks where a prisoner sat immovable while water fell drop by drop upon his head till the torture was more than humanity could bear; and a devilish contrivance of steel, which inclosed a prisoner's head like a shell, and crushed it slowly by means of a screw. It bore the stains of blood that had trickled through its joints long ago, and on one side it had a projection whereon the torturer rested his elbow comfortably and bent down his ear to catch the moanings of the sufferer perishing within.

Of course we went to see the venerable relic of the ancient glory of Venice, with its pavements worn and broken by the passing feet of a thousand years of plebeians and patricians—The Cathedral of St. Mark. It is built entirely of precious marbles, brought from the Orient—nothing in its composition is domestic. Its hoary traditions make it an object of absorbing interest to even the most careless stranger, and thus far it had interest for me; but no further. I could not go into ecstasies over its coarse mosaics, its unlovely Byzantine architecture, or its five hundred curious interior columns from as many distant quarries. Everything was worn out—every block of stone was smooth and almost shapeless with

the polishing hands and shoulders of loungers who
devoutly idled here in by-gone centuries and have died
and gone to the dev—no, simply died, I mean.

Under the altar repose the ashes of St. Mark—and
Matthew, Luke, and John, too, for all I know. Venice
reveres those relics above all things earthly. For
fourteen hundred years St. Mark has been her patron
saint. Everything about the city seems to be named
after him or so named as to refer to him in some way—
so named, or some purchase rigged in some way to
scrape a sort of hurrahing acquaintance with him.
That seems to be the idea. To be on good terms with
St. Mark seems to be the very summit of Venetian
ambition. They say St. Mark had a tame lion, and
used to travel with him, and everywhere that St.
Mark went the lion was sure to go. It was his pro-
tector, his friend, his librarian. And so the Winged
Lion of St. Mark, with the open Bible under his paw,
is a favourite emblem in the grand old city. It casts
its shadow from the most ancient pillar in Venice,
in the Grand Square of St. Mark, upon the throngs
of free citizens below, and has so done for many a
long century. The winged lion is found everywhere;
and doubtless here where the winged lion is, no harm
can come.

St. Mark died at Alexandria, in Egypt. He was
martyred, I think. However, that has nothing to
do with my legend. About the founding of the city
of Venice—say four hundred and fifty years after
Christ—(for Venice is much younger than any other
Italian city), a priest dreamed that an angel told
him that until the remains of St. Mark were brought
to Venice, the city could never rise to high distinction
among the nations; that the body must be captured,
brought to the city, and a magnificent church built

over it; and that if ever the Venetians allowed the Saint to be removed from his new resting-place, in that day Venice would perish from off the face of the earth. The priest proclaimed his dream, and forthwith Venice set about procuring the corpse of St. Mark. One expedition after another tried and failed, but the project was never abandoned during four hundred years. At last it was secured by stratagem, in the year eight hundred and something. The commander of a Venetian expedition disguised himself, stole the bones, separated them, and packed them in vessels filled with lard. The religion of Mahomet causes its devotees to abhor anything that is in the nature of pork, and so when the Christian was stopped by the officers at the gates of the city, they only glanced once into his precious baskets, then turned up their noses at the unholy lard, and let him go. The bones were buried in the vaults of the grand cathedral, which had been waiting long years to receive them, and thus the safety and the greatness of Venice were secured. And to this day there be those in Venice who believe that if those holy ashes were stolen away, the ancient city would vanish like a dream, and its foundations be buried for ever in the unremembering sea.

CHAPTER XXIII

THE Venetian gondola is as free and graceful in its gliding movement as a serpent. It is twenty or thirty feet long, and is narrow and deep like a canoe; its sharp bow and stern sweep upward from the water like the horns of a crescent with the abruptness of the curve slightly modified.

The bow is ornamented with a steel comb with a battle-axe attachment which threatens to cut passing boats in two occasionally, but never does. The gondola is painted black because in the zenith of Venetian magnificence the gondolas became too gorgeous altogether, and the Senate decreed that all such display must cease, and a solemn, unembellished black be substituted. If the truth were known it would doubtless appear that rich plebeians grew too prominent in their affectation of patrician show on the Grand Canal, and required a wholesome snubbing. Reverence for the hallowed Past and its traditions keeps the dismal fashion in force now that the compulsion exists no longer. So let it remain. It is the colour of mourning. Venice mourns.

The stern of the boat is decked over, and the gondolier stands there. He uses a single oar—a long blade, of course, for he stands nearly erect. A wooden peg, a foot and a half high, with two slight crooks or curves in one side of it, and one in the other, projects above the starboard gunwale. Against that peg the gondolier takes a purchase with his oar, changing it at intervals to the other side of the peg, or dropping it into another of the crooks, as the steering of the craft may demand; and how in the world he can back and fill, shoot straight ahead, or flirt suddenly around a corner, and make the oar stay in those insignificant notches, is a problem to me, and a never diminishing matter of interest. I am afraid I study the gondolier's marvellous skill more than I do the sculptured palaces we glide among. He cuts a corner so closely now and then, or misses another gondola by such an imperceptible hair-breadth, that I feel myself " scrooching," as the children say, just as one does when a buggy-wheel grazes his elbow. But he makes all his calcula-

The Innocents Abroad

tions with the nicest precision, and goes darting in and out among a Broadway confusion of busy craft with the easy confidence of the educated hackman. He never makes a mistake.

Sometimes we go flying down the great canals at such a gait that we can get only the merest glimpses into front doors, and again, in obscure alleys in the suburbs, we put on a solemnity suited to the silence, the mildew, the stagnant waters, the clinging weeds, the deserted houses, and the general lifelessness of the place, and move to the spirit of grave meditation.

The gondolier *is* a picturesque rascal for all he wears no satin harness, no plumed bonnet, no silken tights. His attitude is stately; he is lithe and supple; all his movements are full of grace. When his long canoe, and his fine figure towering from its high perch on the stern, are cut against the evening sky, they make a picture that is very novel and striking to a foreign eye.

We sit in the cushioned carriage-body of a cabin, with the curtains drawn, and smoke, or read, or look out upon the passing boats, the houses, the bridges, the people, and enjoy ourselves much more than we could in a buggy jolting over our cobble-stone pavements at home. This is the gentlest, pleasantest locomotion we have ever known.

But it seems queer, ever so queer, to see a boat doing duty as a private carriage. We see business men come to the front door, step into a gondola instead of a street car, and go off down town to the counting-room.

We see visiting young ladies stand on the stoop, and laugh, and kiss good-by, and flirt their fans, and say, " Come soon, now *do*—you've been just as mean as ever you can be—mother's dying to see you—and we've moved into the new house, O such a love of a place!—so convenient to the post-office, and the church, and the Young Men's Christian Association; and we do have such fishing, and such carrying on, and *such* swimming-matches in the back-yard—Oh, you *must* come; no distance at all, and if you go down through by St. Mark's and the Bridge of Sighs, and cut through the alley and come up by the church of Santa Maria dei Frari, and into the Grand Canal, there isn't a *bit* of current—now *do* come, Sally Maria—by-by!" and then the little humbug trips down the steps, jumps into the gondola, says, under her breath, "Disagreeable old thing, I hope she won't!" goes skimming away round the corner; and the other girl slams the street door, and says, "Well, *that* infliction's over, any way; but I suppose I've got to go and see her, tiresome stuck-up thing!" Human nature appears to be just the same all over the world. We see the diffident young man, mild of moustache, affluent of hair, indigent of brain, elegant of costume, drive up to *her* father's mansion, tell his hackman to bail out and wait, start fearfully up the steps and meet " the old gentleman " right on the threshold!—hear him ask what street the new British Bank is in—as if *that* were what he came for—and then bounce into his boat and skurry away with his coward heart in his boots!—see him come sneaking round the corner again directly, with a crack of the curtain open toward the old gentleman's disappearing gondola, and out scampers his Susan, with a flock of little Italian endearments fluttering from her lips, and goes to drive with him in the watery avenues down toward the Rialto.

We see the ladies go out shopping, in the most natural way, and flit from street to street, and from store to store, just in the good old fashion, except that they leave the gondola, instead of a private carriage, waiting at the curbstone a couple of hours for them— waiting while they make the nice young clerks pull down tons and tons of silks, and velvets, and moire antiques, and those things; and then they buy a paper of pins and go paddling away to confer the rest of their disastrous patronage on some other firm. And they always have their purchases sent home just in the good old way. Human nature is *very* much the same all over the world; and it is *so* like my dear native home to see a Venetian lady go into a store and buy ten cents' worth of blue ribbon and have it sent home in a scow. Ah! it is these little touches of nature that move one to tears in these far-off foreign lands.

We see little girls and boys go out in gondolas with their nurses for an airing. We see staid families, with prayer-book and beads, enter the gondola dressed in their Sunday best, and float away to church. And at midnight we see the theatre break up and discharge its swarm of hilarious youth and beauty; we hear the cries of the hackman-gondoliers, and behold the struggling crowd jump aboard, and the black multitude of boats go skimming down the moonlit avenues; we see them separate here and there, and disappear up divergent streets; we hear the faint sounds of laughter and of shouted farewells floating up out of the distance; and then, the strange pageant being gone, we have lonely stretches of glittering water— of stately buildings—of blotting shadows—of weird stone faces creeping into the moonlight—of deserted bridges—of motionless boats at anchor. And over all broods that mysterious stillness, that stealthy quiet, that befits so well this old dreaming Venice.

The Innocents Abroad

We have been pretty much everywhere in our gondola. We have bought beads and photographs in the stores, and wax matches in the Great Square of St. Mark. The last remark suggests a digression. Everybody goes to this vast square in the evening. The military bands play in the centre of it, and countless couples of ladies and gentlemen promenade up and down on either side, and platoons of them are constantly drifting away toward the old Cathedral, and by the venerable column with the Winged Lion of St. Mark on its top, and out to where the boats lie moored; and other platoons are as constantly arriving from the gondolas and joining the great throng. Between the promenaders and the side-walks are seated hundreds and hundreds of people at small tables, smoking and taking *granita* (a first cousin to ice-cream); on the side-walks are more employing themselves in the same way. The shops in the first floor of the tall rows of buildings that wall in three sides of the square are brilliantly lighted, the air is filled with music and merry voices, and altogether the scene is as bright and spirited and full of cheerfulness as any man could desire. We enjoy it thoroughly. Very many of the young women are exceedingly pretty, and dress with rare good taste. We are gradually and laboriously learning the ill-manners of staring them unflinchingly in the face—not because such conduct is agreeable to us, but because it is the custom of the country, and they say the girls like it. We wish to learn all the curious, outlandish ways of all the different countries, so that we can " show-off " and astonish people when we get home. We wish to excite the envy of our untravelled friends with our strange foreign fashions which we can't shake off. All our passengers are paying strict attention to this

The Innocents Abroad

thing, with the end in view which I have mentioned. The gentle reader will never, never know what a consummate ass he can become, until he goes abroad. I speak now, of course, in the supposition that the gentle reader has not been abroad, and therefore is not already a consummate ass. If the case be otherwise, I beg his pardon, and extend to him the cordial hand of fellowship and call him brother. I shall always delight to meet an ass after my own heart when I shall have finished my travels.

On this subject let me remark that there are Americans abroad in Italy who have actually forgotten their mother tongue in three months—forgot it in France. They cannot even write their address in English in a hotel register. I append these evidences, which I copied *verbatim* from the register of a hotel in a certain Italian city—

" John P. Whitcomb, *Etats Unis.*
" Wm. L. Ainsworth, *travailleur* (he meant traveller, I suppose), *Etats Unis.*
" George P. Morton *et fils, d'Amérique.*
" Lloyd B. Williams, *et trois amis, ville de* Boston, *Amérique.*
" J. Ellsworth Baker, *tout de suite de France ; place de naissance Amérique, destination la Grand Bretagne.*"

I love this sort of people. A lady passenger of ours tells of a fellow-citizen of hers who spent eight weeks in Paris, and then returned home and addressed his dearest old bosom friend Herbert as Mr. " Er-bare! " He apologised though, and said, " 'Pon my soul, it is aggravating, but I cahn't help it. I have got so used to speaking nothing but French, my dear Erbare— damme, there it goes again!—got so used to French pronunciation that I cahn't get rid of it ; it is positively annoying, I assure you." This entertaining idiot, whose name was Gordon, allowed himself to be hailed three times in the street before he paid any attention, and then begged a thousand pardons, and said he had grown so accustomed to hearing himself addressed as "M'sieu Gor-r-*dong*," with a roll to the r, that he had forgotten the legitimate sound of his name! He wore a rose in his buttonhole; he gave the French salutation—two flips of the hand in front of the face; he called Paris *Pairree* in ordinary English conversation; he carried envelopes bearing foreign post marks protruding from his breast-pocket; he cultivated a moustache and imperial, and did what else he could to suggest to the beholder his pet fancy that he resembled Louis Napoleon, and in a spirit of thankfulness which is entirely unaccountable, considering the slim foundation there was for it, he praised his Maker that he was *as* he was, and went on enjoying his little life just the same as if he really *had* been deliberately designed and erected by the great Architect of the Universe.

Think of our Whitcombs, and our Ainsworths, and our Williamses writing themselves down in dilapidated French in foreign hotel registers! We laugh at Englishmen when we are at home, for sticking so sturdily to their national ways and customs, but we look back upon it from abroad very forgivingly. It is not pleasant to see an American thrusting his nationality forward *obtrusively* in a foreign land, but oh! it is pitiable to see him making of himself a thing that is neither male nor female, neither fish, flesh, nor fowl—a poor, miserable, hermaphrodite Frenchman.

Among a long list of churches, art galleries, and such things, visited by us in Venice, I shall mention only one—the church of Santa Maria dei Frari. It is about five hundred years old, I believe, and stands on twelve hundred thousand piles. In it lie the body of Canova and the heart of Titian, under magnificent

monuments. Titian died at the age of almost one
hundred years. A plague which swept away fifty
thousand lives was raging at the time, and there is
notable evidence of the reverence in which the great
painter was held, in the fact that to him alone the
state permitted a public funeral in all that season of
terror and death.

In this church, also, is a monument to the doge
Foscari, whose name a once resident of Venice, Lord
Byron, has made permanently famous.

The monument to the doge Giovanni Pesaro, in
this church, is a curiosity in the way of mortuary
adornment. It is eighty feet high and is fronted like
some fantastic pagan temple. Against it stand four
colossal Nubians, as black as night, dressed in white
marble garments. The black legs are bare, and
through rents in sleeves and breeches, the skin, of
shiny black marble, shows. The artist was as ingenious as his funeral designs were absurd. There
are two bronze skeletons bearing scrolls, and two
great dragons uphold the sarcophagus. On high,
amid all this grotesqueness, sits the departed
doge.

In the conventual buildings attached to this church
are the state archives of Venice. We did not see
them, but they are said to number millions of documents. "They are the records of centuries of the
most watchful, observant, and suspicious government
that ever existed—in which everything was written
down and nothing spoken out." They fill nearly
three hundred rooms. Among them are manuscripts
from the archives of nearly two thousand families,
monasteries, and convents. The secret history of
Venice for a thousand years is here—its plots, its
hidden trials, its assassinations, its commissions of

hirelings spies and masked bravoes—food, ready to hand, for a world of dark and mysterious romances.

Yes, I think we have seen all of Venice. We have seen, in these old churches, a profusion of costly and elaborate sepulchre ornamentation such as we never dreamt of before. We have stood in the dim religious light of these hoary sanctuaries, in the midst of long ranks of dusty monuments and effigies of the great dead of Venice, until we seemed drifting back, back, back into the solemn past, and looking upon the scenes and mingling with the peoples of a remote antiquity. We have been in a half-waking sort of dream all the time. I do not know how else to describe the feeling. A part of our being has remained still in the nineteenth century, while another part of it has seemed in some unaccountable way walking among the phantoms of the tenth.

We have seen famous pictures until our eyes are weary with looking at them and refuse to find interest in them any longer. And what wonder, when there are twelve hundred pictures by Palma the Younger in Venice and fifteen hundred by Tintoretto? And behold there are Titians and the works of other artists in proportion. We have seen Titian's celebrated Cain and Abel, his David and Goliath, his Abraham's Sacrifice. We have seen Tintoretto's monster picture, which is seventy-four feet long, and I do not know how many feet high, and thought it a very commodious picture. We have seen pictures of martyrs enough, and saints enough, to regenerate the world. I ought not to confess it, but still, since one has no opportunity in America to acquire a critical judgment in art, and since I could not hope to become educated in it in Europe in a few short weeks, I may therefore as well acknowledge with such apologies as

The Innocents Abroad

may be due, that to me it seemed that when I had seen one of these martyrs I had seen them all. They all have a marked family resemblance to each other, they dress alike, in coarse monkish robes and sandals, they are all bald-headed, they all stand in about the same attitude, and without exception they are gazing heavenward with countenances which the Ainsworths, the Mortons, and the Williamses, *et fils*, inform me are full of "expression." To me there is nothing tangible about these imaginary portraits, nothing that I can grasp and take a living interest in. If great Titian had only been gifted with prophecy, and had skipped a martyr, and gone over to England and painted a portrait of Shakespeare, even as a youth, which we could all have confidence in now, the world down to the latest generations would have forgiven him the lost martyr in the rescued seer. I think posterity could have spared one more martyr for the sake of a great historical picture of Titian's time and painted by his brush—such as Columbus returning in chains from the discovery of a world, for instance. The old masters did paint some Venetian historical pictures, and these we did not tire of looking at, notwithstanding representations of the formal introduction of defunct doges to the Virgin Mary in regions beyond the clouds clashed rather harshly with the proprieties, it seemed to us.

But humble as we are, and unpretending, in the matter of art, our researches among the painted monks and martyrs have not been wholly in vain. We have striven hard to learn. We have had some success. We have mastered some things, possibly of trifling import in the eyes of the learned, but to us they give pleasure, and we take as much pride in our little acquirements as do others who have learned far

more, and we love to display them full as well.
When we see a monk going about with a lion and
looking tranquilly up to heaven, we know that that
is St. Mark. When we see a monk with a book and
a pen, looking tranquilly up to heaven, trying to
think of a word, we know that that is St. Matthew.
When we see a monk sitting on a rock, looking tranquilly up to heaven, with a human skull beside him,
and without other baggage, we know that that is
St. Jerome. Because we know that he always went
flying light in the matter of baggage. When we see
a party looking tranquilly up to heaven, unconscious
that his body is shot through and through with
arrows, we know that that is St. Sebastian. When
we see other monks looking tranquilly up to heaven,
but having no trade-mark, we always ask who those
parties are. We do this because we humbly wish to
learn. We have seen thirteen thousand St. Jeromes,
and twenty-two thousand St. Marks, and sixteen
thousand St. Matthews, and sixty thousand St.
Sebastians, and four millions of assorted monks,
undesignated, and we feel encouraged to believe that
when we have seen some more of these various
pictures, and had a larger experience, we shall begin
to take an absorbing interest in them like our cultivated countrymen from *Amérique*.

Now it does give me real pain to speak in this
almost unappreciative way of the old masters and
their martyrs, because good friends of mine in the
ship—friends who do thoroughly and conscientiously
appreciate them and are in every way competent to
discriminate between good pictures and inferior
ones—have urged me for my own sake not to make
public the fact that I lack this appreciation and this
critical discrimination myself. I believe that what

The Innocents Abroad

I have written and may still write about pictures
will give them pain, and I am honestly sorry for it.
I even promised that I would hide my uncouth
sentiments in my own breast. But alas! I never
could keep a promise. I do not blame myself for
this weakness, because the fault must lie in my
physical organisation. It is likely that such a very
liberal amount of space was given to the organ which
enables me to *make* promises, that the organ which
should enable me to keep them was crowded out.
But I grieve not. I like no half-way things. I had
rather have one faculty nobly developed than two
faculties of mere ordinary capacity. I certainly
meant to keep that promise, but I find I cannot
do it. It is impossible to travel through Italy
without speaking of pictures, and can I see them
through others' eyes?

If I did not so delight in the grand pictures that are
spread before me every day of my life by that monarch
of all the old masters, Nature, I should come to
believe sometimes, that I had in me no appreciation
of the beautiful whatsoever.

It seems to me that whenever I glory to think that
for once I have discovered an ancient painting that
is beautiful and worthy of all praise, the pleasure it
gives me is an infallible proof that it is *not* a beautiful
picture and not in any wise worthy of commendation.
This very thing has occurred more times than I can
mention, in Venice. In every single instance the
guide has crushed out my swelling enthusiasm with
the remark—

"It is nothing—it is of the *Renaissance*."

I did not know what in the mischief the Renaissance was, and so always I had to simply say—

"Ah! so it is—I had not observed it before."

The Innocents Abroad

I could not bear to be ignorant before a cultivated negro, the offspring of a South Carolina slave. But it occurred too often for even my self-complacency, did that exasperating " It is nothing—it is of the *Renaissance*." I said at last—

"*Who* is this Renaissance? Where did he come from? Who gave him permission to cram the Republic with his execrable daubs? "

We learned, then, that Renaissance was not a man; that *renaissance* was a term used to signify what was at best but an imperfect rejuvenation of art. The guide said that after Titian's time, and the time of the other great names we had grown so familiar with, high art declined; then it partially rose again —an inferior sort of painters sprang up, and these shabby pictures were the work of their hands. Then I said, in my heat, that I " wished to goodness high art had declined five hundred years sooner." The Renaissance pictures suit me very well, though sooth to say its school were too much given to painting real men and did not indulge enough in martyrs.

The guide I have spoken of is the only one we have had yet who knew anything. He was born in South Carolina, of slave parents. They came to Venice while he was an infant. He has grown up here. He is well educated. He reads, writes, and speaks English, Italian, Spanish, and French, with perfect facility; is a worshipper of art, and thoroughly conversant with it; knows the history of Venice by heart and never tires of talking of her illustrious career. He dresses better than any of us, I think, and is daintily polite. Negroes are deemed as good as white people in Venice, and so this man feels no desire to go back to his native land. His judgment is correct.

The Innocents Abroad

I have had another shave. I was writing in our front room this afternoon and trying hard to keep my attention on my work and refrain from looking out upon the canal. I was resisting the soft influences of the climate as well as I could, and endeavouring to overcome the desire to be indolent and happy. The boys sent for a barber. They asked me if I would be shaved. I reminded them of my tortures in Genoa, Milan, Como; of my declaration that I would suffer no more on Italian soil. I said "Not any for me, if you please."

I wrote on. The barber began on the doctor. I heard him say—

"Dan, this is the easiest shave I have had since we left the ship."

He said again, presently—

"Why, Dan, a man could go to sleep with this man shaving him."

Dan took the chair. Then he said—

"Why, this is Titian. This is one of the old masters."

I wrote on. Directly Dan said—

"Doctor, it is perfect luxury. The ship's barber isn't anything to him."

My rough beard was distressing me beyond measure. The barber was rolling up his apparatus. The temptation was too strong. I said—

"Hold on, please. Shave me also."

I sat down in the chair and closed my eyes. The barber soaped my face, and then took his razor and gave me a rake that well nigh threw me into convulsions. I jumped out of the chair; Dan and the doctor were both wiping blood off their faces and laughing.

I said it was a mean, disgraceful fraud.

The Innocents Abroad

They said that the misery of this shave had gone so far beyond anything they had ever experienced before, that they could not bear the idea of losing such a chance of hearing a cordial opinion from me on the subject.

It was shameful. But there was no help for it. The skinning was begun and had to be finished. The tears flowed with every rake, and so did the fervent execrations. The barber grew confused, and brought blood every time. I think the boys enjoyed it better than anything they have seen or heard since they left home.

We have seen the Campanile, and Byron's house, and Balbi's, the geographer, and the palaces of all the ancient dukes and doges of Venice, and we have seen their effeminate descendants airing their nobility in fashionable French attire in the Grand Square of St. Mark, and eating ices and drinking cheap wines, instead of wearing gallant coats of mail and destroying fleets and armies, as their great ancestors did in the days of Venetian glory. We have seen no bravoes with poisoned stilettos, no masks, no wild carnival; but we have seen the ancient pride of Venice, the grim Bronze Horses that figure in a thousand legends. Venice may well cherish them, for they are the only horses she ever had. It is said there are hundreds of people in this curious city who never have seen a living horse in their lives. It is entirely true, no doubt.

And so, having satisfied ourselves, we depart to-morrow, and leave the venerable Queen of the Republics to summon her vanished ships, and marshal her shadowy armies, and know again in dreams the pride of her old renown.

The Innocents Abroad

CHAPTER XXIV

SOME of the *Quaker City's* passengers had arrived in Venice from Switzerland and other lands before we left there, and others were expected every day. We heard of no casualties among them, and no sickness.

We were a little fatigued with sight-seeing, and so we rattled through a good deal of country by rail without caring to stop. I took few notes. I find no mention of Bologna in my memorandum book, except that we arrived there in good season, but saw none of the sausages for which the place is so justly celebrated.

Pistoia awoke but a passing interest.

Florence pleased us for a while. I think we appreciated the great figure of David in the grand square, and the sculptured group they call the Rape of the Sabines. We wandered through the endless collections of paintings and statues of the Pitti and Ufizzi galleries, of course. I make that statement in self-defence; there let it stop. I could not rest under the imputation that I visited Florence and did not traverse its weary miles of picture galleries. We tried indolently to recollect something about the Guelphs and Ghibelines, and the other historical cut-throats whose quarrels and assassinations make up so large a share of Florentine history, but the subject was not attractive. We had been robbed of all the fine mountain scenery on our little journey by a system of railroading that had three miles of tunnel to a hundred yards of daylight, and we were not inclined to be sociable with Florence. We had seen the spot, outside the city somewhere, where these people had allowed the bones of Galileo to rest in unconsecrated ground for an age because his great discovery that the world turned around was regarded as a damning heresy by the Church; and we know that long after the world had accepted his theory and raised his name high in the list of its great men, they had still let him rot there. That we had lived to see his dust in honoured sepulture in the church of Santa Croce we owed to a society of *literati*, and not to Florence or her rulers. We saw Dante's tomb in that church also, but we were glad to know that his body was not in it; that the ungrateful city that had exiled him and persecuted him would give much to have it there, but need not hope to ever secure that high honour to herself. Medicis are good enough for Florence. Let her plant Medicis and build grand monuments over them to testify how gratefully she was wont to lick the hand that scourged her.

Magnanimous Florence! Her jewelry marts are filled with artists in mosaic. Florentine mosaics are the choicest in all the world. Florence loves to have that said. Florence is proud of it. Florence would foster this specialty of hers. She is grateful to the artists that bring to her this high credit and fill her coffers with foreign money, and so she encourages them with pensions. With pensions! Think of the lavishness of it. She knows that people who piece together the beautiful trifles die early, because the labour is so confining, and so exhausting to hand and brain, and so she has decreed that all these people who reach the age of sixty shall have a pension after that! I have not heard that any of them have called for their dividends yet. One man did fight along till he was sixty, and started after his pension, but it appeared that there had been a mistake of a year in his family record, and so he gave it up and died.

The Innocents Abroad

These artists will take particles of stone or glass no larger than a mustard seed, and piece them together on a sleeve button or a shirt stud, so smoothly and with such nice adjustment of the delicate shades of colour the pieces bear, as to form a pigmy rose with stem, thorn, leaves, petals complete, and all as softly and as truthfully tinted as though Nature had builded it herself. They will counterfeit a fly, or a high-toned bug, or the ruined Coliseum, within the cramped circle of a breastpin, and do it so deftly and so neatly that any man might think a master painted it.

I saw a little table in the great mosaic school in Florence—a little trifle of a centre table—whose top was made of some sort of precious polished stone, and in the stone was inlaid the figure of a flute, with bell-mouth and a mazy complication of keys. No painting in the world could have been softer or richer; no shading out of one tint into another could have been more perfect; no work of art of any kind could have been more faultless than this flute, and yet to count the multitude of little fragments of stone of which they swore it was formed would bankrupt any man's arithmetic! I do not think one could have seen where two particles joined each other with eyes of ordinary shrewdness. Certainly *we* could detect no such blemish. This table-top cost the labour of one man for ten long years, so they said, and it was for sale for thirty-five thousand dollars.

We went to the Church of Santa Croce, from time to time, in Florence, to weep over the tombs of Michael Angelo, Raphael, and Machiavelli (I suppose they are buried there, but it may be that they reside elsewhere, and rent their tombs to other parties— such being the fashion in Italy), and between times we used to go and stand on the bridges and admire the Arno. It is popular to admire the Arno. It is a great historical creek with four feet in the channel and some scows floating around. It would be a very plausible river if they would pump some water into it. They all call it a river, and they honestly think it *is* a river, do these dark and bloody Florentines. They even help out the delusion by building bridges over it. I do not see why they are too good to wade.

How the fatigues and annoyances of travel fill one with bitter prejudices sometimes! I might enter Florence under happier auspices a month hence and find it all beautiful, all attractive. But I do not care to think of it now at all, nor of its roomy shops filled to the ceiling with snowy marble and alabaster copies of all the celebrated sculptures in Europe—copies so enchanting to the eye, that I wonder how they can really be shaped like the dingy petrified nightmares they are the portraits of. I got lost in Florence at nine o'clock one night, and staid lost in that labyrinth of narrow streets and long rows of vast buildings that look all alike, until towards three o'clock in the morning. It was a pleasant night, and at first there were a good many people abroad, and there were cheerful lights about. Later I grew accustomed to prowling about mysterious drifts and tunnels, and astonishing and interesting myself with coming around corners expecting to find the hotel staring me in the face, and not finding it doing anything of the kind. Later still I felt tired. I soon felt remarkably tired. But there was no one abroad now—not even a policeman. I walked till I was out of all patience and very hot and thirsty. At last, somewhere after one o'clock, I came unexpectedly to one of the city gates. I knew then that I was very far from the hotel. The soldiers thought I wanted to

The Innocents Abroad

leave the city, and they sprang up and barred the way with their muskets. I said—

"Hotel d'Europe."

It was all the Italian I knew, and I was not certain whether that was Italian or French. The soldiers looked stupidly at each other and at me, and shook their heads and took me into custody. I said I wanted to go home. They did not understand me. They took me to the guard house and searched me, but they found no sedition on me. They found a small piece of soap (we carry soap with us now) and I made them a present of it, seeing that they regarded it as a curiosity. I continued to say Hotel d'Europe, and they continued to shake their heads, until at last a young soldier nodding in the corner roused up and said something. He said he knew where the hotel was, I suppose, for the officer of the guard sent him away with me. We walked a hundred or a hundred and fifty miles, it appeared to me, and then *he* got lost. He turned this way and that, and finally gave it up and signified that he was going to spend the remainder of the morning trying to find the city gate again. At that moment it struck me that there was something familiar about the house over the way. It was the hotel!

It was a happy thing for me that there happened to be a soldier there that knew even as much as he did; for they say that the policy of the government is to change the soldiery from one place to another constantly, and from country to city, so that they cannot become acquainted with the people, and grow lax in their duties and enter into plots and conspiracies with friends. My experiences of Florence were chiefly unpleasant. I will change the subject.

At Pisa we climbed up to the top of the strangest

structure the world has any knowledge of—the Leaning Tower. As every one knows, it is in the neighbourhood of one hundred and eighty feet high— and I beg to observe that one hundred and eighty feet reach to about the height of four ordinary three-story buildings piled one on top of the other, and is a very considerable altitude for a tower of uniform thickness to aspire to, even when it stands upright—yet this one leans more than thirteen feet out of the perpendicular. It is seven hundred years old, but neither history nor tradition say whether it was built as it is purposely, or whether one of its sides has settled. There is no record that it ever stood straight up. It is built of marble. It is an airy and a beautiful structure, and each of its eight stories is encircled by fluted columns, some of marble and some of granite, with Corinthian capitals that were handsome when they were new. It is a bell tower, and in its top hangs a chime of ancient bells. The winding staircase within is dark, but one always knows which side of the tower he is on because of his naturally gravitating from one side to the other of the staircase with the rise or dip of the tower. Some of the stone steps are foot-worn only on one end; others only on the other end; others only in the middle. To look down into the tower from the top is like looking down into a tilted well. A rope that hangs from the centre of the top touches the wall before it reaches the bottom. Standing on the summit, one does not feel altogether comfortable when he looks down from the high side; but to crawl on your breast to the verge on the lower side and try to stretch your neck out far enough to see the base of the tower makes your flesh creep, and convinces you for a single moment, in spite of all your philosophy, that the building is falling. You handle yourself very carefully, all the time, under the silly impression that if it is *not* falling, your trifling weight will start it unless you are particular not to "bear down" on it.

The Duomo, close at hand, is one of the finest cathedrals in Europe. It is eight hundred years old. Its grandeur has outlived the high commercial prosperity and the political importance that made it a necessity, or rather a possibility. Surrounded by poverty, decay, and ruin, it conveys to us a more tangible impression of the former greatness of Pisa than books could give us.

The Baptistery, which is a few years older than the Leaning Tower, is a stately rotunda, of huge dimensions, and was a costly structure. In it hangs the lamp whose measured swing suggested to Galileo the pendulum. It looked an insignificant thing to have conferred upon the world of science and mechanics such a mighty extension of their dominions as it has. Pondering in its suggestive presence, I seemed to see a crazy universe of swinging discs, the toiling children of this sedate parent. He appeared to have an intelligent expression about him of knowing that he was not a lamp at all; that he was a Pendulum; a pendulum disguised for prodigious and inscrutable purposes of his own deep devising, and not a common pendulum either, but the old original patriarchal Pendulum—the Adam Pendulum of the world.

This Baptistery is endowed with the most pleasing echo of all the echoes we have read of. The guide sounded two sonorous notes, about half an octave apart; the echo answered with the most enchanting, the most melodious, the richest blending of sweet sounds that one can imagine. It was like a long-

drawn chord of a church organ, infinitely softened by
distance. I may be extravagant in this matter, but
if this be the case, my ear is to blame—not my pen.
I am describing a memory, and one that will remain
long with me.

The peculiar devotional spirit of the olden time,
which placed a higher confidence in outward forms of
worship than in the watchful guarding of the heart
against sinful thoughts, and the hands against sinful
deeds, and which believed in the protecting virtues of
inanimate objects made holy by contact with holy
things, is illustrated in a striking manner in one of the
cemeteries of Pisa.   The tombs are set in soil brought
in ships from the Holy Land ages ago. To be buried
in such ground was regarded by the ancient Pisans
as being more potent for salvation than many masses
purchased of the church and the vowing of many
candles to the Virgin.

Pisa is believed to be about three thousand years
old. It was one of the twelve great cities of ancient
Etruria; that commonwealth which has left so many
monuments in testimony of its extraordinary advance-
ment, and so little history of itself that is tangible
and comprehensible. A Pisan antiquarian gave me
an ancient tear-jug, which he averred was full four
thousand years old. It was found among the ruins
of one of the oldest of the Etruscan cities. He said it
came from a tomb, and was used by some bereaved
family in that remote age when even the Pyramids of
Egypt were young, Damascus a village, Abraham a
prattling infant, and ancient Troy not yet dreamt of,
to receive the tears wept for some lost idol of a household. It spoke to us in a language of its own; and
with a pathos more tender than any words might
bring, its mute eloquence swept down the long roll of

the centuries with its tale of a vacant chair, a familiar footstep missed from the threshold, a pleasant voice gone from the chorus, a vanished form!—a tale which is always so new to us, so startling, so terrible, so benumbing to the senses, and behold how threadbare and old it is! No shrewdly-worded history could have brought the myths and shadows of that old dreamy age before us clothed with human flesh and warmed with human sympathies so vividly as did this poor little unsentient vessel of pottery.

Pisa was a republic in the middle ages, with a government of her own, armies and navies of her own, and a great commerce. She was a warlike power, and inscribed upon her banners many a brilliant fight with Genoese and Turks. It is said that the city once numbered a population of four hundred thousand; but her sceptre has passed from her grasp now, her ships and her armies are gone, her commerce is dead. Her battle-flags bear the mould and the dust of centuries, her marts are deserted, she has shrunken far within her crumbling walls, and her great population has diminished to twenty thousand souls. She has but one thing left to boast of, and that is not much, viz.: she is the second city of Tuscany.

We reached Leghorn in time to see all we wished to see of it long before the city gates were closed for the evening, and then came on board the ship.

We felt as though we had been away from home an age. We never entirely appreciated before what a very pleasant den our state-room is; nor how jolly it is to sit at dinner in one's own seat in one's own cabin, and hold familiar conversation with friends in one's own language. Oh, the rare happiness of comprehending every single word that is said, and knowing that every word one says in return will be understood as well! We would talk ourselves to death now, only there are only about ten passengers out of the sixty-five to talk to. The others are wandering, we hardly know where. We shall not go ashore in Leghorn. We are surfeited with Italian cities for the present, and much prefer to walk the familiar quarter-deck and view this one from a distance.

The stupid magnates of this Leghorn government cannot understand that so large a steamer as ours could cross the broad Atlantic with no other purpose than to indulge a party of ladies and gentlemen in a pleasure excursion. It looks too improbable. It is suspicious, they think. Something more important must be hidden behind it all. They cannot understand it, and they scorn the evidence of the ship's papers. They have decided at last that we are a battalion of incendiary, blood-thirsty Garibaldians in disguise! And in all seriousness they have set a gunboat to watch the vessel night and day, with orders to close down on any revolutionary movement in a twinkling! Police boats are on patrol duty about us all the time, and it is as much as a sailor's liberty is worth to show himself in a red shirt. These policemen follow the executive officer's boat from shore to ship and from ship to shore and watch his dark manœuvres with a vigilant eye. They will arrest him yet unless he assumes an expression of countenance that shall have less of carnage, insurrection, and sedition in it. A visit paid in a friendly way to General Garibaldi yesterday (by cordial invitation) by some of our passengers, has gone far to confirm the dread suspicions the government harbours towards us. It is thought the friendly visit was only the cloak of a bloody conspiracy. These people draw near and watch us when we bathe in the sea from the ship's side. Do they think we are communing with a reserve force of rascals at the bottom?

It is said that we shall probably be quarantined at Naples. Two or three of us prefer not to run this risk. Therefore, when we are rested, we propose to go in a French steamer to Civita Vecchia, and from thence to Rome, and by rail to Naples. They do not quarantine the cars, no matter where they got their passengers from.

CHAPTER XXV

THERE are a good many things about this Italy which I do not understand—and more especially I cannot understand how a bankrupt Government can have such palatial railroad depôts and such marvels of turnpikes. Why, these latter are as hard as adamant, as straight as a line, as smooth as a floor, and as white as snow. When it is too dark to see any other object one can still see the white turnpikes of France and Italy; and they are clean enough to eat from without a table-cloth. And yet no tolls are charged.

As for the railways—we have none like them. The cars slide as smoothly along as if they were on runners. The depôts are vast palaces of cut marble, with stately colonnades of the same royal stone traversing them from end to end, and with ample walls and ceilings richly decorated with frescoes. The lofty gateways are graced with statues, and the broad floors are all laid in polished flags of marble.

These things win me more than Italy's hundred galleries of priceless art treasures, because I can understand the one and am not competent to appreciate the other. In the turnpikes, the railways, the depôts, and the new boulevards of uniform houses in Florence and other cities here, I see the genius of Louis Napoleon, or rather, I see the works of that statesman imitated. But Louis has taken care that in France there shall be a foundation for these improvements — money. He has always the wherewithal to back up his projects; they strengthen France, and never weaken her. Her material prosperity is genuine. But here the case is different. This country is bankrupt. There is no real foundation for these great works. The prosperity they would seem to indicate is a pretence. There is no money in the treasury, and so they enfeeble her instead of strengthening. Italy has achieved the dearest wish of her heart and become an independent State—and in so doing she has drawn an elephant in the political lottery. She has nothing to feed it on. Inexperienced in government, she plunged into all manner of useless expenditure, and swamped her treasury almost in a day. She squandered millions of francs on a navy which she did not need, and the first time she took her new toy into action she got it knocked higher than Gilderoy's kite—to use the language of the Pilgrims.

But it is an ill wind that blows nobody good. A year ago, when Italy saw utter ruin staring her in the face and her greenbacks hardly worth the paper they were printed on, her Parliament ventured upon a *coup de main* that would have appalled the stoutest of her statesmen under less desperate circumstances. They, in a manner, confiscated the domains of the Church. This in priest-ridden Italy! This in a land which has groped in the midnight of priestly superstition for sixteen hundred years! It was a rare good fortune for Italy, the stress of weather that drove her to break from this prison-house.

They do not call it *confiscating* the church property. That would sound too harshly yet. But it amounts to that. There are thousands of churches in Italy, each with untold millions of treasures stored away in its closets, and each with its battalion of priests to be supported. And then there are the estates of the Church—league on league of the richest lands and the noblest forests in all Italy—all yielding immense revenues to the Church, and none paying a cent in taxes to the State. In some great districts the Church owns *all* the property—lands, watercourses, woods, mills, and factories. They buy, they sell, they manufacture, and since they pay no taxes, who can hope to compete with them?

Well, the Government has seized all this in effect, and will yet seize it in rigid and unpoetical reality, no doubt. Something must be done to feed a starving treasury, and there is no other resource in all Italy— none but the riches of the Church. So the Government intends to take to itself a great portion of the revenues arising from priestly farms, factories, etc., and also intends to take possession of the churches and carry them on, after its own fashion and upon its own responsibility. In a few instances it will leave the establishments of great pet churches undisturbed, but in all others only a handful of priests will be retained to preach and pray, a few will be pensioned, and the balance turned adrift.

Pray glance at some of these churches and their embellishments, and see whether the Government is doing a righteous thing or not. In Venice, to-day a city of a hundred thousand inhabitants, there are twelve hundred priests. Heaven only knows how many there were before the Parliament reduced their numbers. There was the great Jesuit Church. Under the old regime it required sixty priests to engineer it—the Government does it with five now, and the others are discharged from service. All about that church wretchedness and poverty abound. At its door a dozen hats and bonnets were doffed to us, as many heads were humbly bowed, and as many hands extended, appealing for pennies—appealing with foreign words we could not understand, but appealing mutely, with sad eyes and sunken cheeks, and ragged raiment, that no words were needed to translate. Then we passed within the great doors, and it seemed that the riches of the world were before us! Huge columns carved out of single masses of marble, and inlaid from top to bottom with a hundred intricate figures wrought in costly verde antique; pulpits of the same rich materials, whose draperies hung down in many a pictured fold, the stony fabric counterfeiting the delicate work of the loom; the grand altar brilliant with polished facings and balustrades of oriental agate, jasper, verde antique, and other precious stones, whose names even we seldom hear; and slabs of priceless lapis lazuli lavished everywhere as recklessly as if the church had owned a quarry of it. In the midst of all this magnificence. the solid gold and silver furniture of the altar seemed cheap and trivial. Even the floors and ceilings cost a princely fortune.

Now, where is the use of allowing all those riches to lie idle, while half of that community hardly know, from day to day, how they are going to keep body and soul together? And where is the wisdom in permitting hundreds upon hundreds of millions of francs to be locked up in the useless trumpery of churches all over Italy, and the people ground to death with taxation to uphold a perishing Government?

As far as I can see, Italy for fifteen hundred years has turned all her energies, all her finances, and all her industry to the building up of a vast array of wonderful church edifices, and starving half her citizens to accomplish it. She is to-day one great museum of magnificence and misery. All the churches in an ordinary American city put together could hardly buy the jewelled frippery in one of her hundred cathedrals. And for every beggar in America, Italy can show a hundred, and rags and vermin to match. It is the wretchedest, princeliest land on earth.

Look at the grand Duomo of Florence—a vast pile, that has been sapping the purses of her citizens for five hundred years, and is not nearly finished yet. Like all other men, I fell down and worshipped it, but when the filthy beggars swarmed around me the contrast was too striking, too suggestive, and I said, " O, sons of classic Italy, *is* the spirit of enterprise, of self-reliance, of noble endeavour, utterly dead within ye? Curse your indolent worthlessness, why don't you rob your church? "

Three hundred happy, comfortable priests are employed in that Cathedral.

And now that my temper is up, I may as well go on and abuse everybody I can think of. They have built a grand mausoleum in Florence, which they built to bury our Lord and Saviour and the Medici family in. It sounds blasphemous, but it is true, and here they *act* blasphemy. The dead and damned Medicis who cruelly tyrannised over Florence and were her curse for over two hundred years, are salted away in a circle of costly vaults, and in their midst the Holy Sepulchre was to have been set up. The expedition sent to Jerusalem to seize it got into trouble, and could not accomplish the burglary, and so the centre of the mausoleum is vacant now. They say the entire mausoleum was intended for the Holy Sepulchre, and was only turned into a family burying-place after the Jerusalem expedition failed—but you will excuse me. Some of those Medicis would have smuggled themselves in sure.—What *they* had not the effrontery to do was not worth doing. Why, they had their trivial, forgotten exploits on land and sea pictured out in grand frescoes (as did also the ancient Doges of Venice) with the Saviour and the Virgin throwing bouquets to them out of the clouds, and the Deity himself applauding from his throne in Heaven! And who painted these things? Why, Titian, Tintoretto, Paul Veronese, Raphael— none other than the world's idols, the " old masters."

Andrea del Sarto glorified his princes in pictures that must save them for ever from the oblivion they merited, and they let him starve. Serve him right. Raphael pictured such infernal villains as Catherine and Marie de Medicis seated in heaven, and conversing familiarly with the Virgin Mary and the angels (to say nothing of higher personages), and yet my friends abuse me because I am a little prejudiced against the old masters, because I fail sometimes to see the beauty that is in their productions. I cannot help but see it now and then, but I keep on protesting against the grovelling spirit that could persuade those masters to prostitute their noble talents to the adulation of such monsters as the French, Venetian, and Florentine Princes of two and three hundred years ago all the same.

The Innocents Abroad

I am told that the old masters had to do these shameful things for bread, the princes and potentates being the only patrons of art. If a grandly gifted man may drag his pride and his manhood in the dirt for bread rather than starve with the nobility that is in him untainted, the excuse is a valid one. It would excuse theft in Washingtons and Wellingtons, and unchastity in women as well.

But somehow I cannot keep the Medici mausoleum out of my memory. It is as large as a church; its pavement is rich enough for the pavement of a King's palace; its great dome is gorgeous with frescoes; its walls are made of — what? Marble? — plaster? — wood?—paper? No. Red porphyry—verde antique —jasper — oriental agate — alabaster — mother-of-pearl—chalcedony—red coral—lapis lazuli! All the vast walls are made wholly of these precious stones, worked in and in, and in together in elaborate patterns and figures, and polished till they glow like great mirrors with the pictured splendours reflected from the dome overhead. And before a statue of one of those dead Medicis reposes a crown that blazes with diamonds and emeralds enough to buy a ship-of-the-line almost. These are the things the Government has its evil eye upon, and a happy thing it will be for Italy when they melt away in the public treasury.

And now— However, another beggar approaches. I will go out and destroy him, and then come back and write another chapter of vituperation.

Having eaten the friendless orphan—having driven away his comrades—having grown calm and reflective at length—I now feel in a kindlier mood. I feel that after talking so freely about the priests and the churches, justice demands that if I know anything good about either I ought to say it. I *have* heard of many things that redound to the credit of the priest-hood, but the most notable matter that occurs to me now is the devotion one of the mendicant orders showed during the prevalence of the cholera last year. I speak of the Dominican friars—men who wear a coarse, heavy brown robe and a cowl, in this hot climate, and go barefoot. They live on alms altogether, I believe. They must unquestionably love their religion to suffer so much for it. When the cholera was raging in Naples; when the people were dying by hundreds and hundreds every day; when every concern for the public welfare was swallowed up in selfish private interest, and every citizen made the taking care of himself his sole object, these men banded themselves together, and went about nursing the sick and burying the dead. Their noble efforts cost many of them their lives. They laid them down cheerfully, and well they might. Creeds mathematically precise, and hair-splitting niceties of doctrine, are absolutely necessary for the salvation of some kinds of souls, but surely the charity, the purity, the unselfishness that are in the hearts of men like these would save their souls though they were bankrupt in the true religion—which is ours.

One of these fat bare-footed rascals came here to Civita Vecchia with us in the little French steamer. There were only half-a-dozen of us in the cabin. He belonged in the steerage. He was the life of the ship, the bloody-minded son of the Inquisition! He and the leader of the marine band of a French man-of-war played on the piano and sang opera turn about; they sang duets together; they rigged impromptu theatrical costumes and gave us extravagant farces and pantomimes. We got along first-rate with the

friar, and were excessively conversational, albeit
he could not understand what we said, and certainly
he never uttered a word that we could guess the
meaning of.

This Civita Vecchia is the finest nest of dirt, vermin
and ignorance we have found yet, except that African
perdition they call Tangier, which is just like it.
The people here live in alleys two yards wide, which
have a smell about them which is peculiar but not
entertaining. It is well the alleys are not wider,
because they hold as much smell now as a person can
stand, and of course, if they were wider they would
hold more, and then the people would die. These
alleys are paved with stone, and carpeted with
deceased cats, and decayed rags, and decomposed
vegetable-tops, and remnants of old boots, all soaked
with dish-water, and the people sit around on stools
and enjoy it. They are indolent, as a general thing,
and yet have few pastimes. They work two or three
hours at a time, but not hard, and then they knock
off and catch flies. This does not require any talent,
because they only have to grab—if they do not get
the one they are after, they get another. It is all the
same to them. They have no partialities. Which-
ever one they get is the one they want.

They have other kinds of insects, but it does not
make them arrogant. They are very quiet, unpretending people. They have more of these kind of
things than other communities, but they do not
boast.

They are very uncleanly—these people—in face,
in person and dress. When they see anybody with
a clean shirt on, it arouses their scorn. The women
wash clothes half the day at the public tanks in the
streets, but they are probably somebody else's. Or

may be they keep one set to wear and another to wash; because they never put on any that have ever been washed. When they get done washing, they sit in the alleys and nurse their cubs. They nurse one ash-cat at a time, and the others scratch their backs against the doorpost and are happy.

All this country belongs to the Papal States. They do not appear to have any schools here, and only one billiard table. Their education is at a very low stage. One portion of the men go into the military, another into the priesthood, and the rest into the shoe-making business.

They keep up the passport system here, but so they do in Turkey. This shows that the Papal States are as far advanced as Turkey. This fact will be alone sufficient to silence the tongues of malignant calumniators. I had to get my passport *vised* for Rome in Florence, and then they would not let me come ashore here until a policeman had examined it on the wharf and sent me a permit. They did not even dare to let me take my passport in my hands for twelve hours, I looked so formidable. They judged it best to let me cool down. They thought I wanted to take the town, likely. Little did they know me. I wouldn't have it. They examined my baggage at the depôt. They took one of my ablest jokes and read it over carefully twice and then read it backwards. But it was too deep for them. They passed it around, and everybody speculated on it awhile, but it mastered them all.

It was no common joke. At length a veteran officer spelled it over deliberately and shook his head three or four times and said that in his opinion it was seditious. That was the first time I felt alarmed. I immediately said I would explain the document, and they crowded around. And so I explained, and explained, and explained, and they took notes of all I said, but the more I explained the more they could not understand it, and when they desisted at last, I could not even understand it myself. They said they believed it was an incendiary document, levelled at the Government. I declared solemnly that it was not, but they only shook their heads and would not be satisfied. Then they consulted a good while; and finally they confiscated it. I was very sorry for this, because I had worked a long time on that joke, and took a good deal of pride in it, and now I suppose I shall never see it any more. I suppose it will be sent up and filed away among the criminal archives of Rome, and will always be regarded as a mysterious infernal machine which would have blown up like a mine and scattered the good Pope all around, but for a miraculous providential interference. And I suppose that all the time I am in Rome the police will dog me about from place to place because they think I am a dangerous character.

It is fearfully hot in Civita Vecchia. The streets are made very narrow and the houses built very solid and heavy and high, as a protection against the heat. This is the first Italian town I have seen which does not appear to have a patron saint. I suppose no saint but the one that went up in the chariot of fire could stand the climate.

There is nothing here to see. They have not even a cathedral, with eleven tons of solid silver archbishops in the back room; and they do not show you any moldy buildings that are seven thousand years old; nor any smoke-dried old fire-screens which are *chef-d'œuvres* of Rubens or Simpson, or Titian or Ferguson, or any of those parties; and they haven't any bottled fragments of saints, and not even a nail from the true cross. We are going to Rome. There is nothing to see here.

CHAPTER XXVI

What is it that confers the noblest delight? What is that which swells a man's breast with pride above that which any other experience can bring to him? Discovery! To know that you are walking where none others have walked; that you are beholding what human eye has not seen before; that you are breathing a virgin atmosphere. To give birth to an idea— to discover a great thought—an intellectual nugget, right under the dust of a field that many a brain-plow had gone over before. To find a new planet, to invent a new hinge, to find the way to make the lightnings carry your messages. To be the *first*—that is the idea. To do something, say something, see something, before *anybody* else—these are the things that confer a pleasure compared with which other pleasures are tame and common-place, other ecstasies cheap and trivial. Morse, with his first message, brought by his servant, the lightning; Fulton, in that long-drawn century of suspense, when he placed his hand upon the throttle-valve and lo, the steamboat moved; Jenner, when his patient with the cow's virus in his blood walked through the small-pox hospitals unscathed; Howe, when the idea shot through his brain that for a hundred and twenty generations the eye had been bored through the wrong end of the needle; the nameless lord of art who laid down his chisel in some old age that is forgotten now, and gloated upon the finished Laocoon; Daguerre, when he commanded the sun, riding in the zenith, to print the landscape upon his insignificant silvered plate, and he obeyed; Columbus, in the Pinta's shrouds, when he swung his hat above a fabled sea and gazed abroad upon an unknown world! These are the men who have really *lived*—who have actually comprehended what pleasure is—who have crowded long lifetimes of ecstasy into a single moment.

What is there in Rome for me to see that others have not seen before me? What is there for me to touch that others have not touched? What is there for me to feel, to learn, to hear, to know, that shall thrill me before it pass to others? What can I discover?—Nothing. Nothing whatsoever. One charm of travel dies here. But if I were only a Roman!— If, added to my own I could be gifted with modern Roman sloth, modern Roman superstition, and modern Roman boundlessness of ignorance, what bewildering worlds of unsuspected wonders I would discover! Ah, if I were only a habitant of the Campagna five and twenty miles from Rome! *Then* I would travel.

I would go to America, and see, and learn, and return to the Campagna and stand before my countrymen an illustrious discoverer. I would say—

" I saw there a country which has no overshadowing Mother Church, and yet the people survive. I saw a government which never was protected by foreign soldiers at a cost greater than that required to carry on the government itself. I saw common men and common women who could read; I even saw small children of common country people reading from books; if I dared think you would believe it, I would say they could write also. In the cities I saw people drinking a delicious beverage made of chalk and water, but never once saw goats driven through their

Broadway or their Pennsylvania Avenue or their
Montgomery Street and milked at the doors of the
houses. I saw real glass windows in the houses of even
the commonest people. Some of the houses are not of
stone, nor yet of bricks; I solemnly swear they are
made of wood. Houses there will take fire and burn,
sometimes—actually burn entirely down, and not
leave a single vestige behind. I could state that for a
truth upon my death-bed. And as a proof that the
circumstance is not rare, I aver that they have a thing
which they call a fire-engine, which vomits forth great
streams of water, and is kept always in readiness, by
night and by day, to rush to houses that are burning.
You would think one engine would be sufficient, but
some great cities have a hundred; they keep men
hired, and pay them by the month to do nothing but
put out fires. For a certain sum of money other men
will insure that your house shall not burn down; and
if it burns they will pay you for it. There are
hundreds and thousands of schools, and anybody
may go and learn to be wise, like a priest. In that
singular country if a rich man dies a sinner, he is
damned; he cannot buy salvation with money for
masses. There is really not much use in being rich
there. Not much use as far as the other world is concerned, but much, very much use, as concerns this;
because there, if a man be rich, he is very greatly
honoured, and can become a legislator, a governor,
a general, a senator, no matter how ignorant an ass
he is—just as in our beloved Italy the nobles hold all
the great places, even though sometimes they are born
noble idiots. There, if a man be rich, they give him
costly presents, they ask him to feasts, they invite him
to drink complicated beverages; but if he be poor and
in debt, they require him to do that which they term

The Innocents Abroad

to " settle." The women put on a different dress almost every day; the dress is usually fine, but absurd in shape; the very shape and fashion of it changes twice in a hundred years; and did I but covet to be called an extravagant falsifier, I would say it changed even oftener. Hair does not grow upon the American women's heads; it is made for them by cunning workmen in the shops, and is curled and frizzled into scandalous and ungodly forms. Some persons wear eyes of glass which they see through with facility perhaps, else they would not use them; and in the mouths of some are teeth made by the sacrilegious hand of man. The dress of the men is laughably grotesque. They carry no musket in ordinary life, nor no long-pointed pole; they wear no wide green-lined cloak; they wear no peaked black felt hat, no leathern gaiters reaching to the knee, no goat-skin breeches with the hair side out, no hob-nailed shoes, no prodigious spurs. They wear a conical hat termed a " nail-kag; " a coat of saddest black; a shirt which shows dirt so easily that it has to be changed every month, and is very troublesome; things called pantaloons, which are held up by shoulders straps, and on their feet they wear boots which are ridiculous in pattern and can stand no wear. Yet dressed in this fantastic garb, these people laughed at *my* costume. In that country books are so common that it is really no curiosity to see one. Newspapers also. They have a great machine which prints such things by thousands every hour.

" I saw common men, there—men who were neither priests nor princes—who yet absolutely owned the land they tilled. It was not rented from the church, nor from the nobles. I am ready to take my oath of this. In that country you might fall from a third-

story window three several times, and not mash either
a soldier or a priest.—The scarcity of such people is
astonishing. In the cities you will see a dozen
civilians for every soldier, and as many for every priest
or preacher. Jews are treated just like human beings,
instead of dogs. They can work at any business they
please; they can sell brand new goods if they want
to; they can keep drug-stores; they can practise
medicine among Christians; they can even shake
hands with Christians if they choose; they can
associate with them, just the same as one human being
does with another human being; they don't have to
stay shut up in one corner of the towns; they can live
in any part of a town they like best; it is said they
even have the privilege of buying land and houses,
and owning them themselves, though I doubt that
myself; they never have had to run races naked
through the public streets, against jackasses, to please
the people in carnival time; there they never have
been driven by the soldiers into a church every
Sunday for hundreds of years to hear themselves and
their religion especially and particularly cursed; at
this very day, in that curious country, a Jew is allowed
to vote, hold office, yea, get up on a rostrum in the
public street and express his opinion of the government if the government don't suit him! Ah! it is
wonderful. The common people there know a great
deal; they even have the effrontery to complain if
they are not properly governed, and to take hold and
help conduct the government themselves; if they had
laws like ours, which give one dollar of every three a
crop produces to the government for taxes, they would
have that law altered: instead of paying thirty-three
dollars in taxes, out of every one hundred they receive,
they complain if they have to pay seven. They are

The Innocents Abroad

curious people. They do not know when they are
well off. Mendicant priests do not prowl among them
with baskets begging for the church and eating up
their substance. One hardly ever sees a minister of
the gospel going around there in his bare feet, with a
basket, begging for subsistence. In that country the
preachers are not like our mendicant orders of friars
—they have two or three suits of clothing, and they
wash sometimes. In that land are mountains far
higher than the Alban mountains; the vast Roman
Campagna, a hundred miles long and full forty broad,
is really small compared to the United States of
America; the Tiber, that celebrated river of ours,
which stretches its mighty course almost two hundred
miles, and which a lad can scarcely throw a stone
across at Rome, is not so long, nor yet so wide, as the
American Mississippi—nor yet the Ohio, nor even the
Hudson. In America the people are absolutely wiser
and know much more than their grandfathers did.
They do not plough with a sharpened stick, nor yet
with a three-cornered block of wood that merely
scratches the top of the ground. We do that because
our fathers did, three thousand years ago, I suppose.
But those people have no holy reverence for their
ancestors. They plough with a plough that is a
sharp, curved blade of iron, and it cuts into the earth
full five inches. And this is not all. They cut their
grain with a horrid machine that mows down whole
fields in a day. If I dared, I would say that sometimes they use a blasphemous plough that works by
fire and vapour and tears up an acre of ground in a
single hour—but—but—I see by your looks that you
do not believe the things I am telling you. Alas!
my character is ruined, and I am a branded speaker
of untruths! "

The Innocents Abroad

Of course we have been to the monster Church of St. Peter, frequently. I knew its dimensions. I knew it was a prodigious structure. I knew it was just about the length of the capitol at Washington— say seven hundred and thirty feet. I knew it was three hundred and sixty-four feet wide, and consequently wider than the capitol. I knew that the cross on the top of the dome of the church was four hundred and thirty-eight feet above the ground, and therefore about a hundred or may be a hundred and twenty-five feet higher than the dome of the capitol.—Thus I had one gauge. I wished to come as near forming a correct idea of how it was going to look as possible; I had a curiosity to see how much I would err. I erred considerably. St. Peter's did not look nearly so large as the capitol, and certainly not a twentieth part as beautiful, from the outside.

When we reached the door, and stood fairly within the church, it was impossible to comprehend that it was a *very* large building. I had to *cipher* a comprehension of it. I had to ransack my memory for some more similes. St. Peter's is bulky. Its height and size would represent two of the Washington capitol set one on top of the other—if the capitol were wider; or two blocks or two blocks and a half of ordinary buildings set one on top of the other. St. Peter's *was* that large, but it could and would not look so. The trouble was that everything in it and about it was on such a scale of uniform vastness that there were no contrasts to judge by—none but the people, and I had not noticed them. They were insects. The statues of children holding vases of holy water were immense, according to the tables of figures, but so was everything else around them. The mosaic pictures in the dome were huge, and were made of thousands and thousands of cubes of glass as large as the end of my little finger, but those pictures looked smooth and gaudy of colour, and in good proportion to the dome. Evidently they would not answer to measure by. Away down toward the far end of the church (I thought it was really clear at the far end, but discovered afterward that it was in the centre, under the dome) stood the thing they call the *baldacchino*—a great bronze pyramidal framework like that which upholds a mosquito bar. It only looked like a considerably magnified bedstead— nothing more. Yet I knew it was a good deal more than half as high as Niagara Falls. It was over- shadowed by a dome so mighty that its own height was snubbed. The four great square piers or pillars that stand equidistant from each other in the church, and support the roof, I could not work up to their real dimensions by any method of comparison. I knew that the faces of each were about the width of a very large dwelling-house front (fifty or sixty feet), and that they were twice as high as an ordinary three- story dwelling, but still they looked small. I tried all the different ways I could think of to compel myself to understand how large St. Peter's was, but with small success. The mosaic portrait of an Apostle who was writing with a pen six feet long seemed only an ordinary Apostle.

But the people attracted my attention after a while. To stand in the door of St. Peter's and look at men down toward its further extremity, two blocks away, has a diminishing effect on them; surrounded by the prodigious pictures and statues, and lost in the vast spaces, they look very much smaller than they would if they stood two blocks away in the open air. I "averaged" a man as he passed me, and watched him as he drifted far down by the *baldacchino* and beyond —watched him dwindle to an insignificant schoolboy, and then, in the midst of the silent throng of human pigmies gliding about him, I lost him. The church had lately been decorated, on the occasion of a great ceremony in honour of St. Peter, and men were engaged now in removing the flowers and gilt paper from the walls and pillars. As no ladders could reach the great heights, the men swung themselves down from balustrades and the capitals of pilasters by ropes, to do this work. The upper gallery which encircles the inner sweep of the dome is two hundred and forty feet above the floor of the church—very few steeples in America could reach up to it. Visitors always go up there to look down into the church, because one gets the best idea of some of the heights and distances from that point. While we stood on the floor one of the workmen swung loose from that gallery at the end of a long rope. I had not supposed before that a man *could* look so much like a spider. He was insignificant in size, and his rope seemed only a thread. Seeing that he took up so little space, I could believe the story then that ten thousand troops went to St. Peter's once to hear mass, and their commanding officer came afterward, and not finding them, supposed they had not yet arrived. But they were in the church, nevertheless—they were in one of the transepts. Nearly fifty thousand persons assembled in St. Peter's to hear the publishing of the dogma of the Immaculate Conception. It is estimated that the floor of the church affords standing room for—for a large number of people; I have forgotten the exact figures. But it is no matter—it is near enough.

They have twelve small pillars in St. Peter's which came from Solomon's Temple. They have also—which was far more interesting to me—a piece of the true cross, and some nails, and a part of the crown of thorns.

Of course we ascended to the summit of the dome,

and of course we also went up into the gilt copper ball which is above it. There was room there for a dozen persons, with a little crowding, and it was as close and hot as an oven. Some of those people who are so fond of writing their names in prominent places had been there before us—a million or two, I should think. From the dome of St. Peter's one can see every notable object in Rome, from the Castle of St. Angelo to the Coliseum. He can discern the seven hills upon which Rome is built. He can see the Tiber, and the locality of the bridge which Horatius kept "in the brave days of old" when Lars Porsena attempted to cross it with his invading host. He can see the spot where the Horatii and the Curatii fought their famous battle. He can see the broad green Campagna, stretching away toward the mountains, with its scattered arches and broken aqueducts of the olden time, so picturesque in their grey ruin, and so daintily festooned with vines. He can see the Alban Mountains, the Apennines, the Sabine Hills, and the blue Mediterranean. He can see a panorama that is varied, extensive, beautiful to the eye, and more illustrious in history than any other in Europe. About his feet is spread the remnant of a city that once had a population of four million souls; and among its massed edifices stand the ruins of temples, columns, and triumphal arches that knew the Cæsars and the noonday of Roman splendour; and close by them, in unimpaired strength, is a drain of arched and heavy masonry that belonged to that older city which stood here before Romulus and Remus were born, or Rome thought of. The Appian Way is here yet, and looking much as it did perhaps when the triumphal processions of the Emperors moved over it in other days, bringing fettered princes from the confines of the earth. We cannot see the long array of chariots and mail-clad men laden with the spoils of conquest, but we can imagine the pageant, after a fashion. We look out upon many objects of interest from the dome of St. Peter's; and last of all, almost at our feet, our eyes rest upon the building which was once the Inquisition. How times changed between the older ages and the new! Some seventeen or eighteen centuries ago, the ignorant men of Rome were wont to put Christians in the arena of the Coliseum yonder and turn the wild beast in upon them for a show. It was for a lesson as well. It was to teach the people to abhor and fear the new doctrine the followers of Christ were teaching. The beasts tore the victims limb from limb, and made poor mangled corpses of them in the twinkling of an eye. But when the Christians came into power, when the holy Mother Church became mistress of the barbarians, she taught them the error of their ways by no such means. No, she put them in this pleasant Inquisition and pointed to the Blessed Redeemer, who was so gentle and so merciful toward all men, and they urged the barbarians to love Him; and they did all they could to persuade them to love and honour Him—first by twisting their thumbs out of joint with a screw; then by nipping their flesh with pincers—red-hot ones, because they are the most comfortable in cold weather; then by skinning them alive a little, and finally by roasting them in public. They always convinced those barbarians. The true religion, properly administered, as the good Mother Church used to administer it, is very, very soothing. It is wonderfully persuasive also. There is a great difference between feeding parties to wild beasts and stirring up their finer feelings in an Inquisition. One is the system of degraded barbarians, the other of enlightened, civilised people. It is a great pity the playful Inquisition is no more.

The Innocents Abroad

I prefer not to describe St. Peter's. It has been done before. The ashes of Peter, the disciple of the Saviour, repose in a crypt under the *baldacchino*. We stood reverently in that place; so did we also in the Mamertine Prison, where he was confined, where he converted the soldiers, and where tradition says he caused a spring of water to flow in order that he might baptise them. But when they showed us the print of Peter's face in the hard stone of the prison wall, and said he made that by falling up against it, we doubted. And when also the monk at the church of San Sebastian showed us a paving-stone with two great footprints in it, and said that Peter's feet made those, we lacked confidence again. Such things do not impress one. The monk said that angels came and liberated Peter from prison by night, and he started away from Rome by the Appian Way. The Saviour met him and told him to go back, which he did. Peter left those footprints in the stone upon which he stood at the time. It was not stated how it was ever discovered whose footprints they were, seeing the interview occurred secretly and at night. The print of the face in the prison was that of a man of common size; the footprints were those of a man ten or twelve feet high. The discrepancy confirmed our unbelief.

We necessarily visited the Forum, where Cæsar was assassinated, and also the Tarpeian Rock. We saw the Dying Gladiator at the capitol, and I think that even we appreciated that wonder of art—as much perhaps as we did that fearful story wrought in marble in the Vatican, the Laocoon. And then the Coliseum.

Everybody knows the picture of the Coliseum; everybody recognises at once that " looped and windowed " bandbox with a side bitten out. Being rather isolated, it shows to better advantage than any other of the monuments of ancient Rome. Even the beautiful Pantheon, whose pagan altars uphold the cross now, and whose Venus, tricked out in consecrated gimcracks, does reluctant duty as a Virgin Mary to-day, is built about with shabby houses and its stateliness sadly marred. But the monarch of all European ruins, the Coliseum, maintains that reserve and that royal seclusion which is proper to majesty. Weeds and flowers spring from its massy arches and its circling seats, and vines hang their fringes from its lofty walls. An impressive silence broods over the monstrous structure where such multitudes of men and women were wont to assemble in other days. The butterflies have taken the places of the queens of fashion and beauty of eighteen centuries ago, and the lizards sun themselves in the sacred seat of the Emperor. More vividly than all the written histories, the Coliseum tells the story of Rome's grandeur and Rome's decay. It is the worthiest type of both that exists. Moving about the Rome of to-day, we might find it hard to believe in her old magnificence and her millions of population; but with this stubborn evidence before us that she was obliged to have a theatre with sitting room for eighty thousand persons and standing-room for twenty thousand more, to accommodate such of her citizens as required amusement, we find belief less difficult. The Coliseum is over one thousand six hundred feet long, seven hundred and fifty wide, and one hundred and sixty-five high. Its shape is oval.

In America we make convicts useful at the same time that we punish them for their crimes. We farm them out and compel them to earn money for the State by making barrels and building roads. Thus we combine business with retribution, and all things

The Innocents Abroad

are lovely. But in ancient Rome they combined religious duty with pleasure. Since it was necessary that the new sect called Christians should be exterminated, the people judged it wise to make this work profitable to the State at the same time, and entertaining to the public. In addition to the gladiatorial combats and other shows, they sometimes threw members of the hated sect into the arena of the Coliseum and turned wild beasts in upon them. It is estimated that seventy thousand Christians suffered martyrdom in this place. This has made the Coliseum holy ground, in the eyes of the followers of the Saviour. And well it might; for if the chain that bound a saint, and the footprints a saint has left upon a stone he chanced to stand upon, be holy, surely the spot where a man gave up his life for his faith is holy.

Seventeen or eighteen centuries ago this Coliseum was *the* theatre of Rome, and Rome was mistress of the world. Splendid pageants were exhibited here, in presence of the Emperor, the great ministers of State, the nobles, and vast audiences of citizens of smaller consequence. Gladiators fought with gladiators, and at times with warrior prisoners from many a distant land. It was *the* theatre of Rome—of the world—and the man of fashion who could not let fall in a casual and unintentional manner something about "my private box at the Coliseum" could not move in the first circles. When the clothing-store merchant wished to consume the corner grocery man with envy, he bought secured seats in the front row and let the thing be known. When the irresistible dry goods clerk wished to blight and destroy, according to his native instinct, he got himself up regardless of expense, and took some other fellow's young lady to the Coliseum, and then accented the affront by cramming her with ice cream between the acts, or by

The Innocents Abroad

approaching the cage and stirring up the martyrs with his whalebone cane for her edification. The Roman swell was in his true element only when he stood up against a pillar and fingered his moustache unconscious of the ladies; when he viewed the bloody combats through an opera-glass two inches long; when he excited the envy of provincials by criticisms which showed that he had been to the Coliseum many and many a time, and was long ago over the novelty of it; when he turned away with a yawn at last, and said—

" *He* a star! handles his sword like an apprentice brigand! he'll do for the country, may be, but he don't answer for the metropolis! "

Glad was the contraband that had a seat in the pit at the Saturday matinée, and happy the Roman street boy who ate his peanuts and guyed the gladiators from the dizzy gallery.

For me was reserved the high honour of discovering among the rubbish of the ruined Coliseum the only playbill of that establishment now extant. There was a suggestive smell of mint-drops about it still, a corner of it had evidently been chewed, and on the margin, in choice Latin, these words were written in a delicate female hand:—

" *Meet me on the Tarpeian Rock to-morrow evening, dear, at sharp seven. Mother will be absent on a visit to her friends in the Sabine Hills.*

CLAUDIA."

Ah, where is that lucky youth to-day, and where the little hand that wrote those dainty lines? Dust and ashes these seventeen hundred years!

Thus reads the bill:—

The Innocents Abroad

ROMAN COLISEUM

UNPARALLELED ATTRACTION!

NEW PROPERTIES! NEW LIONS! NEW GLADIATORS!

Engagement of the renowned

MARCUS MARCELLUS VALERIAN!

FOR SIX NIGHTS ONLY!

The management beg leave to offer to the public an entertainment surpassing in magnificence anything that has heretofore been attempted on any stage. No expense has been spared to make the opening season one which shall be worthy the generous patronage which the management feel sure will crown their efforts. The management beg leave to state that they have succeeded in securing the services of a

GALAXY OF TALENT!

such as has not been beheld in Rome before.

The performance will commence this evening with a

GRAND BROADSWORD COMBAT!

between two young and promising amateurs and a celebrated Parthian gladiator who has just arrived a prisoner from the Camp of Verus.

This will be followed by a grand mortal

BATTLE-AXE ENGAGEMENT!

between the renowned Valerian (with one hand tied behind him) and two gigantic savages from Britain.

After which the renowned Valerian (if he survive) will fight with the broadsword,

LEFT HANDED!

against six Sophomores and a Freshman from the Gladiatorial College!

A long series of brilliant engagements will follow, in which the finest talent of the Empire will take part.

After which the celebrated Infant Prodigy known as

" THE YOUNG ACHILLES "

will engage four tiger-whelps in combat, armed with no other weapon than his little spear!

The whole to conclude with a chaste and elegant

GENERAL SLAUGHTER!

in which thirteen African Lions and twenty-two Barbarian Prisoners will war with each other until all are exterminated.

BOX OFFICE NOW OPEN.

Dress Circle One Dollar; Children and Servants half-price.

An efficient police force will be on hand to preserve order and keep the wild beasts from leaping the railings and discommoding the audience.

Doors open at 7; performance begins at 8.

POSITIVELY NO FREE-LIST.

Diodorus Job Press.

255

The Innocents Abroad

It was as singular as it was gratifying that I was also so fortunate as to find among the rubbish of the arena, a stained and mutilated copy of the *Roman Daily Battle-Axe*, containing a critique upon this very performance. It comes to hand too late by many centuries to rank as news, and therefore I translate and publish it simply to show how very little the general style and phraseology of dramatic criticism has altered in the ages that have dragged their slow length along since the carriers laid this one damp and fresh before their Roman patrons:—

"THE OPENING SEASON.—COLISEUM.—Notwithstanding the inclemency of the weather, quite a respectable number of the rank and fashion of the city assembled last night to witness the debut upon metropolitan boards of the young tragedian who has of late been winning such golden opinions in the amphitheatres of the provinces. Some sixty thousand persons were present, and but for the fact that the streets were almost impassable, it is fair to presume that the house would have been full. His august Majesty the Emperor Aurelius occupied the imperial box, and was the cynosure of all eyes. Many illustrious nobles and generals of the Empire graced the occasion with their presence, and not the least among them was the young patrician lieutenant whose laurels, won in the ranks of the 'Thundering Legion,' are still so green upon his brow. The cheer which greeted his entrance was heard beyond the Tiber!

"The late repairs and decorations add both to the comeliness and the comfort of the Coliseum. The new cushions are a great improvement upon the hard marble seats we have been so long accustomed to. The present management deserve well of the public. They have restored to the Coliseum the gilding, the rich upholstery, and the uniform magnificence which old Coliseum frequenters tell us Rome was so proud of fifty years ago.

"The opening scene last night,—the broadsword combat between two young amateurs and a famous Parthian gladiator who was sent here a prisoner—was very fine. The elder of the two young gentlemen handled his weapon with a grace that marked the possession of extraordinary talent. His feint of thrusting, followed instantly by a happily-delivered blow which unhelmeted the Parthian, was received with hearty applause. He was not thoroughly up in the back-

256

The Innocents Abroad

handed stroke, but it was very gratifying to his numerous friends to know that, in time, practice would have overcome this defect. However, he was killed. His sisters, who were present, expressed considerable regret. His mother left the Coliseum. The other youth maintained the contest with such spirit as to call forth enthusiastic bursts of applause. When at last he fell a corpse, his aged mother ran screaming, with hair dishevelled and tears streaming from her eyes, and swooned away just as her hands were clutching at the railings of the arena. She was promptly removed by the police. Under the circumstances the woman's conduct was pardonable, perhaps, but we suggest that such exhibitions interfere with the decorum which should be preserved during the performances, and are highly improper in the presence of the Emperor. The Parthian prisoner fought bravely and well; and well he might, for he was fighting for both life and liberty. His wife and children were there to nerve his arm with their love, and to remind him of the old home he should see again if he conquered. When his second assailant fell, the woman clasped her children to her breast and wept for joy. But it was only a transient happiness. The captive staggered toward her, and she saw that the liberty he had earned was earned too late. He was wounded unto death. Thus the first act closed in a manner which was entirely satisfactory. The manager was called before the curtain and returned his thanks for the honour done him, in a speech which was replete with wit and humour, and closed by hoping that his humble efforts to afford cheerful and instructive entertainment would continue to meet with the approbation of the Roman public.

" The star now appeared, and was received with vociferous applause and the simultaneous waving of sixty thousand handkerchiefs. Marcus Marcellus Valerian (stage name—his real name is Smith) is a splendid specimen of physical development, and an artist of rare merit. His management of the battle-axe is wonderful. His gaiety and his playfulness are irresistible, in his comic parts, and yet they are inferior to his sublime conceptions in the grave realm of tragedy. When his axe was describing fiery circles about the heads of the bewildered barbarians, in exact time with his springing body and his prancing legs, the audience gave way to uncontrollable bursts of laughter; but when the back of his weapon broke the skull of one and almost in the same instant its edge clove the other's body in twain, the howl of enthusiastic applause that shook the building was the acknowledgment of a critical assemblage that he was a master of the noblest department of his profession. If he has a fault (and we are sorry to even intimate that he has), it is

I

that of glancing at the audience, in the midst of the most exciting moments of the performance, as if seeking admiration. The pausing in a fight to bow when bouquets are thrown to him, is also in bad taste. In the great left-handed combat he appeared to be looking at the audience half the time, instead of carving his adversaries; and when he had slain all the sophomores and was dallying with the freshman, he stooped and snatched a bouquet as it fell, and offered it to his adversary at a time when a blow was descending which promised favourably to be his death-warrant. Such levity is proper enough in the provinces, we make no doubt, but it ill suits the dignity of the metropolis. We trust our young friend will take these remarks in good part, for we mean them solely for his benefit. All who know us are aware that although we are at times justly severe upon tigers and martyrs, we never intentionally offend gladiators.

"The Infant Prodigy performed wonders. He overcame his four tiger whelps with ease, and with no other hurt than the loss of a portion of his scalp. The General Slaughter was rendered with a faithfulness to details which reflects the highest credit upon the late participants in it.

"Upon the whole, last night's performances shed honour not only upon the management, but upon the city that encourages and sustains such wholesome and instructive entertainments. We would simply suggest that the practice of vulgar young boys in the gallery of shying peanuts and paper pellets at the tigers, and saying ' Hi-yi! ' and manifesting approbation or dissatisfaction by such observations as ' Bully for the lion! ' ' Go it, Gladdy! ' ' Boots! ' ' Speech! ' ' Take a walk round the block! ' and so on, are extremely reprehensible when the Emperor is present, and ought to be stopped by the police. Several times last night, when the supernumeraries entered the arena to drag out the bodies, the young ruffians in the gallery shouted, ' Supe! supe! ' and also, ' Oh, what a coat! ' and ' Why don't you pad them shanks? ' and made use of various other remarks expressive of derision. These things are very annoying to the audience.

"A matinee for the little folks is promised for this afternoon, on which occasion several martyrs will be eaten by the tigers. The regular performance will continue every night till further notice. Material change of programme every evening. Benefit of Valerian, Tuesday, 29th, if he lives."

I have been a dramatic critic myself, in my time, and I was often surprised to notice how much more I knew about Hamlet than Forrest did; and it gratifies me to observe, now, how much better my brethren of ancient times knew how a broad-sword battle ought to be fought than the gladiators.

CHAPTER XXVII

So far, good. If any man has a right to feel proud of himself and satisfied, surely it is I. For I have written about the Coliseum, and the gladiators, the martyrs, and the lions, and yet have never once used the phrase " butchered to make a Roman holiday." I am the only free white man of mature age who has accomplished this since Byron originated the expression.

Butchered to make a Roman holiday sounds well for the first seventeen or eighteen hundred thousand times one sees it in print, but after that it begins to grow tiresome. I find it in all the books concerning Rome; and here latterly it reminds me of Judge Oliver. Oliver was a young lawyer, fresh from the schools, who had gone out to the deserts of Nevada to begin life. He found that country, and our ways of life there, in those early days, different from life in New England or Paris. But he put on a woollen shirt and strapped a navy revolver to his person, took to the bacon and beans of the country, and determined to do in Nevada as Nevada did. Oliver accepted the situation so completely that although he must have sorrowed over many of his trials, he never complained—that is, he never complained but once. He, two others, and myself, started to the new silver mines in the Humboldt mountains—he to be Probate Judge of Humboldt county, and we to mine. The distance was two hundred miles. It was dead of winter. We bought a two-horse waggon and put eighteen hundred pounds of bacon, flour, beans, blasting-powder, picks and shovels in it; we bought two sorry-looking Mexican " plugs," with the hair turned the wrong way, and more corners on their bodies than there are on the mosque of Omar; we hitched up and started. It was a dreadful trip; but Oliver did not complain. The horses dragged the waggon two miles from town, and then gave out. Then we three pushed the waggon seven miles, and Oliver moved ahead and pulled the horses after him by the bits. We complained, but Oliver did not. The ground was frozen, and it froze our backs while we slept; the wind swept across our faces and froze our noses. Oliver did not complain. Five days of pushing the waggon by day and freezing by night brought us to the bad part of the journey—the Forty Mile Desert, or the Great American Desert, if you please. Still this mildest-mannered man that ever was had not complained. We started across at eight in the morning, pushing through sand that had no bottom; toiling all day long by the wrecks of a thousand waggons, the skeletons of ten thousand oxen; by waggon-tires enough to hoop the Washington Monument to the top, and ox-chains enough to girdle Long Island; by human graves; with our throats parched always with thirst; lips bleeding from the alkali dust; hungry, perspiring, and very, very weary that when we dropped in the sand every fifty yards to rest the horses, we could hardly keep from going to sleep—no complaints from Oliver; none the next morning at three o'clock, when we got across, tired to death. Awakened two or three nights afterward at midnight, in a narrow cañon, by the snow falling on our faces, and appalled at the imminent danger of being "snowed in," we harnessed up and pushed on till eight in the morning, passed the "Divide" and knew we were saved. No complaints. Fifteen days of hardship and fatigue brought us to the end of the two hundred miles, and the Judge had not complained. We wondered if anything *could* exasperate him. We built a Humboldt house. It is done in this way: You dig a square in the steep base of the mountain, and set up two uprights and top them with two joists. Then you stretch a great sheet of "cotton domestic" from the point where the joists join the hill-side down over the joists to the ground; this makes the roof and the front of the mansion; the sides and back are the dirt walls your digging has left. A chimney is easily made by turning up one corner of the roof. Oliver was sitting alone in this dismal den one night by a sage-bush fire, writing poetry; he was very fond of digging poetry out of himself— or blasting it out when it came hard. He heard an animal's footsteps close to the roof; a stone or two and some dirt came through and fell by him. He grew uneasy and said " Hi!—clear out from there, can't you!"—from time to time. But by and by he fell asleep where he sat, and pretty soon a mule fell down the chimney! The fire flew in every direction, and Oliver went over backwards. About ten nights after that he recovered confidence enough to go to writing poetry again. Again he dozed off to sleep, and again a mule fell down the chimney. This time, about half of that side of the house came in with the mule. Struggling to get up, the mule kicked the candle out and smashed most of the kitchen furniture, and raised considerable dust. These violent awakenings must have been annoying to Oliver, but he never complained. He moved to a mansion on the opposite side of the cañon, because he had noticed the mules did not go there. One night, about eight o'clock, he was endeavouring to finish his poem, when a stone rolled in—then a hoof appeared below the canvas—then part of a cow—the after part. He leaned back in dread, and shouted " Hooy! hooy! get out of this! " and the cow struggled manfully—lost ground steadily —dirt and dust streamed down, and before Oliver could get well away, the entire cow crashed through on to the table, and made a shapeless wreck of everything!

Then, for the first time in his life, I think Oliver complained. He said—

" *This thing is growing monotonous !* "

Then he resigned his judgeship and left Humboldt county. " Butchered to make a Roman holiday " has grown monotonous to me.

In this connection I wish to say one word about Michael Angelo Buonarotti. I used to worship the mighty genius of Michael Angelo—that man who was great in poetry, painting, sculpture, architecture— great in everything he undertook. But I do not want Michael Angelo for breakfast—for luncheon— for dinner—for tea—for supper—for between meals. I like a change occasionally. In Genoa he designed everything; in Milan he or his pupils designed every- thing; he designed the Lake of Como; in Padua, Verona, Venice, Bologna, who did we ever hear of, from guides, but Michael Angelo? In Florence he painted everything, designed everything, nearly, and what he did not design he used to sit on a favourite stone and look at, and they showed us the stone. In Pisa he designed everything but the old shot-tower, and they would have attributed that to him if it had not been so awfully out of the perpendicular. He designed the piers of Leghorn and the custom-house regulations of Civita Vecchia. But here—here it is frightful. He designed St. Peter's; he designed the Pope; he designed the Pantheon, the uniform of the Pope's soldiers, the Tiber, the Vatican, the Coliseum, the Capitol, the Tarpeian Rock, the Barberini Palace, St. John Lateran, the Campagna, the Appian Way, the Seven Hills, the Baths of Caracalla, the Claudian Aqueduct, the Cloaca Maxima — the eternal bore designed the Eternal City, and unless all men and books do lie, he painted everything in it! Dan said the other day to the guide, " Enough, enough, enough! Say no more! Lump the whole thing! say that the Creator made Italy from designs by Michael Angelo! "

I never felt so fervently thankful, so soothed, so tranquil, so filled with a blessed peace, as I did yesterday, when I learned that Michael Angelo was dead.

But we have taken it out of this guide. He has marched us through miles of pictures and sculpture in the vast corridors of the Vatican; and through miles of pictures and sculpture in twenty other palaces; he has shown us the great picture in the Sistine Chapel, and frescoes enough to fresco the heavens—pretty much all done by Michael Angelo. So with him we have played that game which has vanquished so many guides for us—imbecility and idiotic questions. These creatures never suspect; they have no idea of a sarcasm.

He shows us a figure and says: " Statoo brunzo." (Bronze statue.)

We look at it indifferently and the doctor asks: " By Michael Angelo? "

" No—not know who."

The Innocents Abroad

Then he shows us the ancient Roman Forum. The doctor asks: " Michael Angelo? "

A stare from the guide. " No—thousan' year before he is born."

Then an Egyptian obelisk. Again: " Michael Angelo? "

" Oh, *mon Dieu*, genteelmen! Zis is *two* thousan' year before he is born! "

He grows so tired of that unceasing question sometimes, that he dreads to show us anything at all. The wretch has tried all the ways he can think of to make us comprehend that Michael Angelo is only responsible for the creation of a *part* of the world, but somehow he has not succeeded yet. Relief for overtasked eyes and brain from study and sightseeing is necessary, or we shall become idiotic sure enough. Therefore this guide must continue to suffer. If he does not enjoy it, so much the worse for him. We do.

In this place I may as well jot down a chapter concerning those necessary nuisances, European guides. Many a man has wished in his heart he could do without his guide; but knowing he could not, has wished he could get some amusement out of him as a remuneration for the affliction of his society. We accomplished this latter matter, and if our experience can be made useful to others they are welcome to it.

Guides know about enough English to tangle everything up so that a man can make neither head nor tail of it. They know their story by heart— the history of every statue, painting, cathedral, or other wonder they show you. They know it and tell it as a parrot would—and if you interrupt and throw them off the track, they have to go back and begin over again. All their lives long they are employed in showing strange things to foreigners and listening

The Innocents Abroad

to their bursts of admiration. It is human nature to take delight in exciting admiration. It is what prompts children to say " smart " things, and do absurd ones, and in other ways " show off " when company is present. It is what makes gossips turn out in rain and storm to go and be the first to tell a startling bit of news. Think, then, what a passion it becomes with a guide, whose privilege it is, every day to show to strangers wonders that throw them into perfect ecstasies of admiration! He gets so that he could not by any possibility live in a soberer atmosphere. After we discovered this, we *never* went into ecstasies any more—we never admired anything—we never showed any but impassible faces and stupid indifference in the presence of the sublimest wonders a guide had to display. We had found their weak point. We have made good use of it ever since. We have made some of those people savage at times, but we have never lost our own serenity.

The doctor asks the questions generally, because he can keep his countenance, and look more like an inspired idiot, and throw more imbecility into the tone of his voice than any man that lives. It comes natural to him.

The guides in Genoa are delighted to secure an American party, because Americans so much wonder, and deal so much in sentiment and emotion before any relic of Columbus. Our guide there fidgeted about as if he had swallowed a spring mattress. He was full of animation—full of impatience. He said—

" Come wis me, genteelmen!—come! I show you ze letter writing by Christopher Colombo!—write it himself!—write it wis his own hand!—come! "

He took us to the municipal palace. After much impressive fumbling of keys and opening of locks,

The Innocents Abroad

the stained and aged document was spread before us. The guide's eyes sparkled. He danced about us and tapped the parchment with his finger.

" What I tell you, genteelmen! Is it not so? See! handwriting Christopher Colombo!—write it himself!"

We looked indifferent—unconcerned. The doctor examined the document very deliberately, during a painful pause.—Then he said, without any show of interest—

" Ah—Ferguson—what—what did you say was the name of the party who wrote this? "

" Christopher Colombo! ze great Christopher Colombo! "

Another deliberate examination.

" Ah—did he write it himself, or—or how? "

" He write it himself!—Christopher Colombo! he's own handwriting, write by himself! "

Then the doctor laid the document down and said—

" Why, I have seen boys in America only fourteen years old that could write better than that."

" But zis is ze great Christo——"

' I don't care who it is! It's the worst writing I ever saw. Now you mustn't think you can impose on us because we are strangers. We are not fools, by a good deal. If you have got any specimens of penmanship of real merit, trot them out!—and if you haven't, drive on! "

We drove on. The guide was considerably shaken up, but he made one more venture. He had something which he thought would overcome us He said—

" Ah, genteelmen, you come wis me! I show you beautiful, O, magnificent bust Christopher Colombo!— splendid, grand, magnificent! "

The Innocents Abroad

He brought us before the beautiful bust—for it *was* beautiful—and sprang back and struck an attitude.

"Ah, look, genteelmen!—beautiful, grand—bust Christopher Colombo!—beautiful bust, beautiful pedestal!"

The doctor put up his eye-glass—procured for such occasions.

"Ah—what did you say this gentleman's name was?"

"Christopher Colombo!—ze great Christopher Colombo!"

"Christopher Colombo!—the great Christopher Colombo. Well, what did *he* do?"

"Discover America!—discover America, Oh, ze devil!"

"Discover America. No—that statement will hardly wash. We are just from America ourselves. We heard nothing about it. Christopher Colombo—pleasant name—is—is he dead?"

"Oh, corpo di Baccho!—three hundred year!"

"What did he die of?"

"I do not know!—I can not tell."

"Small-pox, think?"

"I do not know, genteelmen!—I do not know *what* he die of."

"Measles, likely?"

"Maybe—maybe—I do *not* know—I think he die of somethings."

"Parents living?"

"Im-posseeble!"

"Ah—which is the bust and which is the pedestal?"

"Santa Maria!—*zis* ze bust!—*zis* ze pedestal!"

"Ah, I see, I see—happy combination—very happy combination, indeed. Is—is this the first time this gentleman was ever on a bust?"

The Innocents Abroad

That joke was lost on the defendant—guides cannot master the subtleties of the American joke.

We have made it interesting to this Roman guide. Yesterday we spent three or four hours in the Vatican, again, that wonderful world of curiosities. We came very near expressing interest, sometimes — even admiration—it was very hard to keep from it. We succeeded though. Nobody else ever did in the Vatican museums. The guide was bewildered—nonplussed. He walked his legs off, nearly, hunting up extraordinary things, and exhausted all his ingenuity on us, but it was a failure; we never showed any interest in anything. He had reserved what he considered to be his greatest wonder till the last— a royal Egyptian mummy, the best preserved in the world perhaps. He took us there. He felt so sure this time, that some of his old enthusiasm came back to him—

" See, genteelmen!—Mummy! Mummy! "

The eye-glass came up as calmly, as deliberately as ever.

" Ah—Ferguson, what did I understand you to say the gentleman's name was? "

" Name?—he got no name!—Mummy!—'Gyptian mummy! "

" Yes, yes. Born here? "

" No! *'Gyptian* mummy! "

" Ah, just so. Frenchman, I presume? "

" No!—*not* Frenchman, not Roman! — born in Egypta! "

" Born in Egypta. Never heard of Egypta before. Foreign locality, likely. Mummy—mummy. How calm he is—how self-possessed. Is, ah—is he dead? "

" Oh, *sacre bleu*, been dead three thousan' year! "

The doctor turned on him savagely—

"Is it ———— is he dead?"

The Innocents Abroad

" Here, now, what do you mean by such conduct as this? Playing us for Chinamen because we are strangers and trying to learn! Trying to impose your vile secondhand carcasses on *us*!—thunder and lightning, I've a notion to—to—if you've got a nice *fresh* corpse, fetch him out!—or by George we'll brain you! "

We made it exceedingly interesting for this Frenchman. However, he has paid us back, partly, without knowing it. He came to the hotel this morning to ask if we were up, and he endeavoured as well as he could to describe us, so that the landlord would know which persons he meant. He finished with the casual remark that we were lunatics. The observation was so innocent and so honest that it amounted to a very good thing for a guide to say.

There is one remark (already mentioned) which never yet has failed to disgust these guides. We use it always, when we can think of nothing else to say. After they have exhausted their enthusiasm pointing out to us and praising the beauties of some ancient bronze image or broken-legged statue, we look at it stupidly and in silence for five, ten, fifteen minutes— as long as we can hold out, in fact—and then ask—

" Is—is he dead? "

That conquers the serenest of them. It is not what they are looking for—especially a new guide. Our Roman Ferguson is the most patient, unsuspecting, long-suffering subject we have had yet. We shall be sorry to part with him. We have enjoyed his society very much. We trust he has enjoyed ours, but we are harassed with doubts.

We have been in the catacombs. It was like going down into a very deep cellar, only it was a cellar which had no end to it. The narrow passages are roughly hewn in the rock, and on each hand as you pass along, the hollowed shelves are carved out, from three to fourteen deep; each held a corpse once. There are names, and Christian symbols, and prayers, or sentences expressive of Christian hopes, carved upon nearly every sarcophagus. The dates belong away back in the dawn of the Christian era, of course. Here, in these holes in the ground, the first Christians sometimes burrowed to escape persecution. They crawled out at night to get food, but remained under cover in the day time. The priest told us that St. Sebastian lived underground for some time while he was being hunted; he went out one day, and the soldiery discovered and shot him to death with arrows. Five or six of the early Popes—those who reigned about sixteen hundred years ago—held their papal courts and advised with their clergy in the bowels of the earth. During seventeen years—from A.D. 235 to A.D. 252—the Popes did not appear above ground. Four were raised to the great office during that period. Four years apiece or thereabouts. It is very suggestive of the unhealthiness of underground graveyards as places of residence. One Pope afterward spent his entire pontificate in the catacombs—eight years. Another was discovered in them and murdered in the episcopal chair. There was no satisfaction in being a Pope in those days. There were too many annoyances. There are one hundred and sixty catacombs under Rome, each with its maze of narrow passages crossing and recrossing each other and each passage walled to the top with scooped graves its entire length. A careful estimate makes the length of the passages of all the catacombs combined foot up nine hundred miles, and their graves number seven millions. We did not go through all the passages of all the cata-

The Innocents Abroad

combs. We were very anxious to do it, and made the necessary arrangements, but our too limited time obliged us to give up the idea. So we only groped through the miserable labyrinth of St. Callixtus, under the Church of St. Sebastian. In the various catacombs are small chapels rudely hewn in the stones, and here the early Christians often held their religious services by dim, ghostly lights. Think of mass and a sermon away down in those tangled caverns underground!

In the catacombs were buried St. Cecilia, St. Agnes, and several other of the most celebrated of the saints. In the catacombs of St. Callixtus, St. Bridget used to remain long hours in holy contemplation, and St. Charles Borroméo was wont to spend whole nights in prayer there. It was also the scene of a very marvellous thing.

" Here the heart of St. Philip Neri was so inflamed with divine love as to burst his ribs."

I find that grave statement in a book published in New York in 1858, and written by " Rev. William H. Neligan, LL.D., M.A., Trinity College, Dublin; Member of the Archæological Society of Great Britain." Therefore, I believe it. Otherwise, I could not. Under other circumstances I should have felt a curiosity to know what Philip had for dinner.

This author puts my credulity on its mettle every now and then. He tells of one St. Joseph Calasanctius whose house in Rome he visited; he visited only the house—the priest has been dead two hundred years. He says the Virgin Mary appeared to this saint. Then he continues—

" His tongue and his heart, which were found after nearly a century to be whole, when the body was disinterred before

The Innocents Abroad

his canonisation, are still preserved in a glass-case, and after two centuries the heart is still whole. When the French troops came to Rome, and when Pius VII. was carried away prisoner, blood dropped from it."

To read that in a book written by a monk far back in the Middle Ages, would surprise no one; it would sound natural and proper; but when it is seriously stated in the middle of the nineteenth century, by a man of finished education, an LL.D., M.A., and an Archæological magnate, it sounds strangely enough. Still I would gladly change my unbelief for Neligan's faith, and let him make the conditions as hard as he pleased.

The old gentleman's undoubting, unquestioning simplicity has a rare freshness about it in these matter-of-fact railroading and telegraphing days. Hear him, concerning the church of Ara Cœli:—

" In the roof of the church, directly above the high altar, is engraved ' *Regina Cœli lactare Alleluia.*' In the sixth century Rome was visited by a fearful pestilence. Gregory the Great urged the people to do penance, and a general procession was formed. It was to proceed from Ara Cœli to St. Peter's. As it passed before the mole of Adrian, now the Castle of St. Angelo, the sound of heavenly voices was heard singing (it was Easter morn), ' *Regina Cœli, lactare ! alleluia ! quia quem meruisti portare, alleluia ! resurrexit sicut dixit ; alleluia ! '* The Pontiff, carrying in his hands the portrait of the Virgin (which is over the high altar and is said to have been painted by St. Luke), answered, with the astonished people, ' *Ora pro nobis Deum, alleluia ! '* At the same time an angel was seen to put up a sword in a scabbard, and the pestilence ceased on the same day. There are four circumstances which *confirm* [1] this miracle : the annual procession which takes place in the western church on the feast of St. Mark; the statue of St. Michael, placed on the mole of Adrian, which has since that time been called the Castle of St. Angelo; the antiphon Regina Cœli, which the Catholic church sings during paschal time; and the inscription in the church."

[1] The italics are mine.—M.T.

The Innocents Abroad

CHAPTER XXVIII

FROM the sanguinary sports of the Holy Inquisition; the slaughter of the Coliseum; and the dismal tombs of the Catacombs, I naturally pass to the picturesque horrors of the Capuchin Convent. We stopped a moment in a small chapel in the Church to admire a picture of St. Michael vanquishing Satan—a picture which is so beautiful that I cannot but think it belongs to the reviled " *Renaissance*," notwithstanding I believe they told us one of the ancient old masters painted it—and then we descended into the vast vault underneath.

Here was a spectacle for sensitive nerves! Evidently the old masters had been at work in this place. There were six divisions in the apartment, and each division was ornamented with a style of decoration peculiar to itself—and these decorations were in every instance formed of human bones! There were shapely arches, built wholly of thigh bones; there were startling pyramids, built wholly of grinning skulls; there were quaint architectural structures of various kinds, built of shin bones and the bones of the arm; on the wall were elaborate frescoes, whose curving vines were made of knotted human vertebræ; whose delicate tendrils were made of sinews and tendons; whose flowers were formed of knee-caps and toe-nails. Every lasting portion of the human frame was represented in these intricate designs (they were by Michael Angelo, I think), and there was a careful finish about the work, and an attention to details that betrayed the artist's love of his labours as well as his schooled ability. I asked the good-natured monk who accompanied us who did this? And he said, " *We* did it "—meaning himself and his brethren upstairs. I could see that the old friar took a high pride in his curious show. We made him talkative by exhibiting an interest we never betrayed to guides.

" Who were these people? "

" We—upstairs—Monks of the Capuchin order— my brethren."

" How many departed monks were required to upholster these six parlours? "

" These are the bones of four thousand."

" It took a long time to get enough? "

" Many, many centuries."

" Their different parts are well separated—skulls in one room, legs in another, ribs in another—there would be stirring times here for a while if the last trump should blow. Some of the brethren might get hold of the wrong leg, in the confusion, and the wrong skull, and find themselves limping, and looking through eyes that were wider apart or closer together than they were used to. You cannot tell any of these parties apart, I suppose? "

" Oh yes, I know many of them."

He put his finger on a skull. " This was Brother Anselmo—dead three hundred years—a good man."

He touched another. " This was Brother Alexander—dead two hundred and eighty years. This was Brother Carlo—dead about as long."

Then he took a skull and held it in his hand, and looked reflectively upon it, after the manner of the gravedigger when he discourses of Yorick.

" This," he said, " was Brother Thomas. He was a young prince, the scion of a proud house that traced its lineage back to the grand old days of Rome well nigh two thousand years ago. He loved beneath his estate. His family persecuted him; persecuted the girl as well. They drove her from Rome; he followed; he sought her far and wide; he found no trace of her. He came back and offered his broken heart at our altar and his weary life to the service of God. But look you. Shortly his father died, and likewise his mother. The girl returned, rejoicing. She sought everywhere for him whose eyes had used to look tenderly into hers out of this poor skull, but she could not find him. At last, in this coarse garb we wear, she recognised him in the street. He knew her. It was too late. He fell where he stood. They took him up and brought him here. He never spoke afterwards. Within the week he died. You can see the colour of his hair—faded, somewhat—by this thin shred that clings still to the temple. "This" [taking up a thigh bone] "was his. The veins of this leaf in the decorations over your head were his finger-joints a hundred and fifty years ago."

This business-like way of illustrating a touching story of the heart by laying the several fragments of the lover before us and naming them, was as grotesque a performance, and as ghastly, as any I ever witnessed. I hardly knew whether to smile or shudder. There are nerves and muscles in our frames whose functions and whose methods of working it seems a sort of sacrilege to describe by cold physiological names and surgical technicalities, and the monk's talk suggested to me something of this kind. Fancy a surgeon, with his nippers lifting tendons, muscles, and such things into view, out of the complex machinery of a corpse, and observing, "Now this little nerve quivers—the vibration is imparted to this muscle—from here it is passed to this fibrous substance; here its ingredients are separated by the

The Innocents Abroad

chemical action of the blood—one part goes to the heart and thrills it with what is popularly termed emotion, another part follows this nerve to the brain and communicates intelligence of a startling character—the third part glides along this passage and touches the spring connected with the fluid receptacles that lie in the rear of the eye. Thus, by this simple and beautiful process, the party is informed that his mother is dead, and he weeps." Horrible!

I asked the monk if all the brethren upstairs expected to be put in this place when they died. He answered quietly—

" We must all lie here at last."

See what one can accustom himself to.—The reflection that he must some day be taken apart like an engine or a clock, or like a house whose owner is gone, and worked up into arches and pyramids and hideous frescoes, did not distress this monk in the least. I thought he even looked as if he were thinking, with complacent vanity, that his own skull would look well on top of the heap, and his own ribs add a charm to the frescoes which possibly they lacked at present.

Here and there, in ornamental alcoves, stretched upon beds of bones, lay dead and dried-up monks, with lank frames dressed in the black robes one sees ordinarily upon priests. We examined one closely. The skinny hands were clasped upon the breast; two lustreless tufts of hair stuck to the skull; the skin was brown and sunken; it stretched tightly over the cheek bones and made them stand out sharply; the crisp dead eyes were deep in the sockets; the nostrils were painfully prominent, the end of the nose being gone; the lips had shrivelled away from the yellow teeth: and brought down to us through the circling years,

and petrified there, was a weird laugh a full century
old!

It was the jolliest laugh, but yet the most dreadful,
that one can imagine. Surely, I thought, it must have
been a most extraordinary joke this veteran produced
with his latest breath, that he has not got done
laughing at it yet.

At this moment I saw that the old instinct was
strong upon the boys, and I said we had better hurry
to St. Peter's. They were trying to keep from
asking, " Is—is he dead? "

It makes me dizzy to think of the Vatican—of its
wilderness of statues, paintings, and curiosities of
every description and every age. The " old masters "
(especially in sculpture) fairly swarm there. I cannot
write about the Vatican. I think I shall never remember anything I saw there distinctly but the
mummies, and the " Transfiguration " by Raphael,
and some other things it is not necessary to mention
now. I shall remember the " Transfiguration "
partly because it was placed in a room almost by
itself; partly because it is acknowledged by all to
be the first oil painting in the world; and partly
because it was wonderfully beautiful. The colours
are fresh and rich, the " expression," I am told, is
fine, the " feeling " is lively, the " tone " is good, the
" depth " is profound, and the width is about four
and a half feet, I should judge. It is a picture that
really holds one's attention; its beauty is fascinating.
It is fine enough to be a *Renaissance*. A remark I
made a while ago suggests a thought—and a hope.
Is it not possible that the reason I find such charms
in this picture is because it is out of the crazy chaos of
the galleries? If some of the others were set apart,
might not they be beautiful? If this were set in the

midst of the tempest of pictures one finds in the long galleries of the Roman palaces, would I think it so handsome? If up to this time I had seen only one " old master " in each palace, instead of acres and acres of walls and ceilings fairly papered with them, might I not have a more civilised opinion of the old masters than I have now? I think so. When I was a schoolboy and was to have a new knife, I could not make up my mind as to which was the prettiest in the show-case, and I did not think any of them were particularly pretty; and so I chose with a heavy heart. But when I looked at my purchase, at home, where no glittering blades came into competition with it, I was astonished to see how handsome it was. To this day my new hats look better out of the shop than they did in it with other new hats. It begins to dawn upon me now, that possibly what I have been taking for uniform ugliness in the galleries may be uniform beauty after all. I honestly hope it is, to others, but certainly it is not to me. Perhaps the reason I used to enjoy going to the Academy of Fine Arts in New York was because there were but a few hundred paintings in it, and it did not surfeit me to go through the list. I suppose the Academy was bacon and beans in the Forty-Mile Desert, and a European gallery is a state dinner of thirteen courses. One leaves no sign after him of the one dish, but the thirteen frighten away his appetite and give him no satisfaction.

There is one thing I am certain of, though. With all the Michael Angelos, the Raphaels, the Guidos, and the other old masters, the sublime history of Rome remains unpainted! They painted Virgins enough, and Popes enough, and saintly scarecrows enough, to people Paradise almost, and these things are all they did paint. " Nero fiddling o'er burning Rome," the assassination of Cæsar, the stirring spectacle of a hundred thousand people bending forward with rapt interest, in the Coliseum, to see two skilful gladiators hacking away each other's lives, a tiger springing upon a kneeling martyr—these and a thousand other matters which we read of with a living interest, must be sought for only in books—not among the rubbish left by the old masters—who are no more, I have the satisfaction of informing the public.

They did paint, and they did carve in marble, one historical scene, and one only (of any historical consequence). And what was it, and why did they choose it particularly? It was the " Rape of the Sabines," and they chose it for the legs and busts.

I like to look at statues, however, and I like to look at pictures also—even of monks looking up in sacred ecstasy, and monks looking down in meditation, and monks skirmishing for something to eat—and therefore I drop ill-nature to thank the papal government for so jealously guarding and so industriously gathering up these things; and for permitting me, a stranger, and not an entirely friendly one, to roam at will and unmolested among them, charging me nothing, and only requiring that I shall behave myself simply as well as I ought to behave in any other man's house. I thank the Holy Father right heartily, and I wish him long life and plenty of happiness.

The Popes have long been the patrons and pre-servers of art, just as our new practical Republic is the encourager and upholder of mechanics. In their Vatican is stored up all that is curious and beautiful in art; in our Patent Office is hoarded all that is curious or useful in mechanics. When a man invents a new style of horse-collar, or discovers a new and superior method of telegraphing, our government issues a patent to him that is worth a fortune; when a man digs up an ancient statue in the Campagna, the Pope gives him a fortune in gold coin. We can make something of a guess at a man's character by the style of nose he carries on his face. The Vatican and the Patent Office are governmental noses, and they bear a deal of character about them.

The guide showed us a colossal statue of Jupiter, in the Vatican, which he said looked so damaged and rusty—so like the God of the Vagabonds—because it had but recently been dug up in the Campagna. He asked how much we supposed this Jupiter was worth? I replied, with intelligent promptness, that he was probably worth about four dollars—maybe four and a half. " A hundred thousand dollars! " Ferguson said. Ferguson said further, that the Pope permits no ancient work of this kind to leave his dominions. He appoints a commission to examine discoveries like this and report upon the value; then the Pope pays the discoverer one-half of that assessed value, and takes the statue. He said this Jupiter was dug from a field which had just been bought for thirty-six thousand dollars, so the first crop was a good one for the new farmer. I do not know whether Ferguson always tells the truth or not, but I suppose he does. I know that an exorbitant export duty is exacted upon all pictures painted by the old masters, in order to discourage the sale of those in the private collections. I am satisfied also that genuine old masters hardly exist at all in America, because the cheapest and most insignificant of them are valued at the price of a fine farm. I proposed to buy a small trifle of a Raphael myself, but the price of it was eighty thousand dollars, the export duty would have made it considerably over a hundred, and so I studied on it awhile and concluded not to take it.

I wish here to mention an inscription I have seen, before I forget it—

" Glory to God in the highest, peace on earth TO MEN OF GOOD WILL! " It may not be good scripture, but it is sound Catholic and human nature.

This is in letters of gold around the apsis of a mosaic group at the side of the *scala santa*, church of St. John Lateran, the Mother and Mistress of all the Catholic churches of the world. The group represents the Saviour, St. Peter, Pope Leo, St. Silvester, Constantine, and Charlemagne. Peter is giving the *pallium* to the Pope, and a standard to Charlemagne. The Saviour is giving the keys to St. Silvester, and a standard to Constantine. No prayer is offered to the Saviour, who seems to be of little importance anywhere in Rome; but an inscription below says, " *Blessed Peter, give life to Pope Leo and victory to King Charles*." It does not say, " *Intercede for us, through the Saviour, with the Father, for this boon*," but " Blessed Peter, *give it* us."

In all seriousness—without meaning to be frivolous—without meaning to be irreverent, and more than all, without meaning to be blasphemous,—I state as my simple deduction from the things I have seen and the things I have heard, that the Holy Personages rank thus in Rome:

First—" The Mother of God "—otherwise the Virgin Mary.

Second—The Deity.

Third—Peter.

Fourth—Some twelve or fifteen canonised Popes and martyrs.

The Innocents Abroad

Fifth—Jesus Christ the Saviour—(but always as an infant in arms).

I may be wrong in this—my judgment errs often, just as is the case with other men's—but it *is* my judgment, be it good or bad.

Just here I will mention something that seems curious to me. There are no " Christ's Churches " in Rome, and no " Churches of the Holy Ghost," that I can discover. There are some four hundred churches, but about a fourth of them seem to be named for the Madonna and St. Peter. There are so many named for Mary that they have to be distinguished by all sorts of affixes, if I understand the matter rightly. Then we have churches of St. Louis, St. Augustine, St. Agnes, St. Callixtus, St. Lorenzo in Lucina, St. Lorenzo in Damaso, St. Cecilia, St. Athanasius, St. Philip Neri, St. Catherine, St. Dominico, and a multitude of lesser saints whose names are not familiar in the world—and away down, clear out of the list of the churches, comes a couple of hospitals: one of them is named for the Saviour and the other for the Holy Ghost!

Day after day and night after night we have wandered among the crumbling wonders of Rome; day after day and night after night we have fed upon the dust and decay of five-and-twenty centuries— have brooded over them by day and dreamt of them by night till sometimes we seemed mouldering away ourselves, and growing defaced and cornerless, and liable at any moment to fall a prey to some antiquary, and be patched in the legs, and " restored " with an unseemly nose, and labelled wrong, and dated wrong, and set up in the Vatican for poets to drivel about and Vandals to scribble their names on for ever and for evermore.

But the surest way to stop writing about Rome is to stop. I wished to write a real " guide-book " chapter on this fascinating city, but I could not do it, because I have felt all the time like a boy in a candy-shop—there was everything to choose from, and yet no choice. I have drifted along hopelessly for a hundred pages of manuscript without knowing where to commence. I will not commence at all. Our pass-ports have been examined. We will go to Naples.

CHAPTER XXIX

THE ship is lying here in the harbour of Naples—quarantined. She has been here several days and will remain several more. We that came by rail from Rome have escaped this misfortune. Of course no one is allowed to go on board the ship or come from her. She is a prison now. The passengers probably spend the long blazing days looking out from under the awnings at Vesuvius and the beautiful city—and in swearing. Think of ten days of this sort of pastime! We go out every day in a boat and request them to come ashore. It soothes them. We lie ten steps from the ship, and tell them how splendid the city is; and how much better the hotel fare is here than anywhere else in Europe; and how cool it is; and what frozen continents of ice cream there are; and what a time we are having cavorting about the country and sailing to the islands in the Bay. This tranquillises them.

ASCENT OF VESUVIUS

I shall remember our trip to Vesuvius for many a day—partly because of its sight-seeing experiences,

but chiefly on account of the fatigue of the journey.
Two or three of us had been resting ourselves among
the tranquil and beautiful scenery of the island of
Ischia, eighteen miles out in the harbour, for two
days; we call it "resting," but I do not remember
now what the resting consisted of, for when we got
back to Naples we had not slept for forty-eight hours.
We were just about to go to bed early in the evening,
and catch up on some of the sleep we had lost, when
we heard of this Vesuvius expedition. There was
to be eight of us in the party, and we were to leave
Naples at midnight. We laid in some provisions for
the trip, engaged carriages to take us to Annunciation,
and then moved about the city, to keep awake, till
twelve. We got away punctually, and in the course
of an hour and a half arrived at the town of Annunciation. Annunciation is the very last place under the
sun. In other towns in Italy the people lie around
quietly and wait for you to ask them a question or do
some overt act that can be charged for; but in
Annunciation they have lost even that fragment of
delicacy; they seize a lady's shawl from a chair and
hand it to her and charge a penny; they open a
carriage door, and charge for it—shut it when you
get out, and charge for it; they help you to take off
a duster—two cents; brush your clothes and make
them worse than they were before—two cents;
smile upon you—two cents; bow with a lickspittle
smirk, hat in hand—two cents; they volunteer all
information, such as that the mules will arrive
presently—two cents—warm day, sir—two cents—
take you four hours to make the ascent—two cents.
And so they go. They crowd you—infest you—
swarm about you, and sweat and smell offensively,
and look sneaking and mean and obsequious. There

is no office too degrading for them to perform for
money. I have had no opportunity to find out anything about the upper classes by my own observation,
but from what I hear said about them I judge that
what they lack in one or two of the bad traits the
canaille have, they make up in one or two others that
are worse. How the people beg!—many of them
very well dressed too.

I said I knew nothing against the upper classes by
personal observation. I must recall it. I had forgotten. What I saw their bravest and their fairest
do last night, the lowest multitude that could be
scraped up out of the purlieus of Christendom would
blush to do, I think. They assembled by hundreds,
and even thousands, in the great Theatre of San
Carlo to do—what? Why simply to make fun of an
old woman—to deride, to hiss, to jeer at an actress
they once worshipped, but whose beauty is faded now,
and whose voice has lost its former richness. Everybody spoke of the rare sport there was to be. They
said the theatre would be crammed because Frezzolini
was going to sing. It was said she could not sing
well now, but then the people liked to see her, anyhow. And so we went. And every time the woman
sang they hissed and laughed—the whole magnificent
house—and as soon as she left the stage they called
her on again with applause. Once or twice she was
encored five and six times in succession, and received
with hisses when she appeared, and discharged with
hisses and laughter when she had finished—then
nstantly encored and insulted again! And how the
high-born knaves enjoyed it! White-kidded gentlemen and ladies laughed till the tears came, and clapped
their hands in very ecstasy when that unhappy old
woman would come meekly out for the sixth time,

with uncomplaining patience, to meet a storm of hisses! It was the cruellest exhibition—the most wanton, the most unfeeling. The singer would have conquered an audience of American rowdies by her brave, unflinching tranquillity (for she answered encore after encore, and smiled and bowed pleasantly, and sang the best she possibly could, and went bowing off, through all the jeers and hisses, without ever losing countenance or temper); and surely in any other land than Italy her sex and her helplessness must have been an ample protection to her—she could have needed no other. Think what a multitude of small souls were crowded into that theatre last night. If the manager could have filled his theatre with Neapolitan souls alone, without the bodies, he could not have cleared less than ninety millions of dollars. What traits of character must a man have to enable him to help three thousand miscreants to hiss, and jeer, and laugh at one friendless old woman and shamefully humiliate her? He must have *all* the vile, mean traits there are. My observation persuades me (I do not like to venture beyond my own personal observation) that the upper classes of Naples possess those traits of character. Otherwise they may be very good people; I cannot say.

ASCENT OF VESUVIUS—CONTINUED

In this city of Naples they believe in and support one of the wretchedest of all the religious impostures one can find in Italy—the miraculous liquefaction of the blood of St. Januarius. Twice a year the priests assemble all the people at the Cathedral, and get out this vial of clotted blood and let them see it slowly dissolve and become liquid—and every day for eight days this dismal farce is repeated, while the priests go among the crowd and collect money for the exhibition. The first day, the blood liquefies in forty-seven minutes—the church is crammed then, and time must be allowed the collectors to get around; after that it liquefies a little quicker and a little quicker every day, as the houses grow smaller, till on the eighth day, with only a few dozens present to see the miracle, it liquefies in four minutes.

And here also they used to have a grand procession of priests, citizens, soldiers, sailors, and the high dignitaries of the City Government, once a year, to shave the head of a made-up Madonna—a stuffed and painted image, like a milliner's dummy—whose hair miraculously grew and restored itself every twelve months. They still kept up this shaving procession as late as four or five years ago. It was a source of great profit to the church that possessed the remarkable effigy, and the ceremony of the public barbering of her was always carried out with the greatest possible éclat and display, the more the better because the more excitement there was about it the larger the crowds it drew and the heavier the revenues it produced; but at last a day came when the Pope and his servants were unpopular in Naples, and the City Government stopped the Madonna's Annual show.

There we have two specimens of these Neapolitans —two of the silliest possible frauds, which half the population religiously and faithfully believed, and the other half either believed also or else said nothing about, and thus lent themselves to the support of the imposture. I am very well satisfied to think the whole population believed in those poor, cheap miracles—a people who want two cents every time they bow to you, and who abuse a woman, are capable of it, I think.

ASCENT OF VESUVIUS—CONTINUED

These Neapolitans always ask four times as much money as they intend to take, but if you give them what they first demand, they feel ashamed of themselves for aiming so low, and immediately ask more. When money is to be paid and received, there is always some vehement jawing and gesticulating about it. One cannot buy and pay for two cents' worth of clams without trouble and a quarrel. One "course" in a two-horse carriage costs a franc—that is law; but the hackman always demands more, on some pretence or other, and if he gets it, he makes a new demand. It is said that a stranger took a one-horse carriage for a course—tariff, half a franc. He gave the man five francs by way of experiment. He demanded more, and received another franc. Again he demanded more, and got a franc—demanded more, and it was refused. He grew vehement—was again refused, and became noisy. The stranger said, "Well, give me the seven francs again, and I will see what I can do;" and when he got them, he handed the hackman half a franc, and he immediately asked for two cents to buy a drink with. It may be thought that I am prejudiced. Perhaps I am. I would be ashamed of myself if I were not.

ASCENT OF VESUVIUS—CONTINUED

Well, as I was saying, we got our mules and horses, after an hour and a half of bargaining with the population of Annunciation, and started sleepily up the mountain, with a vagrant at each mule's tail who pretended to be driving the brute along, but was really holding on and getting himself dragged up instead. I made slow headway at first, but I began to get dissatisfied at the idea of paying my minion five francs to hold my mule back by the tail and keep him from going up the hill, and so I discharged him. I got along faster then.

We had one magnificent picture of Naples from a high point on the mountain side. We saw nothing but the gas lamps, of course—two-thirds of a circle, skirting the great Bay—a necklace of diamonds glinting up through the darkness from the remote distance—less brilliant than the stars overhead, but more softly, richly beautiful—and over all the great city the lights crossed and recrossed each other in many and many a sparkling line and curve. And back of the town, far around and abroad over the miles of level campagna, were scattered rows, and circles, and clusters of lights, all glowing like so many gems, and marking where a score of villages were sleeping. About this time, the fellow who was hanging on to the tail of the horse in front of me and practising all sorts of unnecessary cruelty upon the animal, got kicked some fourteen rods, and this incident, together with the fairy spectacle of the lights far in the distance, made me serenely happy, and I was glad I started to Vesuvius.

ASCENT OF MOUNT VESUVIUS—CONTINUED

This subject will be excellent matter for a chapter, and to-morrow or next day I will write it.

CHAPTER XXX

ASCENT OF VESUVIUS—CONTINUED

" SEE Naples and die." Well, I do not know that one would necessarily die after merely seeing it, but to attempt to live there might turn out a little differently. To see Naples as we saw it in the early dawn from far up on the side of Vesuvius, is to see a picture of wonderful beauty. At that distance its dingy buildings looked white—and so, rank on rank of balconies, windows and roofs, they piled themselves up from the blue ocean till the colossal castle of St. Elmo topped the grand white pyramid and gave the picture symmetry, emphasis, and completeness. And when its lilies turned to roses—when it blushed under the sun's first kiss—it was beautiful beyond all description. One might well say, then, " See Naples and die." The frame of the picture was charming, itself. In front, the smooth sea—a vast mosaic of many colours; the lofty islands swimming in a dreamy haze in the distance; at our end of the city the stately double peak of Vesuvius, and its strong black ribs and seams of lava stretching down to the limitless level campagna—a green carpet that enchants the eye and leads it on and on, past clusters of trees, and isolated houses, and snowy villages, until it shreds out in a fringe of mist and general vagueness far away. It is from the Hermitage, there on the side of Vesuvius, that one should " see Naples and die."

But do not go within the walls and look at it in detail. That takes away some of the romance of the thing. The people are filthy in their habits, and this

The Innocents Abroad

makes filthy streets and breeds disagreeable sights and smells. There never was a community so prejudiced against the cholera as these Neapolitans are. But they have good reason to be. The cholera generally vanquishes a Neapolitan when it seizes him, because, you understand, before the doctor can dig through the dirt and get at the disease the man dies. The upper classes take a sea-bath every day, and are pretty decent.

The streets are generally about wide enough for one waggon, and how they do swarm with people! It is Broadway repeated in every street, in every court, in every alley! Such masses, such throngs, such multitudes of hurrying, bustling, struggling humanity. We never saw the like of it, hardly even in New York, I think. There are seldom any side-walks, and when there are, they are not often wide enough to pass a man on without caroming on him. So everybody walks in the street—and where the street is wide enough, carriages are forever dashing along. Why a thousand people are not run over and crippled every day is a mystery that no man can solve.

But if there is an eighth wonder in the world, it must be the dwelling houses of Naples. I honestly believe a good majority of them are a hundred feet high! And the solid brick walls are seven feet through. You go up nine flights of stairs before you get to the " first " floor. No, not nine, but there or thereabouts. There is a little birdcage of an iron railing in front of every window clear away up, up, up, among the eternal clouds, where the roof is, and there is always somebody looking out of every window— people of ordinary size looking out from the first floor, people a shade smaller from the second, people that look a little smaller yet from the third—and from thence upward they grow smaller and smaller by a regularly graduated diminution, till the folks in the topmost windows seem more like birds in an uncommonly tall martin-box than anything else. The perspective of one of these narrow cracks of streets, with its rows of tall houses stretching away till they come together in the distance like railway tracks; its clothes-lines crossing over at all altitudes and waving their bannered raggedness over the swarms of people below; and the white-dressed women perched in balcony railings all the way from the pavement up to the heavens—a perspective like that is really worth going into Neapolitan details to see.

ASCENT OF VESUVIUS—CONTINUED

Naples, with its immediate suburbs, contains six hundred and twenty-five thousand inhabitants, but I am satisfied it covers no more ground than an American city of one hundred and fifty thousand. It reaches up into the air infinitely higher than three American cities, though, and there is where the secret of it lies. I will observe here, in passing, that the contrasts between opulence and poverty, and magnificence and misery, are more frequent and more striking in Naples than in Paris even. One must go to the Bois de Boulogne to see fashionable dressing, splendid equipages, and stunning liveries, and to the Faubourg St. Antoine to see vice, misery, hunger, rags, dirt—but in the thoroughfares of Naples these things are all mixed together. Naked boys of nine years and the fancy dressed children of luxury; shreds and tatters, and brilliant uniforms; jackass-carts and state-carriages; beggars, princes, and bishops, jostle each other in every street. At six o'clock every evening all Naples turns out to drive on the *Riviere di Chiaja* (whatever that may mean); and for two hours one may stand there and see the motliest and the worst mixed procession go by that ever eyes beheld. Princes (there are more Princes than policemen in Naples—the city is infested with them)—Princes who live up seven flights of stairs and don't own any principalities, will keep a carriage and go hungry; and clerks, mechanics, milliners, and strumpets will go without their dinners and squander the money on a hack-ride in the Chiaja; the rag-tag and rubbish of the city stack themselves up, to the number of twenty or thirty, on a rickety little go-cart hauled by a donkey not much bigger than a cat, and *they* drive in the Chiaja; dukes and bankers in sumptuous carriages and with gorgeous drivers and footmen, turn out also, and so the furious procession goes. For two hours rank and wealth, and obscurity and poverty, clatter along side by side in the wild procession, and then go home serene, happy, covered with glory!

I was looking at a magnificent marble staircase in the King's palace, the other day, which, it was said cost five million francs, and I suppose it did cost half a million, may be. I felt as if it must be a fine thing to live in the country where there was such comfort and such luxury as this. And then I stepped out musing, and almost walked over a vagabond who was eating his dinner on the curbstone—a piece of bread and a bunch of grapes. When I found that this mustang was clerking in a fruit establishment (he had the establishment along with him in a basket) at two cents a day, and that he had no palace at home where he lived, I lost some of my enthusiasm concerning the happiness of living in Italy.

This naturally suggests to me a thought about wages here. Lieutenants in the army get about a dollar a day, and common soldiers a couple of cents. I only know one clerk—he gets four dollars a month. Printers get six dollars and a half a month, but I have heard of a foreman who gets thirteen. To be growing suddenly and violently rich, as this man is, naturally makes him a bloated aristocrat. The airs he puts on are insufferable.

And speaking of wages reminds me of prices of merchandise. In Paris you pay twelve dollars a dozen for Jouvin's best kid gloves; gloves of about as good quality sell here at three or four dollars a dozen. You pay five and six dollars a piece for fine linen shirts in Paris; here and in Leghorn you pay two and a half. In Marseilles you pay forty dollars for a first-class dress coat made by a good tailor, but in Leghorn you can get a full dress suit for the same money. Here you get handsome business suits at from ten to twenty dollars, and in Leghorn you can get an overcoat for fifteen dollars that would cost you seventy in New York. Fine kid boots are worth eight dollars in Marseilles, and four dollars here. Lyons velvets rank higher in America than those of Genoa. Yet the bulk of Lyons velvets you buy in the States are made in Genoa and imported into Lyons, where they receive the Lyons stamp, and are then exported to America. You can buy enough velvet in Genoa for twenty-five dollars to make a five hundred dollar cloak in New York—so the ladies tell me. Of course these things bring me back, by a natural and easy transition, to the

ASCENT OF VESUVIUS—CONTINUED

And thus the wonderful Blue Grotto is suggested

to me. It is situated on the Island of Capri, twenty-two miles from Naples. We chartered a little steamer, and went out there. Of course, the police boarded us, and put us through a health examination, and inquired into our politics, before they would let us land. The airs these little insect Governments put on are in the last degree ridiculous. They even put a policeman on board of our boat to keep an eye on us as long as we were in the Capri dominions. They thought we wanted to steal the grotto, I suppose. It was worth stealing. The entrance to the cave is four feet high and four feet wide, and is in the face of a lofty perpendicular cliff—the sea wall. You enter in small boats, and a tight squeeze it is too. You cannot go in at all when the tide is up. Once within you find yourself in an arched cavern about one hundred and sixty feet long, one hundred and twenty wide, and about seventy high. How deep it is no man knows. It goes down to the bottom of the ocean. The waters of this placid subterranean lake are the brightest, loveliest blue that can be imagined. They are as transparent as plate glass, and their colouring would shame the richest sky that ever bent over Italy. No tint could be more ravishing, no lustre more superb. Throw a stone into the water, and the myriad of tiny bubbles that are created flash out a brilliant glare like blue theatrical fires. Dip an oar, and its blade turns to splendid frosted silver, tinted with blue. Let a man jump in, and instantly he is cased in an armour more gorgeous than ever kingly Crusader wore.

Then we went to Ischia, but I had already been to that island, and tired myself to death " resting " a couple of days and studying human villainy, with the landlord of the Grande Sentinelle for a model. So we went to Procida, and from thence to Pozzuoli, where St. Paul landed after he sailed from Samos: I landed at precisely the same spot where St. Paul landed, and so did Dan and the others. It was a remarkable coincidence. St. Paul preached to these people seven days before he started to Rome.

Nero's Baths, the ruins of Baiæ, the Temple of Serapis; Cumæ, where the Cumæn Sybil interpreted the oracles, the Lake Agnano, with its ancient submerged city still visible far down in its depths—these, and a hundred other points of interest, we examined with critical imbecility, but the Grotto of the Dog claimed our chief attention, because we had heard and read so much about it. Everybody has written about the Grotto del Cane and its poisonous vapours, from Pliny down to Smith, and every tourist has held a dog over its floor by the legs to test the capabilities of the place. The dog dies in a minute and a half; a chicken instantly. As a general thing, strangers who crawl in there to sleep do not get up until they are called; and then they don't either. The stranger that ventures to sleep there takes a permanent contract. I longed to see this grotto. I resolved to take a dog and hold him myself; suffocate him a little, and time him; suffocate him some more, and then finish him. We reached the grotto at about three in the afternoon, and proceeded at once to make the experiments. But now an important difficulty presented itself; we had no dog.

ASCENT OF VESUVIUS—CONTINUED

At the Hermitage we were about fifteen or eighteen hundred feet above the sea, and thus far a portion of the ascent had been pretty abrupt. For the next two miles the road was a mixture—sometimes the ascent was abrupt and sometimes it was not; but one characteristic it possessed all the time—without failure—without modification—it was all uncompromisingly and unspeakably infamous. It was a rough, narrow trail, and led over an old lava flow—a black ocean which was tumbled into a thousand fantastic shapes—a wild chaos of ruin, desolation, and barrenness—a wilderness of billowy upheavals, of furious whirlpools, of miniature mountains rent asunder—of gnarled and knotted, wrinkled and twisted masses of blackness, that mimicked branching roots, great vines, trunks of trees, all interlaced and mingled together; and all these weird shapes, all this turbulent panorama, all this stormy, far-stretching waste of blackness, with its thrilling suggestiveness of life, of action, of boiling, surging, furious motion was petrified!—all stricken dead and cold in the instant of its maddest rioting!—fettered, paralysed, and left to glower at heaven in impotent rage for evermore

Finally, we stood in a level, narrow valley (a valley that had been created by the terrific march of some old time eruption) and on either hand towered the two steep peaks of Vesuvius. The one we had to climb—the one that contains the active volcano—seemed about eight hundred or one thousand feet high, and looked almost too straight-up-and-down for any man to climb, and certainly no mule could climb it with a man on his back. Four of these native pirates will carry you to the top in a sedan chair, if you wish it, but suppose they were to slip and let you fall, is it likely that you would ever stop rolling? Not this side of eternity, perhaps. We left the mules, sharpened our finger nails, and began the ascent I have been writing about so long at twenty minutes to

The Innocents Abroad

six in the morning. The path led straight up a rugged sweep of loose chunks of pumice-stone, and for about every two steps forward we took, we slid back one. It was so excessively steep that we had to stop, every fifty or sixty steps, and rest a moment. To see our comrades we had to look very nearly straight up at those above us, and very nearly straight down at those below. We stood on the summit at last—it had taken an hour and fifteen minutes to make the trip.

What we saw there was simply a circular crater—a circular ditch, if you please—about two hundred feet deep, and four or five hundred feet wide, whose inner wall was about half a mile in circumference. In the centre of the great circus ring thus formed was a torn and ragged upheaval a hundred feet high, all snowed over with a sulphur crust of many and many a brilliant and beautiful colour, and the ditch inclosed this like the moat of a castle, or surrounded it as a little river does a little island, if the simile is better. The sulphur coating of that island was gaudy in the extreme—all mingled together in the richest confusion were red, blue, brown, black, yellow, white—I do not know that there was a colour, or shade of a colour, or combination of colours, unrepresented; and when the sun burst through the morning mists and fired this tinted magnificence, it topped imperial Vesuvius like a jewelled crown!

The crater itself—the ditch—was not so variegated in colouring, but yet, in its softness, richness, and unpretentious elegance, it was more charming, more fascinating to the eye. There was nothing " loud " about its well-bred and well-dressed look. Beautiful? One could stand and look down upon it for a week without getting tired of it. It had the semblance of a pleasant meadow, whose slender grasses and whose velvety mosses were frosted with a shining dust, and tinted with palest green that deepened gradually to the darkest hue of the orange leaf, and deepened yet again into brown, then faded into orange, then into the brightest gold, and culminated in the delicate pink of a new-blown rose. Where portions of the meadow had sunk, and where other portions had been broken up like an ice-floe, the cavernous openings of the one, and the ragged up-turned edges exposed by the other, were hung with a lace-work of soft-tinted crystals of sulphur that changed their deformities into quaint shapes and figures that were full of grace and beauty.

The walls of the ditch were brilliant with yellow banks of sulphur and with lava and pumice-stone of many colours. No fire was visible anywhere, but gusts of sulphurous steam issued silently and invisibly from a thousand little cracks and fissures in the crater, and were wafted to our noses with every breeze. But so long as we kept our nostrils buried in our handkerchiefs there was small danger of suffocation.

Some of the boys thrust long slips of paper down into holes and set them on fire, and so achieved the glory of lighting their cigars by the flames of Vesuvius, and others cooked eggs over the fissures in the rocks and were happy.

The view from the summit would have been superb but for the fact that the sun could only pierce the mists at long intervals. Thus the glimpses we had of the grand panorama below were only fitful and unsatisfactory.

THE DESCENT

The descent of the mountain was a labour of only four minutes. Instead of stalking down the rugged path we ascended, we chose one which was bedded knee-deep in loose ashes, and ploughed our way with prodigious strides that would almost have shamed the performance of him of the seven-league boots.

The Vesuvius of to-day is a poor affair compared to the mighty volcano of Kilauea, in the Sandwich Islands, but I am glad I visited it. It was well worth it.

It is said that during one of the grand eruptions of Vesuvius it discharged massy rocks weighing many tons a thousand feet into the air, its vast jets of smoke and steam ascended thirty miles toward the firmament, and clouds of its ashes were wafted abroad and fell upon the decks of ships seven hundred and fifty miles at sea! I will take the ashes at a moderate discount, if any one will take the thirty miles of smoke, but I do not feel able to take a commanding interest in the whole story by myself.

Descent of Vesuvius

The Innocents Abroad

CHAPTER XXXI

THE BURIED CITY OF POMPEII

THEY pronounce it Pom-*pay*-e. I always had an idea
that you went down into Pompeii with torches, by
the way of damp, dark stairways, just as you do in
silver mines, and traversed gloomy tunnels with lava
overhead and something on either hand like dilapidated prisons gouged out of the solid earth, that
faintly resembled houses. But you do nothing of the
kind. Fully one-half of the buried city, perhaps, is
completely exhumed and thrown open freely to the
light of day; and there stand the long rows of solidly-
built brick houses (roofless) just as they stood eighteen
hundred years ago, hot with the flaming sun; and
there lie their floors, clean-swept, and not a bright
fragment tarnished or wanting of the laboured
mosaics that pictured them with the beasts, and birds,
and flowers which we copy in perishable carpets
to-day; and there are the Venuses, and Bacchuses,
and Adonises, making love and getting drunk in
many-hued frescoes on the walls of saloon and bedchamber; and there are the narrow streets and
narrower sidewalks, paved with flags of good hard
lava, the one deeply rutted with the chariot-wheels,
and the other with the passing feet of the Pompeiians of bygone centuries; and there are the bake-
shops, the temples, the halls of justice, the baths, the
theatres—all clean scraped and neat, and suggesting
nothing of the nature of a silver mine away down in
the bowels of the earth. The broken pillars lying
about, the doorless doorways and the crumbled tops

of the wilderness of walls, were wonderfully suggestive of the " burnt district " in one of our cities, and if there had been any charred timbers, shattered windows, heaps of débris, and general blackness and smokiness about the place, the resemblance would have been perfect. But no—the sun shines as brightly down on old Pompeii to-day as it did when Christ was born in Bethlehem, and its streets are cleaner a hundred times than ever Pompeiian saw them in her prime. I know whereof I speak—for in the great chief thoroughfares (Merchant Street and the Street of Fortune) have I not seen with my own eyes how for two hundred years at least the pavements were not repaired!—how ruts five and even ten inches deep were worn into the thick flag-stones by the chariot-wheels of generations of swindled taxpayers? And do I not know by these signs that Street Commissioners of Pompeii never attended to their business, and that if they never mended the pavements they never cleaned them? And, besides, is it not the inborn nature of Street Commissioners to avoid their duty whenever they get a chance? I wish I knew the name of the last one that held office in Pompeii so that I could give him a blast. I speak with feeling on this subject, because I caught my foot in one of those ruts, and the sadness that came over me when I saw the first poor skeleton, with ashes and lava sticking to it, was tempered by the reflection that maybe that party was the Street Commissioner.

No—Pompeii is no longer a buried city. It is a city of hundreds and hundreds of roofless houses, and a tangled maze of streets where one could easily get lost, without a guide, and have to sleep in some ghostly palace that had known no living tenant since that awful November night of eighteen centuries ago.

The Innocents Abroad

We passed through the gate which faces the Mediterranean (called the " Marine Gate "), and by the rusty, broken image of Minerva, still keeping tireless watch and ward over the possessions it was powerless to save, and went up a long street and stood in the broad court of the Forum of Justice. The floor was level and clean, and up and down either side was a noble colonnade of broken pillars, with their beautiful Ionic and Corinthian columns scattered about them. At the upper end were the vacant seats of the Judges, and behind them we descended into a dungeon where the ashes and cinders had found two prisoners chained on that memorable November night, and tortured them to death. How they must have tugged at the pitiless fetters as the fierce fires surged around them!

Then we lounged through many and many a sumptuous private mansion which we could not have entered without a formal invitation in incomprehensible Latin, in the olden time, when the owners lived there—and we probably wouldn't have got it. These people built their houses a good deal alike. The floors were laid in fanciful figures wrought in mosaics of many-coloured marbles. At the threshold your eyes fall upon a Latin sentence of welcome, sometimes, or a picture of a dog, with the legend " Beware of the Dog," and sometimes a picture of a bear or a faun with no inscription at all. Then you enter a sort of vestibule, where they used to keep the hat-rack, I suppose; next a room with a large marble basin in the midst and the pipes of a fountain; on either side are bedrooms; beyond the fountain is a reception-room, then a little garden, dining-room, and so forth, and so on. The floors were all mosaic, the walls were stuccoed, or frescoed, or ornamented with bas-reliefs, and here and there were statues, large and

The Innocents Abroad

small, and little fish-pools, and cascades of sparkling water that sprung from secret places in the colonnade of handsome pillars that surrounded the court, and kept the flower-beds fresh and the air cool. Those Pompeiians were very luxurious in their tastes and habits. The most exquisite bronzes we have seen in Europe came from the exhumed cities of Herculaneum and Pompeii, and also the finest cameos and the most delicate engravings on precious stones; their pictures, eighteen or nineteen centuries old, are often much more pleasing than the celebrated rubbish of the old masters of three centuries ago. They were well up in art. From the creation of these works of the first, clear up to the eleventh century, art seems hardly to have existed at all—at least no remnants of it are left —and it was curious to see how far (in some things, at any rate,) these old time pagans excelled the remote generations of masters that came after them. The pride of the world in sculptures seem to be the " Laocoon " and the " Dying Gladiator," in Rome. They are as old as Pompeii, were dug from the earth like Pompeii; but their exact age, or who made them, can only be conjectured. But worn, and cracked, without a history, and with the blemishing stains of numberless centuries upon them, they still mutely mock at all efforts to rival their perfections.

It was a quaint and curious pastime, wandering through this old silent city of the dead—lounging through utterly deserted streets where thousands of human beings once bought and sold, and walked and rode, and made the place resound with the noise and confusion of traffic and pleasure. They were not lazy. They hurried in those days. We had evidence of that. There was a temple on one corner, and it was a shorter cut to go between the columns of that

temple from one street to the other than to go around
—and behold that pathway had been worn deep into
the heavy flagstone floor of the building by generations of time-saving feet! They would not go around
when it was quicker to go through. We do that way
in our cities.

Everywhere you see things that make you wonder
how old these old houses were before the night of
destruction came—things too which bring back those
long dead inhabitants and place them living before
your eyes. For instance, the steps (two feet thick—
lava blocks) that lead up out of the school, and the
same kind of steps that lead up into the dress circle
of the principal theatre, are almost worn through!
For ages the boys hurried out of that school, and for
ages their parents hurried into that theatre, and the
nervous feet that have been dust and ashes for
eighteen centuries have left their record for us to read
to-day. I imagined I could see crowds of gentlemen
and ladies thronging into the theatre, with tickets
for secured seats in their hand, and on the wall I
read the imaginary placard, in infamous grammar,
" Positively no Free List, except Members of the
Press!" Hanging about the doorway (I fancied)
were slouchy Pompeiian street-boys uttering slang
and profanity, and keeping a wary eye out for checks.
I entered the theatre, and sat down in one of the long
rows of stone benches in the dress circle, and looked
at the place for the orchestra, and the ruined stage,
and around at the wide sweep of empty boxes, and
thought to myself, " This house won't pay." I tried
to imagine the music in full blast, the leader of the
orchestra beating time, and the " versatile " So-and-
So (who had " just returned from a most successful
tour in the provinces to play his last and farewell

The Innocents Abroad

engagement of positively six nights only, in Pompeii, previous to his departure for Herculaneum,") charging around the stage and piling the agony mountains high—but I could not do it with such a " house " as that; those empty benches tied my fancy down to dull reality. I said, these people that ought to be here have been dead, and still, and mouldering to dust for ages and ages, and will never care for the trifles and follies of life any more for ever—" Owing to circumstances, etc., etc., there will not be any performance to-night." Close down the curtain. Put out the lights.

And so I turned away and went through shop after shop and store after store, far down the long street of the merchants, and called for the wares of Rome and the East, but the tradesmen were gone, the marts were silent, and nothing was left but the broken jars all set in cement of cinders and ashes; the wine and the oil that once had filled them were gone with their owners.

In a bakeshop was a mill for grinding the grain, and the furnaces for baking the bread; and they say that here, in the same furnaces, the exhumers of Pompeii found nice, well-baked loaves, which the baker had not found time to remove from the ovens the last time he left his shop, because circumstances compelled him to leave in such a hurry.

In one house (the only building in Pompeii which no woman is now allowed to enter), were the small rooms and short beds of solid masonry, just as they were in the old times, and on the walls were pictures which looked almost as fresh as if they were painted yesterday, but which no pen could have the hardihood to describe; and here and there were Latin inscriptions—obscene scintillations of wit, scratched

The Innocents Abroad

by hands that possibly were uplifted to Heaven for succour in the midst of a driving storm of fire before the night was done.

In one of the principal streets was a ponderous stone tank, and a water-spout that supplied it, and where the tired, heated toilers from the Campagna used to rest their right hands when they bent over to put their lips to the spout, the thick stone was worn down to a broad groove an inch or two deep. Think of the countless thousands of hands that had pressed that spot in the ages that are gone, to so reduce a stone that is as hard as iron!

They had a great public bulletin board in Pompeii —a place where announcements for gladiatorial combats, elections, and such things, were posted— not on perishable paper, but carved in enduring stone. One lady, who I take it was rich and well brought up, advertised a dwelling or so to rent, with baths and all the modern improvements, and several hundred shops, stipulating that the dwellings should not be put to immoral purposes. You can find out who lived in many a house in Pompeii by the carved stone doorplates affixed to them: and in the same way you can tell who they were that occupy the tombs. Everywhere around are things that reveal to you something of the customs and history of this forgotten people. But what would a volcano leave of an American city if it once rained its cinders on it? Hardly a sign or a symbol to tell its story.

In one of these long Pompeiian halls the skeleton of a man was found, with ten pieces of gold in one hand and a large key in the other. He had seized his money and started toward the door, but the fiery tempest caught him at the very threshold, and he sank down and died. One more minute of precious time would have saved him. I saw the skeletons of a man, a woman, and two young girls. The woman had her hands spread wide apart, as if in mortal terror, and I imagined I could still trace upon her shapeless face something of the expression of wild despair that distorted it when the heavens rained fire in these streets, so many ages ago. The girls and the man lay with their faces upon their arms, as if they had tried to shield them from the enveloping cinders. In one apartment eighteen skeletons were found, all in sitting postures, and blackened places on the walls still mark their shapes and show their attitudes, like shadows. One of them, a woman, still wore upon her skeleton throat a necklace, with her name engraved upon it—JULIE DI DIOMEDE.

But perhaps the most poetical thing Pompeii has yielded to modern research, was that grand figure of a Roman soldier, clad in complete armour, who, true to his duty, true to his proud name of a soldier of Rome, and full of the stern courage which had given to that name its glory, stood to his post by the city gate, erect and unflinching, till the hell that raged around him *burned out* the dauntless spirit it could not conquer.

We never read of Pompeii but we think of that soldier; we cannot write of Pompeii without the natural impulse to grant to him the mention he so well deserves. Let us remember that he was a soldier—not a policeman—and so praise him. Being a soldier he stayed—because the warrior instinct forbade him to fly. Had he been a policeman, he would have stayed also—because he would have been asleep.

There are not half a dozen flights of stairs in Pompeii, and no other evidences that the houses were more than one story high. The people did not live in the clouds, as do the Venetians, the Genoese, and Neapolitans of to-day.

We came out from under the solemn mysteries of this city of the Venerable Past—this city which perished, with all its old ways and its quaint old fashions about it, remote centuries ago, when the Disciples were preaching the new religion, which is as old as the hills to us now—and went dreaming among the trees that grow over acres and acres of its still buried streets and squares, till a shrill whistle and the cry of " *All aboard—last train for Naples!* " woke me up and reminded me that I belonged in the nineteenth century, and was not a dusty mummy, caked with ashes and cinders, eighteen hundred years old. The transition was startling. The idea of a railroad train actually running to old dead Pompeii, and whistling irreverently, and calling for passengers in the most bustling and business-like way, was as strange a thing as one could imagine, and as unpoetical and disagreeable as it was strange.

Compare the cheerful life and the sunshine of this day with the horrors the younger Pliny saw here, the 9th of November, A.D. 79, when he was so bravely striving to remove his mother out of reach of harm, while she begged him, with all a mother's unselfishness, to leave her to perish and save himself.

" By this time the murky darkness had so increased, that one might have believed himself abroad in a black and moon-less night, or in a chamber where all the lights had been extinguished. On every hand was heard the complaints of women, the wailing of children, and the cries of men. One called his father, another his son, and another his wife, and only by their voices could they know each other. Many in their despair begged that death would come and end their distress.

" Some implored the gods to succour them, and some be-

The Innocents Abroad

lieved that this night was the last, the eternal night which should engulf the universe!

"Even so it seemed to me—and I consoled myself for the coming death with the reflection: BEHOLD, THE WORLD IS PASSING AWAY!"

. . . .

After browsing among the stately ruins of Rome, of Baiæ, of Pompeii, and after glancing down the long marble ranks of battered and nameless imperial heads that stretch down the corridors of the Vatican, one thing strikes me with a force it never had before— the unsubstantial, unlasting character of fame. Men lived long lives in the olden time, and struggled feverishly through them, toiling like slaves in oratory, in generalship, or in literature, and then laid them down and died, happy in the possession of an enduring history and a deathless name. Well, twenty little centuries flutter away, and what is left of these things? A crazy inscription on a block of stone, which snuffy antiquaries bother over and tangle up and make nothing out of but a bare name (which they spell wrong)—no history, no tradition, no poetry, nothing that can give it even a passing interest. What may be left of General Grant's great name forty centuries hence? This—in the Encyclopædia for A.D. 5868, possibly:

"URIAH S. (or Z.) GRAUNT—popular poet of ancient times in the Aztec provinces of the United States of British America. Some authors say flourished about A.D. 742; but the learned Ah-ah Foo-foo states that he was a cotemporary of Shark-spyre, the English poet, and flourished about A.D. 1328, some three centuries *after* the Trojan war instead of before it. He wrote 'Rock me to Sleep, Mother.'"

These thoughts sadden me. I will to bed.

THE
CELEBRATED JUMPING FROG
OF CALAVERAS COUNTY
AND OTHER SKETCHES

THE

CELEBRATED JUMPING FROG

OF CALAVERAS COUNTY

In compliance with the request of a friend of mine, who wrote me from the East, I called on good-natured, garrulous old Simon Wheeler, and inquired after my friend's friend, *Leonidas W*. Smiley, as requested to do, and I hereunto append the result. I have a lurking suspicion that *Leonidas W*. Smiley is a myth; that my friend never knew such a personage; and that he only conjectured that, if I asked old Wheeler about him, it would remind him of his infamous *Jim* Smiley, and he would go to work and bore me nearly to death with some infernal reminiscence of him as long and tedious as it should be useless to me. If that was the design, it certainly succeeded.

I found Simon Wheeler dozing comfortably by the bar-room stove of the old, dilapidated tavern in the ancient mining camp of Angel's, and I noticed that he was fat and bald-headed, and had an expression of winning gentleness and simplicity upon his tranquil countenance. He roused up and gave me good-day. I told him a friend of mine had commissioned me to make some inquiries about a cherished companion of his boyhood named *Leonidas W*. Smiley — *Rev. Leonidas W*. Smiley — a young minister of the Gospel, who he had heard was at one time a resident of Angel's Camp. I added that, if Mr. Wheeler could tell me anything

The Jumping Frog

about this Rev. Leonidas W. Smiley, I would feel
under many obligations to him.

Simon Wheeler backed me into a corner and
blockaded me there with his chair, and then sat
me down and reeled off the monotonous narrative
which follows this paragraph. He never smiled,
he never frowned, he never changed his voice from
the gentle-flowing key to which he tuned the initial
sentence, he never betrayed the slightest suspicion
of enthusiasm; but all through the interminable
narrative there ran a vein of impressive earnestness
and sincerity, which showed me plainly that, so far
from his imagining that there was anything ridiculous or funny about his story, he regarded it as a
really important matter, and admired its two heroes
as men of transcendent genius in *finesse*. To me,
the spectacle of a man drifting serenely along through
such a queer yarn without ever smiling, was exquisitely absurd. As I said before, I asked him to
tell me what he knew of Rev. Leonidas W. Smiley,
and he replied as follows. I let him go on in his own
way, and never interrupted him once.

There was a feller here once by the name of *Jim*
Smiley, in the winter of '49—or may be it was the
spring of '50—I don't recollect exactly, somehow,
though what makes me think it was one or the
other is because I remember the big flume wasn't
finished when he first came to the camp; but any
way, he was the curiosest man about always betting
on anything that turned up you ever see, if he
could get anybody to bet on the other side; and
if he couldn't, he'd change sides. Anyway that
suited the other man would suit him—anyway just
so's he got a bet, *he* was satisfied. But still he

The Jumping Frog

was lucky, uncommon lucky; he most always come out winner. He was always ready and laying for a chance; there couldn't be no solit'ry thing mentioned but that feller'd offer to bet on it, and take any side you please, as I was just telling you. If there was a horse-race, you'd find him flush, or you'd find him busted at the end of it; if there was a dog-fight, he'd bet on it; if there was a cat-

"There was a feller here once o' the name o' Jim Smiley."...

fight, he'd bet on it; if there was a chicken-fight, he'd bet on it; why, if there was two birds sitting on a fence, he would bet you which one would fly first; or if there was a camp-meeting, he would be there reg'lar, to bet on Parson Walker, which he judged to be the best exhorter about here, and so he was, too, and a good man. If he even seen a straddle-bug start to go anywheres, he would bet you how long it would take him to get wherever he was going to, and if you took him up, he would foller that straddle-bug to Mexico but what he would find out

The Jumping Frog

where he was bound for and how long he was on the road. Lots of the boys here has seen that Smiley, and can tell you about him. Why, it never made no difference to *him*—he would bet on *any* thing—the dangdest feller. Parson Walker's wife laid very sick once, for a good while, and it seemed as if they warn't going to save her; but one morning he come in, and Smiley asked how she was, and he said she was considerable better—thank the Lord for his inf'nit mercy—and coming on so smart that, with the blessing of Prov'dence she'd get well yet; and Smiley, before he thought, says, "Well, I'll risk two-and-a-half that she don't, anyway."

Thish-yer Smiley had a mare—the boys called her the fifteen-minute nag, but that was only in fun, you know, because, of course, she was faster than that—and he used to win money on that horse, for all she was so slow and always had the asthma, or the distemper, or the consumption, or something of that kind. They used to give her two or three hundred yards' start, and then pass her under way; but always at the fag-end of the race she'd get excited and desperate-like, and come cavorting and straddling up, and scattering her legs around limber, sometimes in the air, and sometimes out to one side amongst the fences, and kicking up m-o-r-e dust, and raising m-o-r-e racket with her coughing and sneezing and blowing her nose—and always fetch up at the stand just about a neck ahead, as near as you could cypher it down.

And he had a little small bull pup, that to look at him you'd think he wan't worth a cent, but to set around and look ornery, and lay for a chance to steal something. But as soon as money was upon him, he was a different dog; his under-jaw'd

The Jumping Frog

begin to stick out like the fo'castle of a steamboat, and his teeth would uncover, and shine savage like the furnaces. And a dog might tackle him, and bully-rag him, and bite him, and throw him over his shoulder two or three times, and Andrew Jackson —which was the name of the pup—Andrew Jackson would never let on but what *he* was satisfied, and hadn't expected nothing else—and the bets being doubled and doubled on the other side all the time, till the money was all up; and then all of a sudden he would grab that other dog jest by the j'int of his hind leg and freeze to it—not chaw, you understand, but only jest grip and hang on till they throwed up the sponge, if it was a year. Smiley always come out winner on that pup, till he harnessed a dog once that didn't have no hind legs, because they'd been sawed off by a circular saw, and when the thing had gone along far enough, and the money was all up, and he come to make a snatch for his pet holt, he saw in a minute how he'd been imposed on, and how the other dog had him in the door, so to speak, and he 'peared surprised, and then he looked sorter discouraged-like, and didn't try no more to win the fight, and so he got shucked out bad. He give Smiley a look, as much as to say his heart was broke, and it was *his* fault for putting up a dog that hadn't no hind legs for him to take holt of, which was his main depend-ence in a fight, and then he limped off a piece and laid down and died. It was a good pup, was that Andrew Jackson, and would have made a name for hisself if he'd lived, for the stuff was in him, and he had genius—I know it, because he hadn't had no opportunities to speak of, and it don't stand to reason that a dog could make such a fight as he could under them circumstances, if he hadn't no

The Jumping Frog

talent. It always makes me feel sorry when I think of that last fight of his'n, and the way it turned out.

Well, thish - yer Smiley had rat - tarriers, and chicken cocks, and tom-cats, and all them kind of things, till you couldn't rest, and you couldn't fetch nothing for him to bet on but he'd match you. He ketched a frog one day, and took him home, and said he cal'klated to edercate him; and so he never done nothing for three months but set in his back yard and learn that frog to jump. And you bet you he *did* learn him, too. He'd give him a little punch behind, and the next minute you'd see that frog whirling in the air like a doughnut—see him turn one summerset, or may be a couple, if he got a good start, and come down flat-footed and all right, like a cat. He got him up so in the matter of catching flies, and kept him in practice so constant, that he'd nail a fly every time as far as he could see him. Smiley said all a frog wanted was education, and he could do most anything—and I believe him. Why, I've seen him set Dan'l Webster down here on this floor—Dan'l Webster was the name of the frog—and sing out, " Flies, Dan'l, flies! " and quicker'n you could wink, he'd spring straight up, and snake a fly off'n the counter there, and flop down on the floor again as solid as a gob of mud, and fall to scratching the side of his head with his hind foot as indifferent as if he hadn't no idea he'd been doin' any more'n any frog might do. You never see a frog so modest and straightfor'ard as he was, for all he was so gifted. And when it come to fair and square jumping on a dead level, he could get over more ground at one straddle than any animal of his breed you ever see. Jumping on a dead level was his strong suit, you understand;

The Jumping Frog

and when it come to that, Smiley would ante up money on him as long as he had a red. Smiley was monstrous proud of his frog, and well he might be, for fellers that had travelled and been every-wheres, all said he laid over any frog that ever *they* see.

Well, Smiley kept the beast in a little lattice box, and he used to fetch him down town some-times and lay for a bet. One day a feller—a stranger in the camp, he was—come across him with his box, and says:

" What might it be that you've got in the box? "

And Smiley says, sorter indifferent like, " It might be a parrot, or it might be a canary, maybe, but it ain't—it's only just a frog."

And the feller took it, and looked at it careful, and turned it round this way and that, and says, " H'm—so 'tis. Well, what's *he* good for? "

" Well," Smiley says, easy and careless, " he's good enough for *one* thing, I should judge—he can outjump any frog in Calaveras county."

The feller took the box again, and took another long, particular look, and give it back to Smiley, and says, very deliberate, " Well, I don't see no p'ints about that frog that's any better'n any other frog."

" Maybe you don't," Smiley says. " Maybe you understand frogs, and maybe you don't understand 'em; maybe you've had experience, and maybe you an't only a amature, as it were. Anyways, I've got *my* opinion, and I'll risk forty dollars that he can outjump any frog in Calaveras county."

And the feller studied a minute, and then says, kinder sad like, " Well, I'm only a stranger here, and I an't got no frog; but if I had a frog, I'd bet you."

The Jumping Frog

And then Smiley says, "That's all right—that's all right—if you'll hold my box a minute, I'll go and get you a frog." And so the feller took the box, and put up his forty dollars along with Smiley's, and set down to wait.

So he set there a good while thinking and thinking to hisself, and then he got the frog out and prised his mouth open and took a teaspoon and filled him full of quail shot—filled him pretty near up to his chin—and set him on the floor. Smiley he went to the swamp and slopped around in the mud for a long time, and finally he ketched a frog, and fetched him in, and give him to this feller, and says:

"Now, if you're ready, set him alongside of Dan'l, with his fore-paws just even with Dan'l, and I'll give the word." Then he says, "One—two—three—jump!" and him and the feller touched up the frogs from behind, and the new frog hopped off, but Dan'l give a heave, and hysted up his shoulders—so—like a Frenchman, but it wan't no use—he couldn't budge; he was planted as solid as an anvil, and he couldn't no more stir than if he was anchored out. Smiley was a good deal surprised, and he was disgusted too, but he didn't have no idea what the matter was, of course.

The feller took the money and started away; and when he was going out at the door, he sorter jerked his thumb over his shoulder—this way—at Dan'l, and says again, very deliberate, "Well, *I* don't see no p'ints about that frog that's any better'n any other frog."

Smiley he stood scratching his head and looking down at Dan'l a long time, and at last he says, "I do wonder what in the nation that frog throw'd off

"He could n't budge; he was planted as solid as a church....."

The Jumping Frog

for—I wonder if there an't something the matter
with him—he 'pears to look mighty baggy, somehow." And he ketched Dan'l by the nap of the
neck, and lifted him up and says, " Why, blame
my cats, if he don't weigh five pound! " and turned
him upside down, and he belched out a double
handful of shot. And then he see how it was, and
he was the maddest man—he set the frog down

a double handful of shot

and took out after that feller, but he never ketched
him. And——

[Here Simon Wheeler heard his name called
from the front yard, and got up to see what was
wanted.] And turning to me as he moved away,
he said: " Just set where you are, stranger, and
rest easy—I an't going to be gone a second."

But, by your leave, I did not think that a con-
tinuation of the history of the enterprising vagabond
Jim Smiley would be likely to afford me much information concerning the Rev. *Leonidas W.* Smiley,
and so I started away.

The Jumping Frog

At the door I met the sociable Wheeler returning, and he button-holed me and recommenced:

"Well, thish-yer Smiley had a yaller one-eyed cow that didn't have no tail, only jest a short stump like a bannanner, and——"

"Oh! hang Smiley and his afflicted cow!" I muttered, good-naturedly, and bidding the old gentleman good day, I departed.

AURELIA'S
UNFORTUNATE YOUNG MAN

THE facts in the following case came to me by letter from a young lady who lives in the beautiful city of San José; she is perfectly unknown to me, and simply signs herself " Aurelia Maria," which may possibly be a fictitious name. But no matter, the poor girl is almost heart-broken by the misfortunes she has undergone, and so confused by the conflicting counsels of misguided friends and insidious enemies, that she does not know what course to pursue in order to extricate herself from the web of difficulties in which she seems almost hopelessly involved. In this dilemma she turns to me for help, and supplicates for my guidance and instruction with a moving eloquence that would touch the heart of a statue. Hear her sad story:

She says that when she was sixteen years old she met and loved, with all the devotion of a passionate nature, a young man from New Jersey, named Williamson Breckinridge Caruthers, who was some six years her senior. They were engaged, with the free consent of their friends and relatives, and for a time it seemed as if their career was destined to be characterised by an immunity from sorrow beyond the usual lot of humanity. But at last the tide of fortune turned; young Caruthers became infected with small-pox of the most virulent type, and when he recovered from his illness his face was pitted like a waffle-mould and his comeliness gone for ever. Aurelia thought to break off the engagement at first, but pity for her unfortunate lover caused her to postpone the marriage-day for a season, and give him another trial.

The very day before the wedding was to have taken place, Breckinridge, while absorbed in watching the flight of a balloon, walked into a well and fractured one of his legs, and it had to be taken off above the knee. Again Aurelia was moved to break the engagement, but again love triumphed, and she set the day forward and gave him another chance to reform.

And again misfortune overtook the unhappy youth. He lost one arm by the premature discharge of a Fourth-of-July cannon, and within three months he got the other pulled out by a carding-machine. Aurelia's heart was almost crushed by these latter calamities. She could not but be deeply grieved to see her lover passing from her by piecemeal, feeling, as she did, that he could not last for ever under this disastrous process of reduction, yet knowing of no way to stop its dreadful career, and in her tearful despair she almost regretted, like brokers who hold on and lose, that she had not taken him at first, before he had suffered such an alarming depreciation. Still, her brave soul bore her up, and she resolved to bear with her friend's unnatural disposition yet a little longer.

Again the wedding-day approached, and again disappointment overshadowed it: Caruthers fell ill with the erysipelas, and lost the use of one of his eyes entirely. The friends and relatives of the bride, considering that she had already put up with more than could reasonably be expected of her, now came forward and insisted that the match should be broken off; but after wavering awhile, Aurelia, with a generous spirit which did her credit, said she had reflected calmly upon the matter, and could not discover that Breckinridge was to blame.

So she extended the time once more, and he broke his other leg.

It was a sad day for the poor girl when she saw the surgeons reverently bearing away the sack whose uses she had learned by previous experience, and her heart told her the bitter truth that some more of her lover was gone. She felt that the field of her affections was growing more and more circumscribed every day, but once more she frowned down her relatives and renewed her betrothal.

Shortly before the time set for the nuptials another disaster occurred. There was but one man scalped by the Owens River Indians last year. That man was Williamson Breckinridge Caruthers, of New Jersey. He was hurrying home with happiness in his heart, when he lost his hair for ever, and in that hour of bitterness he almost cursed the mistaken mercy that had spared his head.

At last Aurelia is in serious perplexity as to what she ought to do. She still loves her Breckinridge, she writes, with truly womanly feeling—she still loves what is left of him—but her parents are bitterly opposed to the match, because he has no property and is disabled from working, and she has not sufficient means to support both comfortably. " Now, what should she do? " she asks with painful and anxious solicitude.

It is a delicate question; it is one which involves the lifelong happiness of a woman, and that of nearly two-thirds of a man, and I feel that it would be

Aurelia's Unfortunate Young Man

assuming too great a responsibility to do more than make a mere suggestion in the case. How would it do to build to him? If Aurelia can afford the expense, let her furnish her mutilated lover with wooden arms and wooden legs, and a glass eye and a wig, and give him another show; give him ninety days, without grace, and if he does not break his neck in the meantime, marry him and take the chances. It does not seem to me that there is much risk, any way, Aurelia, because if he sticks to his infernal propensity for damaging himself every time he sees a good opportunity, his next experiment is bound to finish him, and then you are all right, you know, married or single. If married, the wooden legs and such other valuables as he may possess, revert to the widow, and you see you sustain no actual loss save the cherished fragment of a noble but most unfortunate husband, who honestly strove to do right, but whose extraordinary instincts were against him. Try it, Maria! I have thought the matter over carefully and well, and it is the only chance I see for you. It would have been a happy conceit on the part of Caruthers if he had started with his neck and broken that first; but since he has seen fit to choose a different policy and string himself out as long as possible, I do not think we ought to upbraid him for it if he has enjoyed it. We must do the best we can under the circumstances, and try not to feel exasperated at him.

CURING A COLD

It is a good thing, perhaps, to write for the amusement of the public, but it is a far higher and nobler thing to write for their instruction, their profit, their actual and tangible benefit. The latter is the sole object of this article. If it prove the means of restoring to health one solitary sufferer among my race, of lighting up once more the fire of hope and joy in his faded eyes, of bringing back to his dead heart again the quick, generous impulses of other days, I shall be amply rewarded for my labour; my soul will be permeated with the sacred delight a Christian feels when he has done a good, unselfish deed.

Having led a pure and blameless life, I am justified in believing that no man who knows me will reject the suggestions I am about to make, out of fear that I am trying to deceive him. Let the public do itself the honour to read my experience in doctoring a cold, as herein set forth, and then follow in my footsteps.

When the White House was burned in Virginia, I lost my home, my happiness, my constitution, and my trunk. The loss of the two first-named articles was a matter of no great consequence, since a home without a mother or a sister, or a distant young female relative in it, to remind you, by putting your soiled linen out of sight and taking your boots down off the mantel-piece, that there are those who think about you and care for you, is easily obtained. And I cared nothing for the loss of my happiness, because,

Curing a Cold

not being a poet, it could not be possible that melancholy would abide with me long.

But to lose a good constitution and a better trunk were serious misfortunes.

On the day of the fire my constitution succumbed to a severe cold caused by undue exertion in getting ready to do something. I suffered to no purpose, too, because the plan I was figuring at for the extinguishing of the fire was so elaborate that I never got it completed until the middle of the following week.

The first time I began to sneeze, a friend told me to go and bathe my feet in hot water and go to bed. I did so. Shortly afterward, another friend advised me to get up and take a cold shower-bath. I did that also. Within the hour, another friend assured me that it was policy to "feed a cold and starve a fever." I had both. So I thought it best to fill myself up for the cold, and then keep dark and let the fever starve awhile.

In a case of this kind, I seldom do things by halves; I ate pretty heartily; I conferred my custom upon a stranger who had just opened his restaurant that morning; he waited near me in respectful silence until I had finished feeding my cold, when he inquired if the people about Virginia were much afflicted with colds? I told him I thought they were. He then went out and took in his sign. I started down toward the office, and on the way encountered another bosom friend, who told me that a quart of salt water, taken warm, would come as near curing a cold as anything in the world. I hardly thought I had room for it, but I tried it any how. The result was surprising. I believe I threw up my immortal soul.

Now, as I am giving my experience only for the benefit of those who are troubled with the distemper

Curing a Cold

I am writing about, I feel that they will see the propriety of my cautioning them against following such portions of it as proved inefficient with me, and acting upon this conviction, I warn them against warm salt water. It may be a good enough remedy, but I think it is too severe. If I had another cold in the head, and there was no course left me but to take either an earthquake or a quart of warm salt water, I would take my chances on the earthquake.

After the storm which had been raging in my stomach had subsided, and no more good Samaritans happening along, I went on borrowing handkerchiefs again and blowing them to atoms, as had been my custom in the early stages of my cold, until I came across a lady who had just arrived from over the plains, and who said she had lived in a part of the country where doctors were scarce, and had from necessity acquired considerable skill in the treatment of simple "family complaints." I knew she must have had much experience, for she appeared to be a hundred and fifty years old.

She mixed a decoction composed of molasses, aqua fortis, turpentine, and various other drugs, and instructed me to take a wine-glass full of it every fifteen minutes. I never took but one dose; that was enough; it robbed me of all moral principle, and awoke every unworthy impulse of my nature. Under its malign influence my brain conceived miracles of meanness, but my hands were too feeble to execute them; at that time, had it not been that my strength had surrendered to a succession of assaults from infallible remedies for my cold, I am satisfied that I would have tried to rob the graveyard.

Like most other people I often feel mean, and act accordingly; but until I took that medicine I had

Curing a Cold

never revelled in such supernatural depravity and felt proud of it. At the end of two days I was ready to go to doctoring again. I took a few more unfailing remedies, and finally drove my cold from my head to my lungs.

I got to coughing incessantly, and my voice fell below zero; I conversed in a thundering base, two octaves below my natural tone; I could only compass my regular nightly repose by coughing myself down to a state of utter exhaustion, and then the moment I began to talk in my sleep, my discordant voice woke me up again.

My case grew more and more serious every day. Plain gin was recommended; I took it. Then gin and molasses; I took that also. Then gin and onions; I added the onions, and took all three. I detected no particular result, however, except that I had acquired a breath like a buzzard's.

I found I had to travel for my health. I went to Lake Bigler with my reportorial comrade, Wilson, It is gratifying to me to reflect that we travelled in considerable style; we went in the Pioneer coach, and my friend took all his baggage with him, consisting of two excellent silk handkerchiefs and a daguerreotype of his grandmother. We sailed and hunted and fished and danced all day, and I doctored my cough all night. By managing in this way, I made out to improve every hour in the twenty-four. But my disease continued to grow worse.

A sheet-bath was recommended. I had never refused a remedy yet, and it seemed poor policy to commence then; therefore I determined to take a sheet-bath, notwithstanding I had no idea what sort of arrangement it was.

It was administered at midnight, and the weather

Curing a Cold

was very frosty. My breast and back were bared, and a sheet (there appeared to be a thousand yards of it) soaked in ice-water was wound around me until I resembled a swab for a Columbiad.

It is a cruel expedient. When the chilly rag touches one's warm flesh, it makes him start with sudden violence and gasp for breath just as men do in the death agony. It froze the marrow in my bones and stopped the beating of my heart. I thought my time had come.

Young Wilson said the circumstance reminded him of an anecdote about a negro who was being baptised, and who slipped from the parson's grasp, and came near being drowned. He floundered around, though, and finally rose up out of the water considerably strangled and furiously angry, and started ashore at once spouting water like a whale, and remarking, with great asperity, that "One o' dese days some gen'lman's nigger gwyne to git killed wid jes' such dam foolishness as dis!"

Never take a sheet-bath—never. Next to meeting a lady acquaintance, who, for reasons best known to herself, don't see you when she looks at you, and don't know you when she does see you, it is the most uncomfortable thing in the world.

But, as I was saying, when the sheet-bath failed to cure my cough, a lady friend recommended the application of a mustard plaster to my breast. I believe that would have cured me effectually, if it had not been for young Wilson. When I went to bed, I put my mustard plaster—which was a very gorgeous one, eighteen inches square — where I could reach it when I was ready for it. But young Wilson got hungry in the night, and ate it up. I never saw anybody have such an appetite; I am

Curing a Cold

confident that lunatic would have eaten me if I had been healthy.

After sojourning a week at Lake Bigler, I went to Steamboat Springs, and beside the steam baths, I took a lot of the vilest medicines that were ever concocted. They would have cured me, but I had to go back to Virginia, where, notwithstanding the variety of new remedies I absorbed every day, I managed to aggravate my disease by carelessness and undue exposure.

I finally concluded to visit San Francisco, and the first day I got there, a lady at the Lick House told me to drink a quart of whisky every twenty-four hours, and a friend at the Occidental recommended precisely the same course. Each advised me to take a quart: that made half a gallon. I did so, and still live.

Now, with the kindest motives in the world, I offer for the consideration of consumptive patients the variegated course of treatment I have lately gone through. Let them try it; if it don't cure, it can't more than kill them.

LUCRETIA SMITH'S SOLDIER

I AM an ardent admirer of those nice, sickly war stories which have lately been so popular, and for the last three months I have been at work upon one of that character, which is now completed. It can be relied upon as true in every particular, inasmuch as the facts it contains were compiled from the official records in the War Department of Washington. It is but just, also, that I should confess that I have drawn largely on "*Jomini's Art of War*," the "*Message of the President and Accompanying Documents*," and sundry maps and military works, so necessary for reference in building a novel like this. To the accommodating Directors of the Overland Telegraph Company I take pleasure in returning my thanks for tendering me the use of their wires at the customary rates. And finally, to all those kind friends who have by good deeds or encouraging words, assisted me in my labours upon this story of "Lucretia Smith's Soldier," during the past three months, and whose names are too numerous for special mention, I take this method of tendering my sincerest gratitude.

CHAPTER I

On a balmy May morning in 1861, the little village of Bluemass, in Massachusetts, lay wrapped in the splendour of the newly-risen sun. Reginald de Whittaker, confidential and only clerk in the house of Bushrod & Ferguson, general drygoods and grocery dealers and keepers of the post-office, rose from his bunk under the counter, and shook

Lucretia Smith's Soldier

himself. After yawning and stretching comfortably, he sprinkled the floor and proceeded to sweep it. He had only half finished his task, however, when he sat down on a keg of nails and fell into a reverie. "This is my last day in this shanty," said he. "How it will surprise Lucretia when she hears I am going for a soldier! How proud she will be, the little darling!" He pictured himself in all manner of warlike situations; the hero of a thousand extraordinary adventures; the man of rising fame; the pet of Fortune at last; and beheld himself, finally, returning to his own home, a bronzed and scarred brigadier-general, to cast his honours and his matured and perfect love at the feet of his Lucretia Borgia Smith.

At this point a thrill of joy and pride suffused his system; but he looked down and saw his broom and blushed. He came toppling down from the clouds he had been soaring among, and was an obscure clerk again, on a salary of two dollars and a half a week.

CHAPTER II

At eight o'clock that evening, with a heart palpitating with the proud news he had brought for his beloved, Reginald sat in Mr. Smith's parlour awaiting Lucretia's appearance. The moment she entered, he sprang to meet her, his face lighted by the torch of love that was blazing in his head somewhere and shining through, and ejaculated, "Mine own!" as he opened his arms to receive her.

"Sir!" said she, and drew herself up like an offended queen.

Poor Reginald was stricken dumb with astonishment. This chilling demeanour, this angry rebuff,

337

Lucretia Smith's Soldier

where he had expected the old, tender welcome, banished the gladness from his heart as the cheerful brightness is swept from the landscape when a dark cloud drifts athwart the face of the sun. He stood bewildered a moment, with a sense of goneness on him like one who finds himself suddenly overboard upon a midnight sea, and beholds the ship pass into shrouding gloom, while the dreadful conviction falls upon his soul that he has not been missed. He tried to speak, but his pallid lips refused their office. At last he murmured:

"O Lucretia! what have I done? what is the matter? why this cruel coldness? Don't you love your Reginald any more?"

Her lips curled in bitter scorn, and she replied, in mocking tones:

"Don't I love my Reginald any more? No, I *don't* love my Reginald any more! Go back to your pitiful junk-shop and grab your pitiful yardstick, and stuff cotton in your ears, so that you can't hear your country shout to you to fall in and shoulder arms. Go!" And then, unheeding the new light that flashed from his eyes, she fled from the room and slammed the door behind her.

Only a moment more! Only a single moment more, he thought, and he could have told her how he had already answered the summons and signed the muster-roll, and all would have been well; his lost bride would have come back to his arms with words of praise and thanksgiving upon her lips. He made a step forward, once, to recall her, but he remembered that he was no longer an effeminate drygoods student, and his warrior soul scorned to sue for quarter. He strode from the place with martial firmness, and never looked behind him.

BRIEF BIOGRAPHICAL SKETCH
OF GEORGE WASHINGTON

THIS day, many years ago precisely, George Washington was born. How full of significance the thought! Especially to those among us who have had a similar experience, though subsequently; and still more especially to the young, who should take him for a model, and faithfully try to be like him, undeterred by the frequency with which the same thing has been attempted by American youths before them and not satisfactorily accomplished. George Washington was the youngest of nine children, eight of whom were the offspring of his uncle and his aunt. As a boy, he gave no promise of the greatness he was one day to achieve. He was ignorant of the commonest accomplishments of youth. He could not even lie. But then he never had any of those precious advantages which are within the reach of the humblest of the boys of the present day. Any boy can lie now. I could lie before I could stand—yet this sort of sprightliness was so common in our family that little notice was taken of it. Young George appears to have had no sagacity whatever. It is related of him that he once chopped down his father's favourite cherry-tree, and then didn't know enough to keep dark about it. He came near going to sea once, as a midshipman; but when his mother represented to him that he must necessarily be absent when he was away from home, and that this must continue to be the case until he got back, the sad truth struck him so forcibly that he ordered his trunk ashore, and quietly but firmly refused to serve in the navy and fight

Sketch of George Washington

the battles of his king so long as the effect of it would
be to discommode his mother. The great rule of
his life was, that procrastination was the thief
of time, and that we should always do unto others
somehow. This is the golden rule. Therefore, he
would never discommode his mother.

Young George Washington was actuated in all
things by the highest and purest principles of morality,
justice, and right. He was a model in every way
worthy of the emulation of youth. Young George
was always prompt and faithful in the discharge of
every duty. It has been said of him, by the historian,
that he was always on hand, like a thousand of brick.
And well deserved was this compliment. The
aggregate of the building material specified might
have been largely increased — might have been
doubled, even—without doing full justice to these
high qualities in the subject of this sketch. Indeed,
it would hardly be possible to express in bricks the
exceeding promptness and fidelity of young George
Washington. His was a soul whose manifold excel-
lencies were beyond the ken and computation of
mathematics, and bricks are, at the least, but an
inadequate vehicle for the conveyance of a comprehension of the moral sublimity of a nature so pure as his.

Young George W. was a surveyor in early life—
a surveyor of an inland port—a sort of county
surveyor; and under a commission from Governor
Dinwiddie, he set out to survey his way four hundred
miles through trackless forests, infested with Indians,
to procure the liberation of some English prisoners.
The historian says the Indians were the most de-
praved of their species, and did nothing but lay for
white men, whom they killed for the sake of robbing
them. Considering that white men only travelled

Sketch of George Washington

through the country at the rate of one a year, they were probably unable to do what might be termed a land-office business in their line. They did not rob young G. W.; one savage made the attempt, but failed; he fired at the subject of this sketch from behind a tree, but the subject of this sketch immediately snaked him out from behind the tree and took him prisoner.

The long journey failed of success; the French would not give up the prisoners, and Wash. went sadly back home again. A regiment was raised to go and make a rescue, and he took command of it. He caught the French out in the rain and tackled them with great intrepidity. He defeated them in ten minutes, and their commander handed in his checks. This was the battle of Great Meadows.

After this, a good while, George Washington became Commander-in-Chief of the American armies, and had an exceedingly dusty time of it all through the Revolution. But every now and then he turned a Jack from the bottom and surprised the enemy. He kept up his lick for seven long years, and hazed the British from Harrisburg to Halifax—and America was free! He served two terms as President, and would have been President yet if he had lived—even so did the people honour the Father of his Country. Let the youth of America take his incomparable character for a model, and try it one jolt, anyhow. Success is possible—let them remember that—success is possible, though there are chances against it.

I could continue this biography with profit to the rising generation, but I shall have to drop the subject at present, because of other matters which must be attended to.

A
TOUCHING STORY OF GEORGE WASHINGTON'S BOYHOOD

IF it please your neighbour to break the sacred
calm of night with the snorting of an unholy trombone, it is your duty to put up with his wretched
music and your privilege to pity him for the unhappy
instinct that moves him to delight in such discordant
sounds. I did not always think thus: this consideration for musical amateurs was born of certain disagreeable personal experiences that once followed
the development of a like instinct in myself. Now
this infidel over the way, who is learning to play on
the trombone, and the slowness of whose progress
is almost miraculous, goes on with his harrowing
work every night, uncursed by me, but tenderly
pitied. Ten years ago, for the same offence, I would
have set fire to his house. At that time I was a prey
to an amateur violinist for two or three weeks, and
the sufferings I endured at his hands are inconceivable.
He played " Old Dan Tucker," and he never played
anything else; but he performed that so badly that
he could throw me into fits with it if I were awake,
or into a nightmare if I were asleep. As long as
he confined himself to " Dan Tucker," though, I
bore with him and abstained from violence; but
when he projected a fresh outrage, and tried to do
" Sweet Home," I went over and burnt him out.
My next assailant was a wretch who felt a call to

play the clarionet. He only played the scale, however, with his distressing instrument, and I let him run the length of his tether also; but finally, when he branched out into a ghastly tune, I felt my reason deserting me under the exquisite torture, and I sallied forth and burnt him out likewise. During the next two years I burnt out an amateur cornet player, a bugler, a bassoon-sophomore, and a barbarian whose talents ran in the base-drum line.

I would certainly have scorched this trombone man if he had moved into my neighbourhood in those days. But as I said before, I leave him to his own destruction now, because I have had experience as an amateur myself, and I feel nothing but compassion for that kind of people. Besides, I have learned that there lies dormant in the souls of all men a penchant for some particular musical instrument, and an unsuspected yearning to learn to play on it, that are bound to wake up and demand attention some day. Therefore, you who rail at such as disturb your slumbers with unsuccessful and demoralising attempts to subjugate a fiddle, beware! for sooner or later your own time will come. It is customary and popular to curse these amateurs when they wrench you out of a pleasant dream at night with a peculiarly diabolical note; but seeing that we are all made alike, and must all develop a distorted talent for music in the fulness of time, it is not right. I am charitable to my trombone maniac; in a moment of inspiration he fetches a snort, sometimes, that brings me to a sitting posture in bed, broad awake and weltering in a cold perspiration. Perhaps my first thought is, that there has been an earthquake; perhaps I hear the trombone, and my next thought is, that suicide and the silence of the grave would be a happy release from this nightly agony; perhaps the old instinct comes strong upon me to go after my matches; but my first cool, collected thought is, that the trombone man's destiny is upon him, and he is working it out in suffering and tribulation; and I banish from me the unworthy instinct that would prompt me to burn him out.

After a long immunity from the dreadful insanity that moves a man to become a musician in defiance of the will of God that he should confine himself to sawing wood, I finally fell a victim to the instrument they call the accordeon. At this day I hate that contrivance as fervently as any man can, but at the time I speak of I suddenly acquired a disgusting and idolatrous affection for it. I got one of powerful capacity, and learned to play "Auld Lang Syne" on it. It seems to me, now, that I must have been gifted with a sort of inspiration to be enabled, in the state of ignorance in which I then was, to select out of the whole range of musical composition the one solitary tune that sounds vilest and most distressing on the accordeon. I do not suppose there is another tune in the world with which I could have inflicted so much anguish upon my race as I did with that one during my short musical career.

After I had been playing "Lang Syne" about a week, I had the vanity to think I could improve the original melody, and I set about adding some little flourishes and variations to it, but with rather indifferent success, I suppose, as it brought my landlady into my presence with an expression about her of being opposed to such desperate enterprises. Said she, "Do you know any other tune but that, Mr. Twain?" I told her, meekly, that I did not. "Well, then," said she, "stick to it just

George Washington's Boyhood

as it is; don't put any variations to it, because it's rough enough on the boarders the way it is now."

The fact is, it was something more than simply "rough enough" on them; it was altogether too rough; half of them left, and the other half would have followed, but Mrs. Jones saved them by discharging me from the premises.

I only stayed one night at my next lodging-house. Mrs. Smith was after me early in the morning. She said, " You can go, sir; I don't want you here; I have had one of your kind before—a poor lunatic, that played the banjo and danced breakdowns, and jarred the glass all out of the windows. You kept me awake all night, and if you was to do it again, I'd take and mash that thing over your head!" I could see that this woman took no delight in music, and I moved to Mrs. Brown's.

For three nights in succession I gave my new neighbours " Auld Lang Syne," plain and unadulterated, save by a few discords that rather improved the general effect than otherwise. But the very first time I tried the variations the boarders mutinied. I never did find anybody that would stand those variations. I was very well satisfied with my efforts in that house, however, and I left it without any regrets; I drove one boarder as mad as a March hare, and another one tried to scalp his mother. I reflected, though, that if I could only have been allowed to give this latter just one more touch of the variations, he would have finished the old woman.

I went to board at Mrs. Murphy's, an Italian lady of many excellent qualities. The very first time I struck up the variations, a haggard, careworn, cadaverous old man walked into my room and stood

345

beaming upon me a smile of ineffable happiness.
Then he placed his hand upon my head, and looking
devoutly aloft, he said with feeling unction, and in a
voice trembling with emotion, " God bless you, young
man! God bless you! for you have done that for
me which is beyond all praise. For years I have
suffered from an incurable disease, and knowing my
doom was sealed and that I must die, I have striven
with all my power to resign myself to my fate, but
in vain—the love of life was too strong within me.
But Heaven bless you, my benefactor! for since I
heard you play that tune and those variations, I
do not want to live any longer—I am entirely resigned—I am willing to die—in fact, I am anxious
to die." And then the old man fell upon my neck
and wept a flood of happy tears. I was surprised
at these things; but I could not help feeling a little
proud at what I had done, nor could I help giving the
old gentleman a parting blast in the way of some
peculiarly lacerating variations as he went out at the
door. They doubled him up like a jack-knife, and the
next time he left his bed of pain and suffering he was
all right, in a metallic coffin.

My passion for the accordeon finally spent itself
and died out, and I was glad when I found myself
free from its unwholesome influence. While the
fever was upon me, I was a living, breathing calamity
wherever I went, and desolation and disaster followed
in my wake. I bred discord in families, I crushed
the spirits of the light-hearted, I drove the melancholy
to despair, I hurried invalids to premature dissolution,
and I fear me I disturbed the very dead in their
graves. I did incalculable harm, and inflicted untold
suffering upon my race with my execrable music;
and yet to atone for it all, I did but one single blessed

George Washington's Boyhood

...ct, in making that weary old man willing to go to his ...ong home.

Still, I derived some little benefit from that ...ccordeon; for while I continued to practise on it, ...I never had to pay any board—landlords were ...lways willing to compromise, on my leaving before ...he month was up.

Now, I had two objects in view in writing the ...oregoing, one of which was to try and reconcile ...people to those poor unfortunates who feel that ...they have a genius for music, and who drive their ...neighbours crazy every night in trying to develop ...and cultivate it; and the other was to introduce an ...admirable story about Little George Washington, ...who could Not Lie, and the Cherry-Tree—or the ...Apple-Tree—I have forgotten now which, although ...it was told me only yesterday. And writing such ...a long and elaborate introductory has caused me ...to forget the story itself; but it was very touching.

ADVICE FOR GOOD LITTLE GIRLS

GOOD little girls ought not to make mouths at their teachers for every trifling offence. This kind of retaliation should only be resorted to under peculiarly aggravating circumstances.

If you have nothing but a rag doll stuffed with saw-dust, while one of your more fortunate little playmates has a costly china one, you should treat her with a show of kindness, nevertheless. And you ought not to attempt to make a forcible swap with her unless your conscience would justify you in it, and you know you are able to do it.

You ought never to take your little brother's " chawing-gum " away from him by main force: it is better to rope him in with the promise of the first two dollars and a half you find floating down the river on a grindstone. In the artless simplicity natural to his time of life, he will regard it as a perfectly fair transaction. In all ages of the world this eminently plausible fiction has lured the obtuse infant to financial ruin and disaster.

If at any time you find it necessary to correct your brother, do not correct him with mud—never on any account throw mud at him, because it will soil his clothes. It is better to scald him a little; for then you attain two desirable results—you secure his immediate attention to the lesson you are inculcating, and, at the same time, your hot water

Advice for Good Little Girls

will have a tendency to remove impurities from his person—and possibly the skin also, in spots.

If your mother tells you to do a thing, it is wrong to reply that you won't. It is better and more becoming to intimate that you will do as she bids you, and then afterwards act quietly in the matter according to the dictates of your better judgment.

You should ever bear in mind that it is to your kind parents that you are indebted for your food and your nice bed and your beautiful clothes, and for the privilege of staying home from school when you let on that you are sick. Therefore you ought to respect their little prejudices and humour their little whims, and put up with their little foibles, until they get to crowding you too much.

Good little girls should always show marked deference for the aged. You ought never to " sass " old people—unless they " sass " you first.

CONCERNING CHAMBERMAIDS

AGAINST all chambermaids, of whatsoever age or nationality, I launch the curse of bachelordom! Because:

They always put the pillows at the opposite end of the bed from the gas-burner, so that while you read and smoke before sleeping (as is the ancient and honoured custom of bachelors), you have to hold your book aloft, in an uncomfortable position, to keep the light from dazzling your eyes.

When they find the pillows removed to the other end of the bed in the morning, they receive not the suggestion in a friendly spirit; but, glorying in their absolute sovereignty, and unpitying your helplessness, they make the bed just as it was originally, and gloat in secret over the pang their tyranny will cause you.

Always after that, when they find you have transposed the pillows, they undo your work, and thus defy and seek to embitter the life that God has given you.

If they cannot get the light in an inconvenient position any other way, they move the bed.

If you pull your trunk out six inches from the wall, so that the lid will stay up when you open it, they always shove that trunk back again. They do it on purpose.

If you want the spittoon in a certain spot, where it will be handy, they don't, and so they move it.

They always put your other boots into inaccessible

Concerning Chambermaids

places. They chiefly enjoy depositing them as far under the bed as the wall will permit. It is because this compels you to get down in an undignified attitude and make wild sweeps for them in the dark with the boot-jack, and swear.

They always put the match-box in some other place. They hunt up a new place for it every day, and put up a bottle, or other perishable glass thing, where the box stood before. This is to cause you to break that glass thing, groping in the dark, and get yourself into trouble.

They are for ever and ever moving the furniture. When you come in, in the night, you can calculate on finding the bureau where the wardrobe was in the morning. And when you go out in the morning, if you leave the slop-bucket by the door and rocking-chair by the window, when you come in at midnight, or thereabouts, you will fall over that rocking-chair, and you will proceed toward the window and sit down in that slop-tub. This will disgust you. They like that.

No matter where you put anything, they are not going to let it stay there. They will take it and move it the first chance they get. It is their nature. And besides, it gives them pleasure to be mean and contrary this way. They would die if they couldn't be villains.

They always save up all the old scraps of printed rubbish you throw on the floor, and stack them up carefully on the table, and start the fire with your valuable manuscripts. If there is any one particular old scrap that you are more down on than any other, and which you are gradually wearing your life out trying to get rid of, you may take all the pains you possibly can in that direction, but it won't be of any use, because they will always fetch that old scrap back

Concerning Chambermaids

and put it in the same old place again every time. It does them good.

And they use up more hair-oil than any six men. If charged with purloining the same, they lie about it. What do they care about a hereafter? Absolutely nothing.

If you leave the key in the door for convenience sake, they will carry it down to the office and give it to the clerk. They do this under the vile pretence of trying to protect your property from thieves; but actually they do it because they want to make you tramp back downstairs after it when you come home tired, or put you to the trouble of sending a waiter for it, which waiter will expect you to pay him something. In which case I suppose the degraded creatures divide.

They keep always trying to make your bed before you get up, thus destroying your rest and inflicting agony upon you; but after you get up, they don't come any more till next day.

They do all the mean things they can think of, and they do them just out of pure cussedness, and nothing else.

Chambermaids are dead to every human instinct.

I have cursed them in behalf of outraged bachelordom. They deserve it. If I can get a bill through the Legislature abolishing chambermaids, I mean to do it.

THE TEMPLE PRESS, PRINTERS, LETCHWORTH